ATTRACTING CAPITAL FROM ANGELS

HOW THEIR MONEY—AND THEIR EXPERIENCE—CAN HELP YOU BUILD A SUCCESSFUL COMPANY

BRIAN E. HILL
and
DEE POWER

JOHN WILEY & SONS, INC.

Published by John Wiley & Sons, Inc., New York.
Published simultaneously in Canada.

Library of Congress Cataloging in Publication Data:
Hill, Brian E. (Brian Edward), 1955–
Attracting capital from angels : how their money—and their experience—can help you build a successful company/Brian E. Hill and Dee Power.
p. cm.
Includes index.
ISBN 0-471-03620-X (cloth : alk. paper)
1. Angels (Investors) 2. Venture capital. 3. New business enterprises—Finance.
I. Power, Dee. II. Title.
HG4751 H548 2001
658.15'224—dc21 2001045610

Printed in the United States of America

10 9 8 7 6 5 4 3 2 1

Preface

Hundreds of angel investors, entrepreneurs, and experts contributed to *Attracting Capital from Angels* through short question-and-answer sessions, surveys, and in-depth interviews. The angels are from all parts of the United States. Some have been investing for many years; others have limited investing experience; a few have founded angel networks. The angels interviewed or surveyed were for the most part accredited and have invested in more than one company. Some of the names you will recognize as they have achieved a certain visibility within the venture capital and private equity community.

Fifty accredited investors completed our survey and gave us a picture of the average angel investor, but please remember: If you are an entrepreneur looking for investors, don't rely on generalizations. Angels vary widely in personalities, investment preferences, and desired involvement.

All the angels we talked to, whether they preferred to remain anonymous or allowed themselves to be identified, provided valuable input and advice.

Seventeen professionals in the fields of law, accounting, marketing, public relations, and other disciplines contributed their expertise and added immeasurably to the value of the book. You can find out more about them in the Appendix.

Acknowledgments

The first people to thank are our fathers, Owen L. Hill and Harry D. Power, who viewed writing as something exciting to do.

In one sense, this book was begun when we sat down to put the words on paper in mid-2001. In another, it is the product of a 15-year journey of working with, observing, and listening to entrepreneurs and angel investors as they went about pursuing the entrepreneurial dream. Along the way we visited the high towers of the finance district as well as quiet labs on the wrong side of town where one person tinkered on a technology alone. We met heroes, swashbuckling risk takers, geniuses, thieves, philosophers, and a few people who just seemed pretty much insane.

We included many of their stories in the following pages, and just as importantly tried to incorporate a sense of the zeal with which they chased after this elusive dream. At times the process of growing a venture seemed grand, other times it seemed down and dirty.

All the players in this arena—investors, entrepreneurs, and experts in the law and finance—were extraordinarily willing to take the time to talk with us about the fascinating subject of how individuals finance early-stage companies. A few people even sat down and answered our questions with thoughtful essays, hoping that others would be able to learn from their experiences, ideas, and accumulated wisdom.

So, apart from the first two people we mentioned, we don't have a specific one or two or five people to thank for helping us complete this project. They number in the hundreds; they are out there right now, working late, getting closer to building something big. It is past midnight, and their lights remain on.

Creating a great enterprise starts with possessing a rare gift—the vision to see the future. We would never claim to have that gift ourselves, but we can confidently make this assertion: Entrepreneurship is alive and well, and it is most definitely a dream worth going after with all of your energy, now and always.

Contents

Foreword

Bob Bozeman

The amount of help that entrepreneurs can gain from the angel community continues to grow. Funding is more difficult than ever. Starting a business is more complex than ever. Economically demanding times make finding constructive angels that much more challenging. The advice and tips in *Attracting Capital from Angels* are, therefore, invaluable.

I really like the structure and breadth of this book. The detail exposition is well done—especially when contrasting the different angels' experiences within the narrative and with each other.

The advice is not just for start-ups or neophytes. The book is a companion to resources and approaches to helping a business in all phases of development. It's also a great manual for people who want to share their knowledge (and invest capital) as angels. Most angels rely on their entrepreneurial experiences of building businesses to give aid and support to new entrepreneurs. However, the information in *Attracting Capital from Angels* can prepare these newly winged angels for the demanding range of advice and support required today.

I plan on recommending *Attracting Capital from Angels* to every entrepreneur I run into in the future who asks for mentoring sources.

Great job!

Bob Bozeman
General Partner, Angel Investors, LP
www.svangel.com

Foreword

Randy Haykin

Life used to be so simple. In 1983, at the ripe old age of 23 and straight out of undergraduate work at Brown University, I was asked to join a firm called Sphere Technology, based in Providence, Rhode Island. The firm's founders, Harvey Silverman, Jeffrey Weiss, and Bill Kirk, hired me into my first entrepreneurial job as assistant to the president—to help in creating a business plan, financials, and presentation materials. I quickly learned that fund-raising was a difficult and tricky task—the pitch to potential hires was truly different from the pitch to angels and very different from the story we gave the venture capitalists.

During this first introduction to the world of entrepreneurs, angels, and high finance VCs, we had few tools at our disposal. As entrepreneurs, we simply asked everyone we knew for money. How I wish I had been given some practical guidance on how to locate, pitch, and receive funding. The closest thing I could find at the time was a book called *Business Planning Guide* published by a little firm in New Hampshire called Upstart Publishing. It offered hints on constructing a plan, but *nothing* on how to pitch it, whom to pitch it to, where to find financial backers, and how to raise big bucks.

Today I have a better appreciation for these things—but it took *years* in the school of hard knocks to learn the tricks of the trade. In 1988 I began my management career at Apple Computer, and by 1995 I had landed a role as part of the founding team at Yahoo Inc. as vice president for sales and marketing. Later, I formed Interactive Minds and began work with over four dozen entrepreneurial start-ups around the country, assisting many of them in building their plans, building their teams, and finding funding. During this period, we often acted as an angel investor and mentor to the entrepreneurs—a practice I still follow today. In 1997, our team formed iMinds Ventures (www.iminds.com)—our first venture capital fund. Today, iMinds Ventures has $75 million under management and has made 25 investments in early-stage start-up companies. Our fund works with scores of angels; in fact, 120 or so of them have provided capital to us, and nearly all of our investments have one or more angels involved. Over the years, my perspective on venture financing has grown as a result of seeing the issues from three unique sides: the entrepreneurial view, the angel view, and the venture capital view.

Upon reading Brian Hill and Dee Power's first book on fund-raising, called *Inside Secrets to Venture Capital* (John Wiley & Sons, 2001), I was struck with how well the authors had captured the trials and tribulations of the entrepreneur who seeks venture capital to fund his or her company. The book does an excellent job of portraying many different fronts of the venture capital world—including practical tips on how to find and impress venture capitalists, how to prepare the "Wow" factor for them, and how to bring home the bacon.

But understanding venture capital isn't enough for most entrepreneurs, and I was left with a question: Since most early-stage companies are too raw to receive funding from larger venture capitalists—especially these days when the stock market dive of 2000–2001 has forced VCs to become incredibly cautious about gambling on "the next hot idea," preferring instead to see a finished, shipping product, a strong team, customers, and revenue before funding a company—how do entrepreneurs fund the initial development of their companies?

Attracting Capital from Angels, the latest research from Brian Hill and Dee Power, provides some good answers to these issues. The book strikes home for many of us in the venture industry for these reasons:

- Angels and venture capitalists are completely different—yet understanding their differences and approaches can be critical to the success of your business. The comparison offered by Hill and Power in *Attracting Capital from Angels* will help you sort out the best approach to funding and growing your business.
- The angel landscape is complex—angels are hard to locate, and they are each unique in their needs, approaches, and motivations.

Sometimes they travel in packs. Hill and Power shed some light on how to understand the sheep and the herds.

- Entrepreneurs often complain to us, "We know there are angels out there in them thar hills, but we're not quite sure where to start digging." Finding and attracting angel capital is a difficult, time-consuming, and frustrating task. The helpful hints in *Attracting Capital from Angels* on how to locate angels can save hundreds or even thousands of painful hours that can instead be allocated to running the business.
- My philosophy about good books (and good movies) is that if you can receive one snippet of assistance or insight, it is worth your time and money. *Attracting Capital from Angels*, like its predecessor, offers practical advice from the mouths of the angels (and VCs) themselves—potentially saving readers hundreds of phone calls trying to figure out these truths for themselves.

Frankly, as a venture capitalist, I believe that any book that can potentially help entrepreneurs I'm working with find shortcuts to raising money could mean saving hundreds of hours that could actually be spent *building* the business (i.e., making a product, hiring a team, getting customers lined up—you know, all those relatively easy and "trivial" tasks of entrepreneurship).

So, sit back and enjoy reading *Attracting Capital from Angels*. It may be the best step you take this year in building your business . . . and perhaps the most rewarding.

RANDY HAYKIN
Entrepreneur, Angel, and Venture Capitalist
Managing Director, iMinds Ventures
San Francisco, California
www.iminds.com

WHAT IS AN ANGEL AND WHAT DO ANGELS WANT?

CHAPTER 1

The Fascinating World of Angel Investors

It's really this simple: Angel investors are the start-up entrepreneur's best friend. Wealthy individuals, or angel investors as they have come to be known, are by far the most important source of capital for early-stage ventures, and as such are vital contributors to our economy's continued growth and prosperity.

Financial angels have earned their wings through prior business success, accumulating wealth and wisdom that they re-deploy in ventures founded by the next generation of entrepreneurs. They willingly, even cheerfully, assume financial risks that would frighten off even some of the most experienced venture capital firms.

Remarkably, they take these risks not only in search of great rewards, but also because of an unshakable belief in the viability—and necessity—of entrepreneurship. And they invest many times at the very earliest stage of a venture, when there is little more there than the dream of an entrepreneur. They come in at the most exciting and confounding era in a company's development, when the outcome is very much in doubt.

They serve as coach, mentor, champion, white knight, and hero, helping the company along through good times and bad. Their guiding principle is that uniquely American vision that tomorrow is undoubtedly going to be better than today. Very often, theirs is an amazingly clear vision, based on the success angels have achieved with these investments.

Equally remarkably, these angels are often people who have just completed a lifetime journey of long hours, worry, never-ending problems, huge responsibilities, disappointment, and elation in order to build their own company. So what do they do? They sell their company, then turn around and seek to experience it all again from the start-up stage.

For the typical entrepreneur, angels represent the most attainable source of capital. Angels are not just the best friend; they sometimes are the only friend on the lonely entrepreneurial road.

Who Are Angels?

Angel investors are definitely a Nation of Individuals (and colorful characters). The most common type of angels are generally thought to be older businesspeople who may have sold the companies they started, and now put money in early-stage companies as a kind of hobby/investment opportunity. But this is certainly not the only type. With angel investors, generalizations are elusive and hazardous.

A relatively recent phenomenon is a younger group of high-tech millionaires who have decided to reinvest some of their winnings from taking their own companies public. The stock market correction of late 2000–2001 notwithstanding, the boom in the market over the last years of the 1990s sent the assets of many upper-middle-class individuals up to levels that allowed them to join the ranks of wealthy individuals. With the optimism born of dizzying stock market gains, many of these people decided to become angels as well.

We are even seeing a recent phenomenon of not-so-rich individuals who are trying to crack into venture investing indirectly, by buying public shares in entities that, in turn, put capital into early-stage deals.

ANGELS AND THE WORLD THEY OPERATE IN

Who would be best able to describe the world of angel investing, the financing of early-stage ventures?

Charles Darwin?

Horatio Alger?

Lewis Carroll?

Should we view this marketplace as survival of the fittest, in which all the ideas and management teams do battle against one another, until the best ones—the ones with the highest potential returns and likelihood for success—emerge the winners and get capital? A marketplace in which, at the end of the day, the companies who should get capital, usually do?

Or is the marketplace for start-up capital a place where pluck and perseverance—the ability to pick yourself up and dust yourself off—continue on despite repeated dead ends and disappointments, and are rewarded with the ultimate result of successfully finding investors? Are the stories of successful entrepreneurs heartwarming and uniquely American?

Or is it best viewed through the looking glass, a strangely alien, disorganized world where serendipity, chance meetings, and the secret password of "whom you know" determine who will get capital, where rational analysis gives way to gut instinct? Is this strange world a place where you want to get in, get your capital, and then get out and return home as soon as possible?

In this book, you will see examples of all three, and a key question is investigated: Is it possible to find rules or guidelines an entrepreneur can rely on when seeking angel capital, or is every situation completely different because every company is different, as is every angel investor?

We believe that to understand angels, it helps to look at them up against their more visible and well-publicized counterparts, the venture capital firms (VCs), because the behavior and investment interests of angels are shaped by an important difference with VCs:

Angels invest **their own money** they or their families and companies have **earned.**

VCs invest money they have **raised** from **other financial institutions and wealthy individuals.**

Thus, we can use this general definition of angel investors: A person, partnership, or corporation that uses his, her, or its own funds to invest in private companies, which are often early-stage companies but not exclusively. This is in contrast to venture capital firms that raise money from institutions (pension funds, insurance companies) and sometimes from wealthy individuals, and then invest the money on behalf of these limited partners in primarily later-stage companies (but, again, not exclusively). Venture capitalists, then, are really money managers. Angels put their own (usually hard-earned) money at risk. Angels have created wealth in the past in their own entrepreneurial ventures and now put a portion of the wealth to use in building another entrepreneur's company. They make the money, then they manage it. Venture capitalists invest private equity as a full-time job. Most angels only devote a portion of their time to making and watching over these investments.

Entrepreneurs who want to raise money successfully from angels have to keep these facts mind, because most of the advice that entrepreneurs read or hear about regarding raising capital is primarily applicable to working with venture capital firms. Venture capital firms are much more well known. They are interviewed more often, and their activity and methods are easier to observe.

Although some standardization is emerging as a result of the formation of angel groups that invest as a unit, the negotiation and due-diligence process with angels varies widely with the angels themselves. This implies that, from the entrepreneur's point of view, gaining an understanding of the angel as an individual, prior to taking money from the angel, is an important factor in determining whether the partnership with the angel will be successful.

Do They Have Cell Phones in the Clouds?

In our book, *Inside Secrets to Venture Capital*, one entrepreneur observed, "VCs are like UFOs, everyone talks about them but they are seldom seen."

If that's the case about VCs, then financial angels are very well named: The angels depicted in art and literature are spiritual beings that are immortal, not easy to find, may be all around us but are typically unseen. They serve as guardians or advisors to mere mortals, and exhibit virtues such as goodness and selflessness.

Financial angels know they are mortal, but they hope to build enterprises that will live on after they are gone. Financial angels are not easy to find, certainly, but we pass them on the street every day, even in small towns in rural areas. The most competent financial angels take their role as advisors very seriously. Are they good and selfless? That's a tough one.

If you set about to help someone and in the process greatly enhance your own wealth, are you selfless?

Medieval angelology tells us there are nine levels or orders of these beings. If we were to create an order or ranking of financial angels, how would we do it? Would we base it on:

How old they are?

How much money they have?

How easy they are to work with?

How frequently they make investments?

How skilled they are at advising companies?

How fast they act in making investment decisions?

How successful they have been in their own business?

How knowledgeable they are about your industry, or market?

How well connected they are with other investors, including venture capitalists?

The highest angel from the entrepreneur's standpoint would be one who can comfortably write a check for the full amount of capital the company needs, provides positive support but does not try to get too involved in running the company, can zip through the due-diligence process in 30 days, has a great deal of practical wisdom to provide based on his or her own considerable success, understands the company's market enough to share the entrepreneur's enthusiasm about the venture, and is already thinking about the perfect venture capital firm to bring in for the second stage of the company's financing.

Does this highest, perfect angel exist? Sure. You will meet several of them in this book. They are just referred to as angels, though. They were far too modest to let us designate them as perfect. That's part of the reason they deserve the designation. If someone in the financial world has to tell you how great they are, they probably aren't.

THERE IS A DARK SIDE TO WATCH OUT FOR

If you have read the preceding paragraphs, right about now you may be hearing in your head the theme music from the old TV series, *The Saint*, and expecting the halo to appear over Simon Templar's head.

Before we conclude that he is representative of angel investors, we might want to switch channels and go over to the contemporary TV series, *Angel.* The hero on that program is a vampire who tries to do the right thing and help little, suffering people, but sometimes he lets his unnatural affinity for blood get the better of him. At his worst, though, he is still generally a far cry better than his archrivals, a consortium of guys in dark suits who work out of a high-rise and try to take over the world.

Substitute the words *investor*, *start-up entrepreneurs*, *greed*, and *venture capitalists* and you pretty much get the idea that whenever you are out there looking for capital, it pays to watch your back.

Just as *Angel* works in a shadowy world where seemingly attractive people with absolutely perfect hair can turn into horrible demons right before your eyes, the true motives of angels are many times unseen until much later in the transaction. Fortunately, bad angels do some things that tend to give themselves away before it's too late for the entrepreneur to escape. Their unwillingness to meet with you before dusk is one example. Nobody's that busy.

Risk Capital and Ultrarisk Capital: Not Investments for the Faint of Heart

Funding of early-stage companies involves a high degree of risk, as we all know. The capital that VC firms raise for their funds is sometimes called risk capital to reflect this reality. But venture funds also employ a number of strategies to mitigate the risk. The investments they make are often a blend of early-stage—even seed-stage—companies, and later stage, the Series B or Series C round of financing, as it is sometimes called. These investments would be made to help already successful companies expand and hopefully dominate their markets, and they are, therefore, significantly lower in risk.

Venture funds also spend time and money to get their names known, to, in effect, create a brand image for the fund that allows them to receive a large number of deals, and hopefully the best quality deals. Venture funds also have experienced staff members who know how to evaluate the growth potential of a given company thoroughly prior to funding it. Venture funds rely on complex legal agreements and complicated deal structures to protect their investment and allow them a certain degree of control over the direction of the enterprise.

Angel investments, then, should be called ultrarisk capital. Angels often provide the very first funding a company gets—when few milestones have been reached, and the company has not in any way demonstrated that its business model will be successful. Sometimes, they put money into a deal that is not even a company yet; it is just one or more individuals with the vision of a company in their minds.

When we asked the question, "Why do you want to be an angel?" we got nearly the same answer every time, whether we talked to angels, managers of angel networks, attorneys who represent angels, and even, sometimes reluctantly, venture capitalists. Angels get involved because many of them are highly successful with these investments. They frequently make tremendous returns on their investments and get the added psychic satisfaction of contributing to the growth of a company, and even of helping their community and nation. And they have fun doing it.

Angels succeed. That is the lesson you learn when you study this field of investing. But why do they succeed, how do they do it, and how can an entrepreneur tap into this large and growing source of funding? We hope to provide the answers to these questions in this book.

EARLY-STAGE INVESTING IS WHERE THE RETURNS ARE

Why do angels concentrate their activity on early/seed-stage investments? They know that's where you make the highest rate of return.

We tend to think of the last five years as the red-hot period for private-equity investing, and the 28.3 percent return that all private equity earned, as shown on Table 1.1, certainly bears that out. But look at how early/seed-stage investors did over the last five years—a return of more than 65 percent, and more than double that earned by later-stage private-equity investors.

For those wealthy enough to play in this arena, those who won't be that adversely affected even if the company they invest in turns out to be a bust, it can certainly be an exhilarating experience when you succeed. If you held an investment for five years and it earned 65 percent annually, your $100,000 investment would be worth $1.2 million.

Table 1.1 Venture Economics
U.S. Private Equity Performance Index (PEPI) as of 12/31/2000

	1 Year	*3 Year*	*5 Year*	*10 Year*	*20 Year*
Early/seed	51.20%	93.70%	65.50%	35.80%	23.80%
Later stage	19.90%	31.70%	31.10%	25.20%	18.30%
All private equity	20.00%	30.30%	28.30%	22.10%	19.30%

Angels love start-ups just as much as start-ups love angels. It's easy to see why!

WHERE ENTREPRENEURS GO WRONG IN THEIR SEARCH FOR ANGELS

Despite the fact that angel capital is relatively plentiful and, as we will see, in some cases easier to obtain than capital from venture capital firms, entrepreneurs make some of the same mistakes when seeking capital from angels that they make when approaching VCs.

First and foremost, they do not realize that getting angel capital requires an investment of significant time and effort on the entrepreneur's part. Let's look at the day's schedule for a typical harried founder of an early-stage company:

The Entrepreneur's To-Do List

8:15 A.M.	Meet with attorney to finalize patent application
11:00 A.M.	Look at office space with realtor
12:15 P.M.	Go to OfficeMax and buy supplies
1:25 P.M.	Finish installing new printer on computer
2:00 P.M.	Interview CFO candidate
3:30 P.M.	Raise $1.5 million from angels

Unfortunately, many entrepreneurs assign the same degree of difficulty to each of these tasks. And notice how this entrepreneur left raising capital until the end, when all the other chores were done. The fact is that many founders of start-up companies end up feeling as though their full-time job is raising money, and as a result, a lot of other important tasks get pushed aside while they are out chasing dollars. Part of this is due to the entrepreneurs' lack of planning in their capital search, and going about it incorrectly. Part is due to the nature of the process and the barriers that are erected between the entrepreneurs and their prize: the elusive angel dollars.

AN ANGEL IS MUCH MORE THAN A PERSON WITH A CHECKBOOK

Innovation and job creation come mainly from small enterprises; these small enterprises are early-stage companies that have taken off. It is critical that we create a more efficient equity-capital formation marketplace to enable these companies to flourish. Many entrepreneurs are still limited to family-and-friends capital. Although it is great that some entrepreneurs have these sources ready to be tapped, they do not really fill the needs of most early-stage ventures, which need:

- Capital
- Experience
- Contacts

The true angel can provide all these, and all are critical to the success of an early-stage venture. Many angels make the case that the experience and contacts they provide actually add more value than the capital they provide.

WHY ANGELS ARE INCREASINGLY VITAL

The published numbers for capital invested and number of investments done by VC firms is somewhat misleading because a number of the investments is skewed by follow-on investments in companies, expansion capital rather than start-up capital.

One reason angels have prospered is a simple supply/demand equation: The number of quality start-up ideas has risen much faster than the number of professional venture funds (and the number of venture-fund partners available to analyze deal flow). Angels fill this void very eagerly. The average size of investment done by VC firms has risen dramatically over the last five years, to reach nearly $16 million in 2002, by some estimates, meaning that companies with smaller needs for capital are, for all intents and purposes, shut off from obtaining capital from VC firms.

The very earliest-stage companies often have incomplete management teams and need a great deal of mentoring assistance. The partners of VC firms, whose time is spread over many tasks, cannot usually provide the intensive assistance these companies need. Angels may be better able to do this, but it depends on their interest level, other commitments angels may have including their own companies, and the simple fact of whether they get a kick out of mentoring.

Chapter Summary

- Angel investors are the most important source of capital for early-stage ventures.
- Angels are individuals who invest their own money, which they have earned.
- Angels have diverse backgrounds and motivations for investing.
- Angels know and are willing to accept the fact that they are taking great risks.
- Historically, early-stage investments achieve the highest rates of return.
- Angels provide companies with experience and business contacts as well as capital.
- Angels help make the market for private equity more efficient around the United States.
- Angels provide vision.

CHAPTER

2

Trends in Angel Investing

The Climate Today: A Return to Reason

Wall Street gurus say that fear (of being left behind) and greed (wanting more than the other guy) drive the stock market. What drives the private-equity markets? Why are there upswings and downswings in investor interest? What affects supply and demand of angel capital?

In 1999 and 2000 there was a flood tide of new business ideas all seeking investors. Both venture capitalists and angels seemed literally to be throwing money at anything related to the Internet. We saw the strange phenomenon that Internet companies were valued on the number of visitors they could attract to their Web sites, not on how much revenue they could generate from those users. Valuations became ridiculous in some cases. Then it all changed, as many Internet ventures were deemed failures, and by early 2001 we went back to basics, viewing enterprises as entities that were built slowly and carefully. Some of the less viable business concepts simply dried up and blew away without even ever getting started. Venture investors became much more careful about where they put their money, and in some cases stopped investing altogether. On the other hand there was less competition, in sheer numbers of business plans, for the investor's attention. A significant number of entrepreneurs simply stopped looking for capital, sometimes because of the mistaken belief that none was available anymore.

It is not difficult to predict that the much-maligned dot.coms will make a slow but steady comeback, fueled by both the sheer numbers of consumers gravitating to the Net to explore the idea of shopping there, and the incredible will of these entrepreneurs to succeed. They have faced rejection and even ridicule of their business concepts by venture capitalists. The "I'll show them they were wrong" attitude drives a significant number of entrepreneurs toward their goals. Revenge is a powerful motive in real-life business as well as in fiction. These Net entrepreneurs will simply scale down their business models and grow more slowly, but many will be at least moderate successes.

Angels who had been investing prior to the wild period of speculation in the late 1990s through 2000 have by no means given up on angel investing. Many see this as a better climate for serious angel investors. Entrepreneurs are willing to accept significantly lower valuations. Angels aren't inundated with scores of low-quality deals that were formed mainly to take advantage of the dot.com frenzy. And, as some of the newbie angels become disillusioned and leave the market, there is less competition for the more patient angels seeking out the best deals.

When Will Angel Investing Again Take Flight?

A parallel between angels and VC firms is how they have reacted to the downturn by deciding to spend more time nursing their existing investments along rather than chasing down new ones. Several angel groups that had put together large funds and had become relatively high profile, abruptly decided not to raise additional funding for further ventures in mid-2001.

When and if they see meaningful progress being made by the companies they have already committed funds to, angels and VC firms should be willing to get back to looking at new investments with more enthusiasm. Some observers have argued that VC firms are waiting for the initial public offering (IPO) market to return to health before they make new investments. In other words, they want to cash out of existing deals, generate a return for their limited partners, then redeploy the funds. So, the symbiotic relationship between angels and VC firms looks like this:

> VC firms need the IPO market to come back before they look for new deals; they'll just work on fixing the ailing members of their portfolio.
>
> Angels need follow-on funding from VC firms to take their companies to the next level. They will wait until the VC firms come back in with follow-on funding before they commit to new investments. They'll just work on helping their existing investments achieve some performance milestones.

But statistics show that VC firms exit very few investments through IPO. Most exit through merger or acquisition. So, are we really waiting for large corporations to find these smaller companies attractive acquisitions again? But, large corporations' stocks have dropped along with the smaller ones. Not as fast perhaps, but billions upon billions of equity have disappeared. A lower equity value would tend to cause a corporation to cut back on its acquisition activity.

So are we really waiting here for another roaring bull market on the Dow and NASDAQ before angel investing can pick up again? The lesson seems to be that the financial markets are a remarkably interconnected web. A vibration on one end is felt at the ends of thousands of other strands. The Old Economy, the New Economy, and the New, New Economy are a lot more alike than we think or than we are told.

Some observers see a potential storm brewing as some of the more ill-advised angel investments that took place during the frenzied period begin to run out of capital, find a second round of funding is unavailable to them, and eventually fail. Will there be litigation by angry angels who believe fast-talking entrepreneurs bilked them out their money? Will this lead to negative publicity that scares would-be angels from testing the waters? Experienced angels, and particularly venture capitalists, know that they are going to have deals with poor rates of return or those that fail altogether. They nurse their wounds, try to learn from the experience, and keep investing. But for angels who fail in their first dot.com investment, how will they react?

And even if angels have not lost the money they put into a given start-up, they may have realized that they probably won't be earning the +100 percent compound rate of return they thought they would when they jumped on the Internet investment bandwagon. Their disenchantment will translate into an unwillingness to do further deals. That trend is a particularly disturbing one, because the reality is that exit strategies and rates of return have merely gone back to more normal, historical levels. It doesn't mean that investing in early-stage companies has suddenly become an unprofitable activity.

Another way of looking at the whole process of starting, building, and then exiting a venture is to liken it to a long conveyor belt in an assembly line. At one end, you add the raw ingredients of a company: capital, management, and a product or technology. Then as the little company goes along the line, a number of new people join in and work on the company. These could be additions to the management team, venture capital firms or other sources of second-stage capital, advisors, or strategic partners. The company eventually looks more and more like a successful company, and moves toward the end of the line, the exit, which could involve being taken public or being acquired.

At any given time, there are only so many people and resources to work on the assembly line. If the conveyor belt slows down and fewer companies exit, it means new companies cannot be added to the assembly line as quickly. When the line again speeds up to a normal pace, then more entrepreneurs are invited to add their companies to the system.

Note that a slowdown on the pace of the assembly line does not mean that the workers on the line have all quit and gone home. The assembly process may simply have become more complex, with each little company requiring more attention as it goes down the line.

Perhaps it might have helped if, during the frenzied period of investment in start-ups, our assembly line had employed a few more quality control inspectors to pull the obviously defective companies off the line before they got too far along and used up a lot of time and money.

ADVICE FROM AN ANGEL

Tom Horgan, AZTEC Venture Networks, San Diego, CA

Have you noticed any change in Angels' interest level after the stock market entered a bearish phase in 2001? "No, the appetite is steady. The individuals in our group are substantially wealthy enough. They have made their money preboom, it is not new money. The realization is that we will probably see a dramatic reduction in business plans. Interestingly enough, we have not seen that yet.

"We are still looking. There is a belief that if new technologies are significant enough, there will be a need for them. The returns may not be quite as high.

"One thing we do like is that valuations have become reasonable again and management that we're seeing have gotten their senses again."

Have the more ridiculous deals, or weaker companies, dropped out of the competition for capital? "Yes. The crazy element is gone. Collectively, we view this as a good thing all around."

ADVICE FROM AN ANGEL

Barry Moltz, Co-founder, Prairie Angels, www.prairieangels.org

How much have angels backed off after the dot.com bubble burst in 2000? "The environment is getting more difficult. Wealth in America has dissipated as the stock markets have declined. For the first time in 55 years America's wealth dropped. The result is the average angel who was putting in $100,000 today is putting in 50; the guy who was putting in 50 now is putting in 25; and the guy who was putting in 25 is out of the game. People's commitments have dropped by about 50 percent. The angel group that we started in Chicago in 1999 (Prairie Angels) initially was looking at making investments of $1 million; we're looking at investments of $350 thousand to $500 thousand in individual deals now."

The point is, though, you're still investing. "We're trying to, but we're not investing in anything that is related to the Internet or software. The first investment that the organization is going to do is one that provides shock absorbers for metal bending equipment for the auto industry. Another one that was very popular at the last meeting was a company that provides microbes that eat sewage."

Going back to basics then. Really back to basics in the latter case. "The other aspect is that we're expecting the companies to be further along than we were a year or two ago. We're expecting the companies to have customers and revenue, and to have proven their concept already."

The entrepreneur looking for capital must have reached certain milestones. "Much more than in the past. Very few businesses can get funded with just two guys and a business plan."

ADVICE FROM A VENTURE CAPITALIST WHO IS AN ANGEL

Frank A. McGrew IV, Managing Director, Paradigm Capital Partners, Memphis, TN, www.memphisangels.com

Have the individual angels lost interest to some extent in doing this type of financing, since the financial markets have declined and the IPO activity dropped? "When we started the Memphis Angels, we never really did the pure dot.coms. In fact, our first investment, which was in late 2000, was a fiber optic buildout with our local utility here in Memphis. What's been interesting is the angels have stepped outside what I expected their appetite would be for investing. They've actually increased their commitment to this category because valuations have changed.

"In late 1999 a later-stage company may have thought its valuation was $50 million, whereas today it may only be single digits. Some of the angels that thought they only wanted to do early stage companies now have the opportunity to do some later stage companies at very attractive prices."

ADVICE FROM AN ANGEL

Bob Bozeman, General Partner, Angel Investors LP, www.svangel.com

How has angel investing changed in the last 10 years? "In Silicon Valley, I think the angel investing model got a jolt forward because of so much wealth being created by the Internet world. People made good money there, got their money out and, because they were so young, started to reapply the money back into what they really knew, the Internet space. That's why there was so much froth there. The last five years were really good years for the public markets, and the public markets created a lot of wealth everywhere. Those entrepreneurs that wanted to reapply themselves again and again were the best of the angel community. The venture capital firms started to get so much money that they needed help at that earlier stage, so there was a hand-in-glove movement that helped everybody."

Does angel investing closely follow that of venture capital firms? "Look at it this way: for angels, on the one hand a neutron bomb went off because the value of the equities they held went down so much. And on the other hand, if they were going to be bold and do some start-up funding only to find that there's no follow-up funding for their opportunities, their money is out there dangling in the wind at a very high risk. So, I think they've had tremendous pressures to just go into a shell like the VCs have done."

When do you think this rough climate will end? "The end game really dictates that. When the IPO markets pick up again, that's when the whole chain starts moving through again. You have a group of planes that took off that thought they would land with an IPO during the frothy period. All of a sudden, all the VCs became air traffic controllers. And the angels became an extension of that. Every time they fueled up a plane to take off, they'd look out and see, this has no destination. So everyone's waiting for the order to come back, when planes can take off and land according to a scheduling process.

"For angel investors, the negative effect is that they are going to lose a lot of money. There's risk because those planes that fall out of the sky because of lack of fueling will have passengers on board that are going to go down with the plane. I think the froth period was too extreme. That's why you have support levels in all markets. You get back to the point where you take stock and say, things aren't that bad. Here's the stuff we can learn from and now let's push it up back to where it should be."

ANGELS AND THE NET

It is clear that the Internet will continue to shape the financial world just as it has transformed other areas of our lives.

ADVICE FROM AN ANGEL

Craig W. Johnson, Chairman, Venture Law Group, www.vlg.com

How do you see the Internet changing angel investing? "I think the Internet is simply a method of facilitating the transfer of a great deal of information. I find it is possible for an angel investor to cast a much wider net in terms of investment opportunities, and, more importantly, to perform due diligence on a company and an industry much more quickly than ever before.

"It used to be the case that many angels had limited visibility of the competitive landscape. But now competitive analysis of potential investments can be completed in a matter of minutes. I think angel investors tend to be better informed today. The Internet has made it possible to see many more investment opportunities. Garage.com is one example of an organization that has made it possible for wealthy individuals to reach out. On the other hand, I think that angel investing is primarily a face-to-face business, and although the Internet can facilitate putting people together, investment decisions are almost always made on the basis of eyeball-to-eyeball meetings between investors and entrepreneurs. It really comes down to an act of commitment or an act of trust or faith on the part of the investor that the entrepreneurial team is on the right track, and will make the investor more money than he puts in. You are really betting on the team to execute on the vision. The basic concept of the company, the industry, the opportunity can be much more easily researched on the Internet, but the gut decision to make the decision happens only after the entrepreneur and the investor meet."

The Environment of Angel Investing Is Constantly Changing . . . And Will Continue to Do So

Angel investing is not a static market; it is an evolutionary one, and has seen tremendous growth and volatility in the past decade. In some way it has even greater mood swings than the public equity markets.

ADVICE FROM AN EXPERT

Angel Investing Has Evolved in the Last Decade

Quinn Williams, Partner, Snell & Wilmer Law Offices, www.swlaw.com

For years, traditional angel investing involved one or more notable business types inviting their friends to participate in a promising new deal. Rarely was the management team asked to make a presentation to the prospective investors, rather it was the strength of the sponsors' reputations that other investors relied upon in joining the funding groups. As a result, angel investment was often a secret process based exclusively on who you knew, not how good your deal was.

However, the last decade has seen dramatic changes in the angel investing process, resulting in significant growth in the amount of angel investment funding, which can be traced to these main factors:

Increased Number as Well as Size of Venture Capital Funds. The venture capital industry has gone through a historic increase in the amount of capital under management by venture capitalists during the last 10 years. Now it is routine for new funds to approach a billion dollars in size. This has dramatically increased the demand for venture backable deals. In the rush to get this money out, many VC [firms] skipped the diligence process and deal-review discipline and often funded deals based solely on work and reputation of other VC funds promoting the deal. The current size of VC funds has stressed the deal supply chain. The effect of these mega funds has created a definite gap opportunity for angels because most funds have raised their per-deal size and involved their stage of funding to a later larger round. Angels are now required to fund the early stage and development rounds until a VC round can be justified on a size of investment and valuation basis.

Unparalleled Growth in Capital Markets. In the last seven to eight years, we have witnessed one of the highest growth rates in the capital markets in history. This has fostered an appetite for additional new issuances of equity which has stimulated venture fund creation and overall demand for equity capital. Demographics and tax policy played a leading role in stimulating this market activity. The resultant wealth created has increased both the number and pool of angel funds looking for private equity.

Structural Formation Angel Networks. Angel investing started to take on a formal structure in the late 1990s. The Band of Angels of Silicon Valley, which was begun by Hans Severiens, was typical of the types of groups. The emergence of the Internet/on-line groups led to the development of more open architecture so that promising entrepreneurs could have access based upon the quality of their deal, not necessarily their business contacts. In addition to on-line services, the emergence of the equity capital conferences and incubators, both for-profit and nonprofit, provided alternative networked communities in which investors and angels could be introduced. As a result of this structural change, investors seeking angel investment were required to develop presentation skills, fill out their board of directors, and develop well thought out executive summaries as required by the structure of these angel groups.

Angel Investor Environment. The result of all these forces is that angel investment is at an all-time record high. As we began the new millennium, most angel groups now require some exit strategy with a 50 percent targeted rate of return. The enormity of the appetite of VC funds under management will require angels to help fill the need for new deals. As a result, many promoters will be attempting to structure the angel business. These finders will sample local Angel Networks. National networks using the Internet will also grow. Off Road Capital and Garage.com are examples of networks that seek to provide deal flow to high net-worth investors looking for that "Home Run." Inevitably, the appetite of the capital markets will return to consume quality angel deals and put them in the pipeline for VC investment.

More than ever, the entrepreneurs seeking capital will need to evolve their skills to meet these changes; the success of entrepreneurial educational programs, such as bootcamps, will remain a popular education format. Also, sophistication of angels helps them understand that angel investment is just a bridge hopefully to a later VC round. The changes to the VC market now require that angels first discern which companies will be venture backable before they invest. Although only fools predict the future, I expect that many VC firms and angel networks will partner and develop formal sponsoring/referral relationships to compete for and assist the top entrepreneurs in accessing the capital markets. Angel Investing has become a central component in the venture capital new deal supply chain. It will continue to evolve and be shaped by the changes of the VC market requirements and the hopeful entrepreneurs that need access to it.

ADVICE FROM AN ANGEL

Lore Harp McGovern

How has angel investing changed since you have gotten involved, and what do you see for the future? "Deal flow is still very strong today. Three or four years ago, when we were in incredible economic well-being, people funded opportunities without really thinking about the potential success; they believed all these companies were going to go IPO and multiples were going through the roof. Raising money was relatively easy, even getting second rounds. Starting about a year and a half ago, that scenario changed. Companies that met all the criteria that investors typically set, had a very difficult time getting that second round of funding.

"What I am seeing now is much more caution. The whole process of due diligence has become more prevalent. People take more time to check things out. Valuations have come down. Investors are expecting profitability. It has come full cycle and we are back to basics.

"I think one of the keys for making investments today is to make sure you work with some VC firms and keep them involved right from the start. Angels do the grunt work and take the major, major risk in getting the company launched. But knowing that you have a relationship with a firm that is willing to watch the process and then step up to the plate for Series B is very important.

"I am very diversified in my investment. I did not do a lot of dot.com stuff, I did real technologies. I look at something where you build real value, where you build a real asset."

Chapter Summary

- We have seen rampant optimism in early-stage investing in 1999 and 2000, followed by a swing to widespread pessimism in 2001. As valuations of early-stage companies have returned to more normal levels, so has angel investor enthusiasm returned to more normal, but healthy levels. Serious angels are still investing, but with a greater degree of caution.
- The dollar amount of angel investment should get a boost from new investment vehicles that make it easier for individuals to participate.
- The Internet is facilitating the flow of information, making analysis of industries and companies easier for angels.

CHAPTER

3

What Is an Angel Investor?

Several studies have been completed in the area of angel research, most notably by the Center for Venture Research, University of New Hampshire, Marakon Associates, and Harvard University. Most of these studies have researched angel investors by querying the CEO of the company that the angels have invested in, or by sending questionnaires to the management of angel networks, angel alliances, or matching services to describe their members' preferences.

The angel survey information presented here and throughout the other chapters of this book is based on a survey completed by our company, Profit Dynamics, in mid- to late 2001. Individuals who have been known to invest in private companies were asked to complete a survey of 10 questions, two of which were essay-type questions, and the remainder multiple-choice or ranking. The survey also asked for age, education level, whether the individual completing the survey was accredited as defined by the Securities and Exchange Commission, and the average amount invested per company per investment made.

The 50 individuals completing the survey resided in various geographic areas of the country including Southern and Northern California, Pacific Northwest, Southwest, Midwest, the South, and the East Coast. Although it is known that nearly all the respondents were male, at least two females participated.

Demographics

ACCREDITED

Of the 50 angels, 48 said they were accredited, and 2 declined to answer the question.

THE AVERAGE AMOUNT OF INVESTMENT

The average amount invested by the individual angel is $72,000. The range most often given was between $20,000 and $35,000, with the highest range of $250,000 to $500,000.

AVERAGE AGE OF AN ANGEL

The average age of the respondents was 49. More precisely, 54 percent were between the ages of 46 and 55, 25 percent were between the ages of 36 and 45, 13 percent were between the ages of 56 and 65, 4 percent were between the ages of 66 and 75, and 4 percent were between the ages of 25 and 35 years old. The youngest angel was 25. No angel admitted to being older than 75.

EXPERIENCE IN INVESTING

Of the angels 78 percent had more than five years of experience investing in private companies, 11 percent had less than 1 year of experience, and 11 percent had from 3 to 4 years of experience.

EDUCATION LEVEL

Of the respondents 75 percent had graduate degrees, an additional 17 percent had graduated from college, and 8 percent had at least attended college.

Other attributes, such as how long it takes an angel to close a deal, the expected return on investment, how angels value a transaction, and what angels feel is the most critical mistake entrepreneurs make in their business plan, are covered in the relevant chapters.

Angels are amazingly active in private equity investing:

- They invested over $40 billion in about 50,000 companies for the year ended June 2000.
- As many as 3 million people in the United States have made an angel investment.
- Nearly two-thirds of funding for new enterprises is obtained from angels.[1]

The ranks of angel investors have been growing markedly in recent years, and they are likely to continue to grow in the future. New angels appear each day, created by the amazing and enduring prosperity of the American economy. In 1998, by contrast to the year 2000 figures, angels had invested $20 billion in 30,000 companies. And these numbers are lower than reality; a lot of angel investments simply are difficult to count because these are private transactions that receive no publicity and are not recorded in the way that real estate transactions are, for example.

Other Angel Characteristics

It is difficult to generalize about a group of people that differ so in age, background, location, and investment experience. A few things do emerge when you view angels as a group:

They pursue companies in a wide sphere of industries, although technology companies are popular.

They invest all over the country; there are pockets of concentrated angel investment, such as Silicon Valley, but in general angels are widely dispersed.

[1]*Source*: Center for Venture Research at University of New Hampshire.

Most of them are active to a degree in the companies they invest in. Entrepreneurs who hope that angel investors just purchase equity and then go away are not being realistic. Entrepreneurs who recognize the need for help, and welcome the participation of the angel investor, are much more likely to complete a transaction with an angel.

ADVICE FROM AN ANGEL

Luis Villalobos, Founder and Director, Tech Coast Angels, www.techcoastangel.com

What misconceptions do entrepreneurs have about angel investors? "One is that angels want to take over their business. The other would be that angels want a huge part of the equity. In our case, we explain to entrepreneurs that because of the large number of deals we do, the last thing we want is to take an active role in the management of the company. We can be active as directors or advisors, but we don't have the time or inclination to get involved beyond that. Most of us have been entrepreneurs ourselves, and we understand the difference between being an advisor and being involved in management."

The Amount of Angel Capital Available Has Barely Been Tapped

According to some estimates, there are 6 million individuals in the United States that qualify as accredited investors, who, by definition, are people with net worth that exceeds $1 million.

Let's suppose the average size of their investment portfolio were $1.5 million, probably a conservative assumption. Let's further suppose these investors decided to put a reasonable and prudent 10 percent of their assets into private-equity investments, at the rate of 2 percent per year, reinvested every five years.

The result: $180 billion per year would be available for angel investing in each year, about five times the amount that takes place today. No entrepreneur would be able to say, "there's no money out there."

According to data from Venture Economics and the National Venture Capital Association, VC firms invested in just 7,000 companies in 2000. Angels were involved with 50,000 companies, VC firms with one-seventh as many. The difference is even more striking when you consider that only 28 percent of the investments made by venture capitalists were in early-stage companies—the market that angels clearly concentrate on. More striking still when you again consider it is virtually impossible to count all the angel deals done in a given year because they are private transactions that may involve a relatively small amount of money.

They may be called angels, but they definitely do not have their heads in the clouds. They are, for the most part, experienced, pragmatic business people on a mission to build small companies into large ones and along the way make money, hopefully lots of it.

And who are these angel investors, anyway?

- Bored retired guys looking for something to do?
- Philanthropic individuals who want to help younger entrepreneurial people succeed?
- Blind squirrels in search of an acorn?
- Rich people who want to socialize with other rich people?
- Smooth operators who want to take over an unsuspecting entrepreneur's company?
- Greedy people who want to earn the return on investment they hear the venture capitalists do?
- People who want to share their experience and wisdom?
- People who are so wealthy they have money to throw away on risky deals?
- Community leaders who want to help build local businesses?

THEIR NAME DOESN'T NECESSARILY DESCRIBE THEIR ACTIONS

Does the term *angel* itself lead to erroneous conclusions, and exaggerated expectations regarding how these investors really operate? Many angels hate using the term angel to describe their investment activity. It sounds too ethereal, and they see themselves as decidedly down to earth. Perhaps a better term would be Active Financial Partner (AFP), because many times that's what they really are. They are usually actively involved in companies they invest in, they provide financing and financial assistance, and they view the relationship with the entrepreneur as one of partnership. They are also sometimes called wealthy individuals, but that isn't totally correct either, because many of these invest through entities such as family partnerships, or even through their own corporations. *Accredited investor* is another term, but that really relates more to specific criteria about their financial capability rather than describing what they are.

Angels also don't like the term *angel* because it conveys an image of someone who watches over you and then swoops in when there is trouble. They are trying to avoid trouble and make money. They don't really want the image of a winged rescuer.

ADVICE FROM AN ANGEL

Steve Miller, Co-founder, Prairie Angels, www.prairieangels.org,

Could you give us a profile of the background of the angels in Prairie Angels? "It's interesting. In Chicago we have a mix of new money—people who have started high-tech companies and been successful in selling them—and there's also older money. One interesting twist we have in Chicago, and I'm certainly an example of that, is second generations of successful family businesses. We have several folks in our group who are the sons of people who have started companies that became quite successful and made the families wealthy."

They are a younger group, then, and they bring a lot of energy to the table as well as money. "Yes. Most of us are in our thirties and early forties. So we had operating experience with our family businesses. And I'm talking about significant family businesses with revenues in the hundreds of millions and billions of dollars. So these are not mom and pop ice cream shops. Like good angels should, we have the expertise to do more than write a check. We can roll up our sleeves and help the company based on our experience and our contacts."

Does this younger generation of angels relate a little better to the entrepreneurs? "I think that we do, because we are closer in age. We speak the same language. We grew up with computers as second nature. Technology has been a part of our lives, whereas with the older generation that is not necessarily the case. So they are more skeptical of technology."

Are there professional people like doctors, lawyers involved, or people from industry? "There are several lawyers that are involved. One interesting section of the group comes from the Chicago Board of Trade and other financial exchanges. There are a lot of folks who made significant money trading; and these folks by nature are somewhat . . . whatever the opposite of risk averse is."

Is There an Angel Out There for Everyone?

No. Even angels are not necessarily attracted to all types of companies. Their interest level still depends on many of the same factors venture capitalists look at—potential growth of the company, profit margins, size of the market, the possibility of exiting the investment with a high rate of return. The corner yogurt shop is not a good candidate for angel investment; family and friends are a better alternative—someone who knows you. These people can balance the risk vs. reward and make the equation work for them: Part of the reward they will receive is just in helping you succeed. The angel investor who is a stranger, after all, is not so concerned with your success from a personal standpoint. Angels still need this growth-and-profitability potential in order to assume the risk of putting money in your early-stage company.

ADVICE FROM AN ANGEL

Ian Patrick Sobieski, Ph.D., Managing Member, Band of Angels, www.bandangels.com

Can you tell us about the membership of The Band of Angels? "The Band of Angels is a hybrid early-stage venture organization made up of 150 high net worth individuals and a $50 thousand venture fund. The angel group was started in 1995 and admits only those who have started or run high-technology companies. The average age of a member is 58 years old, though the youngest is 36 and the oldest is 75. The membership is made up of a cross-section of high-technology categories, from biotech to semiconductor, from networking software to Internet consumer businesses."

Capital allows you to start your company. This is what entrepreneurs often think the importance of obtaining outside investment from angels is. Actually, however, capital allows you to grow your business at an accelerated rate. This growth rate creates equity value. Growth that creates equity value is what is on the minds of investors.

We have had many entrepreneurs come to us with very small-scale ideas, and ask, "Where can I find an angel?" Every entrepreneur, it seems, is convinced they need an angel investor, everyone thinks they can go out and get one. It is very difficult for many of them to grasp the fact that angels share many of the characteristics of venture capitalists in the scope of opportunities available to them.

ADVICE FROM AN ANGEL

Greg Cobb, Managing Partner, Arizona Angels Investors Network, www.arizonaangels.com

Can you tell us about the membership of Arizona Angels? "It was established in January 1999, and has grown to over 100 members. The average age is probably around 55 years or so, I believe our youngest member is 31 and our oldest 70, so there's quite a range. Our members come from generally three types of industries: (1) finance (commercial banking, investment banking, venture capital, etc.); (2) technology (start-ups and established companies); and (3) traditional industries (manufacturing, real estate, etc.). Most of the members have been involved in private investing for a number of years. All have been successful business people. We target members with knowledge, contacts, and capital. Since 1999 Arizona Angels has invested approximately $3.5 million in 7 companies with over $15M in additional capital raised."

ADVICE FROM AN EXPERT

Cliff J. Grant, President, LocalFund.com, Inc., Billings, MT, www.localfund.com

Mr. Grant's company provides infrastructure for Montana Private Capital Network, an on-line forum matching angels with Montana entrepreneurs.

Could you characterize the background of the angels in your group? "Our investors are typically high-net worth individuals who have either returned to their hometowns or states or have lived there most of their lives. They are typically business owners. Most are successful entrepreneurs. Almost none are retired, but they are still active in the local business community. Age range is typically 40 to 55. Almost all are male; however, I know many who get input from their wives and share the investing experience with them."

Chapter Summary

- An "average angel" is someone 49 years of age, well educated, who has been investing five years or more and puts over $70 thousand in each individual deal.
- Angel investors have greatly increased their level of activity over the last five years.
- Angel groups' memberships in some cases have a high-tech focus, others have broader backgrounds including finance, professional services, and low-tech Old Economy industries. Most groups have a number of members who have founded companies that became large and successful, truly leaders of the U.S. economy.

CHAPTER

4

Why Do People Want to Be Angels?

What can be said is that angels have a complex set of objectives for getting involved with early-stage companies, and the entrepreneur has to get a feel for what these are because they vary widely by individual.

Some angels want to create a job for themselves out of the investment, or a job for their sons or daughters.

Some want to be part of the club that is making investments, and then can tell colleagues: "Hey, Bob, let me tell you about this great new wireless deal I'm in."

Some get a thrill out of seeing a company they assist blossom into a success.

Some do want to earn a rate of return like they've heard the venture capitalists have been earning.

Many believe the lessons they have learned operating their own companies can be successfully applied to new situations; the knowledge is, therefore, valuable because it is transferable.

Dinner and a Show

Some angels in angel networks are clearly involved for the social aspects, a kind of interactive dinner theater for rich people, where the entrepreneurs are paraded in and make their presentation, and the investors then take turns asking hard questions. When you take away the social aspects, you remove an important feature of this whole angel-investment process. Angels also tend to rely on their peers for validation of a potential investment. Being part of an angel group provides each member with great networking opportunities as well, the chance to meet other successful, even celebrated entrepreneurs who are their peers.

Many of the groups admit members with great care, like posh country clubs, so there is much prestige associated in being invited into the group. It is a wonder the angels don't get lockers with their names on them, where they can keep extra pairs of shoes.

To Pass Along Hard-Won Knowledge

Many angels believe that they have valuable positive and negative experiences to share with others. The chance to mentor others is high on the list of most frequently cited reasons for getting involved in this activity. With some angels, it is expressed almost as though they are doing charity work or service to the community. They are quite sincere about the importance of passing on what they have learned. It is also interesting to note that the angel enjoys passing along the experience and advice regardless of whether the advice is heeded by the entrepreneur starting the new company.

ADVICE FROM AN ANGEL

Barry Moltz, Co-founder, Prairie Angels, www.prairieangels.org

What attracted you to being an angel? "I've had both success and failure as an entrepreneur, and I guess I was driven to take that experience and help people, so hopefully they wouldn't make some of the same mistakes I've made along the way. I was a little bit burned out at running my own businesses, so I wanted to see how I would do as an advisor rather than an operator. I was seeking to build those skills. But I know sometime I'll go back to being the operator of a company."

ADVICE FROM AN ANGEL

Lore Harp McGovern

Why did you want to become an angel investor? "To apply the experiences I have gathered in the last 25 years in running technology-related companies. I felt I could bring a lot to the table in terms of experience and I had the resources to invest, so I got enthusiastically involved in angel investments."

How long have you been doing this? "For the last four years I have made investments in 15 companies, although I have made investments in small companies for the last 10 or 15 years."

Get 'Em While They're Hot

At the firm's earliest stage, valuation of the company is typically at its lowest. For the investor with the iron stomach, who can digest the high degree of risk this investing entails, you purchase a larger chunk of equity for the best price you ever will be able to. If the company is successful, this large chunk of equity will translate into a tremendous return on your invested capital.

It is also the chance to get in on the next hot technology. This can be extremely exciting, when you sit in a room with the other investors and the founding management team, and begin to explore just how fast the company could grow. Angel investing can be almost like a thrill ride at the amusement park, except they don't strap you in quite as securely as they do at Magic Mountain.

ADVICE FROM AN ANGEL

Brent Townshend

What is your motivation for being an angel investor? "For me, I am interested in start-up companies, and have been involved in building companies from the start-up stage myself. I enjoy helping out other people who are doing the same thing. I try to be useful in both funding and advising."

What is the excitement of being involved in early-stage companies? "The most interesting thing I find is being exposed to new ideas and seeing how different people approach the process of starting a company. You get a lot of young people doing this (entrepreneurship) who are full of energy. In some cases they are trying to tackle problems that are too hard, but they don't know they are too hard, so they do it anyway and they succeed."

Some of Our Best Friends Are Greedy

What about angels who are just in it for the money, instead of to help the entrepreneur or for other seemingly altruistic reasons? Some angels are very up front about their motivation: making 10 times their money and then selling out. Have a nice life, company founder, but I'm outta here. They are not mentors or guardians of the entrepreneurial dream. It's all about cash.

The problem is that excessive greed tends to make people chase after things, but then become quickly disillusioned when the results are not as fabulous as planned. Greedy people tend to be less patient with entrepreneurs. You could argue that flighty angels are better than none at all. But it seems as though greed brings people into this marketplace, but the less tangible rewards of watching the *process* of the company growing and succeeding keep them there.

Angels cannot be like day traders who enthusiastically go long one day, and sell short the next because of some whispered bad news about the company. The ability to hang in there is a vital characteristic of angel investors.

The Need to Stay in the Game

It can be difficult to turn the reins of a company you built over to the new owners when you sell it. The next best thing to starting a new venture of your own is to participate in the birth of a company founded by someone else. Almost all of these former owners or founders of successful companies have lived lives of more than 80-hour work weeks. Boredom can set in quickly for these people once they sell their companies. This highlights a potential peril for the entrepreneur bringing in angel investors: Can a person used to running the show let someone else be in the limelight?

ADVICE FROM AN ANGEL

Ian Patrick Sobieski, Ph.D., Managing Member, Band of Angels, www.bandangels.com

Why does a wealthy individual want to be an angel? "They want to stay in the game, but not stay up to 2 A.M. anymore. They are much less interested in the financial reward from doing this. The amount of money they put into these kinds of angel investments is their hobby money. Their accountants wouldn't let them put a substantial portion of their wealth into these kinds of risky private equities. So, financial reward—a tenfold return—is more of a trophy to put on a shelf than a way of increasing personal wealth. As such, they differ dramatically from the common conception of angel investors that has cropped up recently with the Internet technology bubble: people who were trying to make a quick buck. Folks who had a few million dollars in net worth and would put $1 million into early-stage deals with the hope of getting $10 million out at the end of that. Really jumping to the next level of wealth. That's not what our angels are about, but it's what some angels are about.

"What drives angels into this kind of business is as variable as the many variables that constitute an individual's personality. Fundamentally, it is because angels are investing their own money, so they are the only people they have to answer to. Venture capitalists are much more uniform in their attitude, because they are investing other people's money and the terms under which they do that are pretty uniform across the country, so you can always understand their motivation and why they are in the business."

ADVICE FROM AN ANGEL

David Burwen

What was your motivation to want to invest in early-stage companies? "I was a founding executive of a successful start-up that went public in 1996. A year later I realized that I was getting tired of the 80-to-100-hour start-up workweeks. However, I didn't want my life to be simply play—going out, buying things, and traveling. I wanted to have a more fulfilling and interesting life with a higher purpose. To do this, I decided to devote 50 percent of my time to helping entrepreneurs build new companies; I think this adds significant value to our society by creating new jobs and technologies that can improve people's lives. I targeted 20 percent of my time to doing community service projects, especially working to improve public education. For the remaining time I wanted to play. I hadn't had much time for international adventure traveling and wanted the opportunity to do this while my body was still capable of such activities."

MONEY DOESN'T MAKE THEIR WORLD GO 'ROUND

It may seem odd to us that someone who invests their money would say that the rate of return is not of primary concern. In the world of publicly traded stocks, performance is everything. We love our stocks when they go up; we get very mad at them when they go down. Angels are very different: The experienced ones remain committed to their investments in good times and bad. The angels cannot really calculate their profits until much later, as long as five years later. In the meantime, they look to other measurements of the company's progress, such as revenue growth, or establishing important strategic partnerships. For a long time, investors just watch as their money is spent.

THE STIMULATION OF MANY ACTIVITIES AT ONCE

We've all found ourselves at one time or another bored or stagnating in our job. It becomes routine, the same thing every day. Angels do not suffer from this malady, particularly those who juggle a number of ventures at once, in different industries. Keeping up with it all becomes a major challenge, and the same angel who thought he was trading in 80-hour work weeks for a 20-hour/month hobby, may find that working with a half-dozen start-ups at once can seem like a full time job.

ADVICE FROM AN ANGEL

Steve Harari

What made you want to become an angel investor? "The excitement of being able to work in multiple ventures simultaneously instead of being locked into one company—which had really been my background. I spent 20 years in industry working at executive positions. The chance to work with four or five management teams simultaneously was a diversity that I thought would be very interesting."

Has it turned out that way? "Yes it has, it has been fascinating. I might differentiate myself from some other angels because I'm doing this full time. It's not a hobby or something on the side. I'm doing it 40 to 50 hours per week. Probably the majority of angels you will meet are semiretired or they have a day job and do this part time."

ADVICE FROM AN ANGEL

Bob Bozeman, General Partner, Angel Investors, LP
www.svangel.com

What motivates a person to become an angel investor? "There is money to be made. But the psychic rewards of entrepreneurship are huge. I think the problems of building a small business are really like a board game with thousands of possible moves. All the different personalities you are dealing with, all the market demands that you are dealing with. All the things you have to tweak to make it all work are really fabulous.

"People who love business love entrepreneurism because it is business at its best."

WHY WOULD YOU, A WEALTHY PERSON, NOT WANT TO BE AN ANGEL?

There are so many fun, challenging, exciting aspects to angel investing, it is a wonder more millionaires don't get involved in this activity. But this isn't for everyone.

There are many wealthy people who are risk averse, either by their basic nature or because they are at the time of their life when they want to relax and not worry about things as volatile as venture investing. They have worked hard all their lives, have 15 pairs of plaid pants in their closet, and think it's time they finally went golfing.

Many wealthy people (wisely) decline to get involved in angel investing simply because they do not have the acquired business wisdom to judge the merits or potential of a start-up company.

The need to be in control may make them uncomfortable with this area of investing.

Liquidity is also of concern for many people. Many wealthy people find it comforting to have their assets in investment vehicles that can be quickly liquidated or converted into something else in a matter of days or even hours. A five-year holding period for an investment, as many early-stage ventures entail, makes them very uncomfortable.

Entrepreneurs are sometimes very surprised to find, when they contact well-known business people in their community about investing in their ventures, that these people are not the least bit interested, and decline before listening to the pitch. No amount of convincing will change their minds, either.

Chapter Summary

- Angels are motivated by many things, but surprisingly, money is not the most important.
- Not all wealthy people are potential angel candidates.

CHAPTER

5

The Challenges of Being an Angel

The Angel's Challenges Are Myriad

Let's look at this from the angel's standpoint for a moment. It is very hard to find quality deals. There is more risk to this type of investing than investing in publicly traded securities. You have to stay in the investment much longer; it is not liquid, you can't just call up your broker and sell. It is more hassle to perform due diligence and close the deal. There are negotiations and legal fees involved. You have to watch the investment after closing, and lend a hand to the company to help it grow, and even more of a hand if it struggles. If you are one of 10 people who each put up $100,000, how much real clout do you have in the strategic direction of the company?

In other words, everything about being an angel is a challenge. The entrepreneur may say, "So what, why do I care if it is hard to be an angel?" The entrepreneur needs to care because if he can employ some strategies to make the investor's task easier, he can improve his chances of finding capital.

Finding Good Deals

ADVICE FROM AN ANGEL

Steve Harari

How do you find the companies you invest in? "I use every conceivable means. I have worked diligently to establish a network. This included belonging to angel groups, such as Band of Angels. I keep close affiliations with Stanford University, where I was an alum from the business school. And from the various companies I have worked with, the entrepreneurs have referred me to other entrepreneurs. And the last company I was the CEO of spawned, maybe, a dozen new ventures itself. So it's been a combination of many different sources."

We have heard angels remark with a sigh, "I just haven't had a lot of deals come across my desk lately." This is an example of the less proactive type of angel who views deal flow as a matter of chance, or at least out of his or her control. What is the chance a given entrepreneur could ever find this particular low-profile angel? With venture capital firms, it is not only easy to find them in published directories and online databases, but it is possible to find readily what types of deals they have done in the past to see how well yours matches up with their criteria. Many angels, and certainly their investment preferences, remain a mystery to entrepreneurs.

Mr. Harari's statement, "I use every conceivable means," is interesting because it is precisely the same advice we always give entrepreneurs when they ask how to find angels. Use every means you can think of: networking at events, going through professionals who work with angels, ask intermediaries for assistance. The goal is to have as wide a net as possible. Investors have just as difficult a time finding you as you have finding them. And the problem is, as they widen their net to catch the big tuna, they net a lot of deals that smell as though they are already dead. The angel's challenge is to create a network that will bring them the cream-of-the-crop deals.

Assuming you have a prime opportunity, how can you, the entrepreneur, make it less challenging for the angel to find you?

Angels fly in formation, so you need to meet the lead angels in your area.

Analyzing the Opportunity

ADVICE FROM AN ANGEL

Steve Miller, Co-founder, Prairie Angels, www.prairieangels.org

What if an angel has made his or her money in the meat packing business, and decides to jump on the high-technology bandwagon. How do angels even begin to analyze technologies they have no background in? "To me, and I practice what I preach, the most effective and successful angel investors will be the ones who invest in what they know, so that somebody who made their money in meat packing should invest in new meat-packing technologies. They probably wouldn't have as much fun or be as successful if they invest in say, new wireless technologies, because they don't know anything about that. They can't add any value to that opportunity above and beyond the check they can write. My motivation is to invest in what I know, work at building great companies based on my experience, and invest that experience alongside my money. I don't invest in things I don't know about."

Steve Miller's strategy is to stay close to home, both geographically and in the type of company he chose to get involved with. Venture capitalists approach due diligence in a very formal, even standardized way, and they have the contacts in place to check out everything about the company—the technology, the management team's background, the company's claims about the size of the market. Angels often have a more intuitive approach based on talking with members of the management team. Venture capitalists are so structured in how they conduct due diligence that many entrepreneurs are a little bit frightened of them. Therefore, many entrepreneurs are more comfortable discussing their company with angels, who seem more like fellow entrepreneurs.

How can you help make this easier for angels? Approach the angels with the same degree of preparedness you would if you were meeting with a large VC firm. Practice your presentation and make sure you can answer the questions the angels are likely to ask. Give them names of people they can contact to quickly verify the information contained in your business plan.

It helps as well to find out whether the angels have deep knowledge of your market space or technology. If not, you may have to have more material available to help educate them. Because they do not have staffs to gather all of this material, you can motivate angels a little bit more if you do some of this work for them.

The ideal situation, as Steve Miller noted above, is to find angels who know a lot about your industry. They can more readily ratify the strength of the opportunity than those who are just learning about your industry for the first time.

Learning How to Be an Angel. Or, Now I've Landed a Good Company, What Do I Do with It?

Can you dabble at angel investing? The short answer is no. It takes an education process in the techniques of deal selection and evaluation and a willingness to roll up your sleeves and assist the companies. There are lots of resources available for mentoring companies. More are needed for mentoring angels, to help make them comfortable with the process of investing in early-stage companies.

Venture conferences around the nation now regularly feature sessions that address how to get started as an angel investor. The Oregon Entrepreneurs Forum, for example, hosts an annual conference on angel investing. These are particularly useful in places outside the VC hubs, such as Silicon Valley and the Northeast, where angels congregate and have natural opportunities for networking and sharing knowledge.

Why is this important for the entrepreneur? An angel who is experienced, or takes the time to learn how to successfully be an angel, will likely be a better partner for an entrepreneur than a newbie angel who is just jumping into the market because he has heard you can make a lot of money. If it is clear from the meetings that the angel talks the language of deal making fluently, it can make the whole process run more smoothly and professionally.

Experienced angels, who have had perhaps a few successes as well as failures, are also better choices because you do not have to worry that they don't understand the risks they are taking. They are less likely to become disenchanted if the company takes longer to develop than planned. Experienced investors know that it almost always takes longer for a company to develop than planned.

ADVICE FROM AN ANGEL

Ian Patrick Sobieski, Ph.D., Managing Member, Band of Angels, www.bandangels.com

What are the difficulties in getting started as an angel? "The reason many potential angels around the country don't get involved is because they don't have the expertise to analyze deal flow, and even if they did, they probably wouldn't get good deal flow. Success depends on a combination of: what do you know, and how can you bring that to bear on the investments you make, and how are you going to find good investments?

"We're very blessed in Silicon Valley because this is a hotbed of innovation, with the combination of the universities, the capital markets, and the good weather, we attract the best and the brightest. There are few other concentrations like this around the country. We have a good fertile bed for deals, and so if you are a person who knows something about technology, then you can count on being able to get these deals. I don't know what we would do if we were stuck in Duluth."

What are some of the challenges of being an angel, especially an organized group? "The challenges we face are exactly the challenges an institutional venture capitalist faces: filtering the wheat from the chaff at the front end, negotiating a set of terms that align the incentives of the investors and the entrepreneur, and then mentoring that deal, taking care of it, post-deal management is what I call it. That is managing the growth of the company, husbanding its resources, holding management accountable to milestones, and making the tough executive decisions that need to be made on the board of directors to help manage the progress of the company. To do that you need expertise, so the challenge is to bring to bear the right amount of capital under the right terms under the right amount of supervision."

Finding Angels to Co-Invest with You

In many instances, an entrepreneur will find one willing angel who can put in a portion of the capital the company needs. Then the problem becomes how to round up the other ones. This task can fall upon the shoulders of the first, or lead, angel, because he or she typically has contacts with other potential investors. The angel must be an advocate for the company, and present it to other angel candidates. For the entrepreneur, the key here is to be extremely candid with the lead angel about the pluses and minuses of the venture. The lead investor is already in the entrepreneur's corner, and does not expect everything about the venture to be perfect. But if the lead investor goes around and presents a deal to friends and colleagues, a deal that turns out to have serious flaws that are revealed in subsequent due diligence, the entrepreneur may lose the lead investor as well because he loses face with his friends and colleagues.

The tacit endorsement of the lead angel is a precious asset for the entrepreneur to have, and should not be squandered through the entrepreneur's lack of candidness.

One entrepreneur who has started multiple technology companies told us about the terrible struggle he had to raise start-up capital from angels for a venture that ultimately was extremely successful. On his next venture, in which he was also an investor, he called upon the same angels, and received commitments from them almost immediately with much less due diligence being conducted on the new venture by the angel investors. They were eager to join in with an angel they had "won" with before.

Minimizing Woes after the Close

We have emphasized that angels can contribute greatly to the development of the company after they put the money in. Entrepreneurs, though, worry that the angel will push his way into the day-to-day operations of the company, and differences in operating philosophy will result in friction.

Angels, for their part, will say they have no intention of butting in. They just want to be helpful. However, anyone who invests a significant amount of money in a company has a clear sense of ownership—even possessiveness about it. Isn't it human nature to want to butt in at least a little bit, especially if the company is struggling?

ADVICE FROM AN ANGEL

Barry Moltz, Co-founder, Prairie Angels, www.prairieangels.org

What are the challenges an angel faces after the deal closes? "To trust the management team and let them run their business. Do not overmanage them, but try to add positive advice and positive alliances and do whatever you can to help the business. Ultimately, you are investing in their idea and their management team, and there isn't much you can do to control the situation. So you have to maintain that trust. You have to know when to step over that line and when not to. You have to remember that you are the advisor, not the CEO or the CFO."

What if the opposite occurs, and the angel who promised all these contacts and mentoring assistance disappears after the close? A director of one highly regarded angel network said this about the best angels: "When they wake up in the morning they say, 'How can I help this company?' "

The entrepreneur and the angel have a delicate balancing act to work on after the deal closes: How much help is too much, and how much is not enough?

Portfolio Strategy

In order to purchase enough equity in a company to be an important contributor, you must invest a large amount of capital, say $150,000. But, in order to diversify, you need to put money in a number of companies, let's say half a dozen. Diversification helps you minimize risk, because any single investment may turn out to be a bust, bomb, or whatever term you want to use to describe losing all the capital you put in. In a typical asset-allocation model, you might want to allocate 5 to 10 percent of your available capital to high-risk investments. In order to put $150,000 in each of six companies and only use 10 percent of your capital, you would need a total asset base of $9 million! Not that many people have an asset base that large, and not that many angels do either. They usually have fewer investments or they do not put as much as $150,000 in any one deal.

The angel, then, makes the choice to accept more risk from having a smaller number of deals, or more risk because they own such a small amount of the company that they have little impact. The entrepreneur needs to understand this and make an effort to keep all the investors as informed as possible about the company's accomplishments, setbacks, and outlook. Knowledge is in itself a means of lowering at least the perceived risk. When we invest in a publicly traded security, do we really know what is going on in that company? Of course not. By the time a small investor learns anything, the market has usually already reflected the information in the stock price. But angels, with more at risk and at higher risk, absolutely have to be kept informed.

Chapter Summary

- Angel investing is not easy, and the angel faces many challenges.
- It is difficult to find good deals.
- It takes skill and experience to know how to analyze deals.
- Many angels are not schooled in the fundamentals of this type of activity.
- It is often incumbent upon angels to find other angels to bring into a deal.
- Angels must know when and how much assistance to give the company after the deal closes.
- Angels have to constantly try to manage risk.

CHAPTER

6

Angels Compared to Venture Capitalists

Many Times, They Both Get Involved

Everyone seems to have returned to the old-fashioned view that building a company is a marathon of three to seven years, rather than some kind of sprint where the fleet of foot try to be first to market and take the company public in 18 months. If you look at a company's development from a capital standpoint, it is really more of a relay race than a marathon.

You start with small preseed capital from the entrepreneur, the entrepreneur's friends and family, or sometimes even the entrepreneur's VISA cards. The total investment might be $50,000. The major contribution of these investors is usually moral support.

These early investors pass the baton to angels, who might put in a total of $1 million and oversee the company as it reaches certain milestones of product development and introduction.

Professional venture capitalists get the baton next. They have the capability of investing $5 million on up to $50 million, or whatever the company needs. Venture capitalists are experts at strategic guidance from a less hands-on standpoint than angels normally provide.

Angels and venture capitalists are intertwined, and must—sometimes with a certain amount of conflict—work together. They look over each other's shoulder to some degree. Angels pause as well when venture capitalists slow down their investment. Early in 2001, venture capitalists began working more on their existing portfolio companies, putting in additional rounds of capital and fixing their problems instead of putting so much attention on finding new deals. The enthusiasm of the venture capitalists seems to rub off on angels. If we are in a period of intense speculation, or soaring ROIs for venture capitalists, the angels become substantially more enthusiastic as well.

You Know They're Out There, But Where?

In our first book, *Inside Secrets to Venture Capital*, we talked about how there is a wide gulf between the entrepreneur and the venture capitalist: The two don't understand each other that well. This chasm is magnified when we look at the typical entrepreneur who says, "I need an angel investor." Angels are mysterious, elusive, hidden behind high walls. There is no national directory of active angel investors, like there are several excellent directories of venture capital firms. Angels would find it abhorrent to be asked to be listed in a published directory. They need to have a degree of separation from entrepreneurs, in order to prevent being inundated with business plans and phone calls.

Even when these investors join angel networks, outsiders cannot find out who the members of the network are. You can attend any number of conferences around the country and hear partners in VC firms speak about how to approach venture capitalists, how to prepare to meet with venture capitalists, how venture capitalists evaluate deals. Angel investors are not nearly so visible, and so information pertaining to their methods and thought processes is also not readily available.

Imagine going on a hunting trip, being blindfolded, and not told what big game you are hunting for; your guide just says, "You'll know it when you see it." Is the animal dangerous? Am I going to be eaten alive? How fast does this creature run? Do they run in packs?

"You'll find out when you get there," says the guide.

You just might elect to stay in your tent. So it is with the search for angel investors. New species of angels are discovered all the time. Here's one now—the mentor capitalist.

ADVICE FROM A MENTOR CAPITALIST

Bill Krause, Mentor Capitalist

What is the difference between a mentor capitalist and a venture capitalist? "There have been three potential sources of funding for entrepreneurs. The first was angel investing. The second was venture investing. The third was mentor capital, filling the gap between the other two. The gap existed because angels had money but not field operating experience. Many angels were individuals who were fortunate to come into some wealth as a result of being associated with a successful company in some functional level, either vice president of sales, of marketing, or engineering, but not necessarily in the CEO role. For the most part, angels are somewhat like dilettantes: Although they have money, they are not necessarily disciplined in how they spend their time. Nonetheless they are sources of funding for entrepreneurs.

"There are exceptions to the rule, obviously. My next door neighbor is a former COO of Hewlett-Packard. He is an exceptional individual investor. So there are exceptions to this characterization I painted."

When you get involved with a company, do you typically invest in the company? "Yes, but I and my colleagues do not portray ourselves as funding sources. I only get involved in projects when I serve on the board, and I use that as a disciplining mechanism to be selective about what I do. I have to think enough of the entrepreneurs and the business concept to commit enough time to serve on the board. You can only be on so many boards, so it limits the number of projects you can be involved with."

You used the word "professional." What do you mean by that? "As distinguished from angel investors or more formalized versions of angel investors. I'm a limited partner in a firm called Angel Investors. I don't view that as a professional venture firm. I'm also a member of a group called Band of Angels. I don't view that as a professional venture investor. The people I'm talking about are the people you would know—Kleiner Perkins, Sequoia, Mayfield, Interwest.

"On the other hand, the venture capitalists during recent years were raising billion-dollar funds, and, therefore, they were not available to invest enough time in very early-stage companies. So this created a gap between what venture investors were doing with investments of $8 to $10 million versus what angels were doing.

"The mentor capitalists' most significant value added is their experience, which allows them to offer advice, counsel, and coaching. This is even more valuable than the capital."

ADVICE FROM AN ANGEL

Ian Patrick Sobieski, Ph.D., Managing Member, Band of Angels, www.bandangels.com

Is it to correct to say that angels are more diversified in their investments than VCs? "They may not invest in high-tech or what we typically think of as the showcase example of the 'garage' start-up; they might invest in the local McDonald's franchise, or the roller rink, or the trendy restaurant downtown or the restoration of the artsy theater. Those are all angels—individuals that invest their money.

"Angels, by some numbers, invest a total amount of money larger than formal venture capital industry, the institutional venture capital industry. Most of that money does not go into high-tech startups that get fed into the venture capital channel. Most of that money goes into other things. The amount of money going into high-tech equity is only a small part of that total."

ADVICE FROM AN EXPERT—WHO IS ALSO AN ANGEL

The Differences Between Angel Investors and Venture Capitalists

J. Casey McGlynn, Partner, Wilson Sonsini Goodrich & Rosati Law Firm, www.wsgr.com, General Partner, Angel Investors, LP, www.svangel.com

Angel investors and venture capitalists have some things in common: for instance, both are actively looking for start-up companies in which to invest. Both usually provide a level of service as well, getting involved with the entrepreneurs they are backing and helping them manage and grow the company. Both are looking for sizeable returns on their investments.

But that's where the similarities end; in truth, there are far more differences between angel investors and venture capitalists.

For starters, venture capitalists are professional money managers. Although most also have some of their own money invested in their funds, the vast majority of their investment capital comes from other sources, mostly large institutional investors such as pension funds and university endowments. Their job is to maximize returns for their investors. Most successful venture capitalists have been working in the industry for a decade or more and have a lot of experience choosing, valuing, and nurturing their investments.

As investment professionals, venture capitalists have developed sophisticated systems for analyzing and managing their investments. They've got associates doing due diligence on potential deals, and relationships with investment bankers and others in the capital markets to provide additional sources of financing for their portfolio companies. They have access to top-flight legal counsel to help them structure investments. With the exception of venture capitalists who specialize in seed funding or late-stage investing, they are usually expecting to make additional investments in their companies as they mature and need more capital, and they have the capital available to make those investments.

By contrast, angel investors are almost always acting as private investors using their own money to fund their investments. They may bring substantial industry knowledge and may even have professional investment experience, but their role is fundamentally to act as individuals. Their ability to do due diligence is likely to be limited.

Valuing a private company is, by definition, harder than valuing a publicly traded company, and angel investors are at a disadvantage in determining valuations compared to venture capitalists, because angels are generally involved in fewer deals than venture capitalists. Start-up companies doing deals with angel investors are less likely to have access to experienced corporate attorneys who know how to properly structure their private equity arrangement, which can lead to problems down the road as new investors are added or the company is sold. And angels generally do not have the deep pockets start-up companies need to support them all the way to scale and profitability.

So my advice to entrepreneurs looking for start-up financing is simple: if you have a choice, get funding from professional venture capitalists before accepting angel investments.

But what if you don't have a choice? What if you've already tried getting funding from venture capitalists, or you are in an industry that venture capitalists don't fund? In that case, here are some suggestions:

- If you can't get funding from a venture capitalist, try to pitch your deal to an organized group of angel investors, such as Silicon Valley's Band of Angels or the TriState Investment Group in North Carolina's Research Triangle. These groups reduce the risk associated with angel investing, because their membership is diversified and they have some resources to conduct due diligence. You're also more likely to find a business mentor in a large group than in one-on-one meetings.
- If you accept angel investment, try to get enough capital to make it to a meaningful business milestone, such as finishing product development. If you don't, you may have a hard time convincing future investors to commit the additional capital you need.
- Negotiate the angel investment so that it is as plain and "vanilla" as possible. It's okay to give angel investors preferred stock, but avoid loading up the deal with the special terms that venture capitalists sometimes demand, like liquidation preferences and registration rights. Complex private equity deals are

a red flag for future investors, who fear being treated worse than earlier investors.

- Try to do your deal with an experienced angel investor. This has many obvious advantages, but one that is often overlooked is that an experienced investor is more likely to propose a simple, workable investment structure. Typically, the more inexperienced the investor, the worse the deal is structured.

Angel investing has many benefits and has been a tremendous source of investment capital for start-up companies. But it is important for entrepreneurs and company management to be clear about the risks and benefits associated with angel investing, and the key differences between having angel investors as your business partners and having professional venture capitalists.

One Has to Invest, One Wants to Invest

Venture capitalists are under relentless pressure to perform because they go out and raise money from institutions based on past performance, and based on the real or implied promise to meet or exceed the rates of return they have achieved in the past. Venture capitalists are also under pressure to exit investments and realize returns for their limited partners. This leads to what many observers considered to be a fevered rush to take companies public prematurely in the speculative times of 1999–2000, and in normal times it leads venture capitalists to allocate a larger portion of their investing activity to later-stage companies—those with proven business models and generating revenue, those closer to an exit event. Angels do not have any of these constraints, other than their personal financial advisors telling them they are crazy for putting money into start-ups. Angels in fact may prefer to get involved with the company at its earliest stages because more equity is available for purchase at a lower price and there is greater opportunity for them to shape the strategy and development of the business.

ADVICE FROM AN ANGEL

Ian Patrick Sobieski, Ph.D., Managing Member, Band of Angels, www.bandangels.com

Is it true angels don't pay as much attention to financial projections as VCs? "Angels, by rule, are almost always in a company that is very early stage. At this stage detailed financials are not worth the paper they are written on. It's a good exercise for the company to go through, because it helps them understand their business better, and it is fair for an angel to try to analyze the financials to understand the market size, but to go through financials with a fine tooth comb on a company that is early stage, is to become distracted, and you can miss the forest for the trees. And every one of these early-stage companies will have problems: they won't have a CEO or will have a really challenged sales-channel problem; it can be unclear whether their technology will work or whether their patent position is secure. If you want to say no, you can find any number of reasons. Therefore, criticism of angels is really just another way of saying that, because they invest very early, they don't have a complete and clear picture of what it is they are investing in. Problems can crop up later that can seem obvious in hindsight, but that is part of the game, the nature of the stage of the investment."

Anything One Can Do, the Other Does Better

One area where venture capitalists have a clear edge over angels—especially according to venture capitalists—is in their ability to select investments, analyze them, and decide which ones have the best potential. This is simply because the venture capitalist does this as a full-time job and understands what to look for and what to avoid. It is a considerable, even phenomenal, accomplishment for an entrepreneur to pass through all the hoops, the extensive due-diligence process, and be one of only several investments a venture capitalist firm makes out of 1,000 companies who contact the firm each year. The odds are much better to attract angel capital, given the business concept and the management team are sound.

But angels often do as well as venture capitalists from a return-on-investment standpoint. Part of this is because angels often invest at an earlier stage, and, therefore, when they hit a winner they are compensated for taking additional risk by earning a higher return than if they invested at a later stage. But it may also be that many experienced, dedicated angels devote enough time to this activity to allow them to be successful.

Venture capitalists and angels sometimes view one another with a certain degree of suspicion that can border on hostility. Some venture capitalists like to refer to their investment as *professional money* or the *professional round*, which comes after the earlier, presumably amateur round from angel investors. But is that characterization really fair? We think most angels would beg to differ that their money is not professional, given the fact they earned it in the first place, in the harsh competitive marketplace. The conflicts between these two groups run rather deep. In our many conversations with both of these groups, we came away with the impression that some angels view venture capitalists as being greedy, rate-of-return-oriented individuals, purely finance people, whose blood does not run quite as warm. Angels view themselves as people whose primary concern is helping the company, with rate of return a secondary consideration. Angels also take venture capitalists to task for having a kind of arrogance about them, somewhat like the way people who have attended prestigious private universities look down on others who earned their degrees at state universities.

Venture capitalists have a number of complaints with angels, including:

Angels aren't always the great advisors for businesses that they claim to be.

Angels lack even a basic understanding of how to value an early-stage company, so their perception of valuation keeps the company from being able to bring in venture capital at a later stage.

Venture capitalists have a structured, professional approach to funding companies. Angels on the other hand are in the game for the social aspects, often performing shoddy due diligence on companies and investing in dumb deals just because one of their cronies decided to.

Angels inject ego and personal rancor into financial transactions.

So, it appears that each party agrees that the other party has a big ego problem. At least we've found some common ground, which we clearly need, because at some point in a company's development, it may have both angels and venture capitalists involved as investors, strange bedfellows as they may appear to be.

A number of venture capitalists are willing to disparage the deal-selection strategies that angels use. But simple mathematics tells us that the truly successful angels are at least as proficient at choosing deals as the professional venture capitalists. Why is this? Simply because the angel invests in a smaller number of deals. Their portfolio, in order to generate superior rates of return, must contain a higher percentage of winners, or at least fewer failures.

Let's suppose a VC fund makes a total of 10 investments, and the results are:

4 write-offs, 0 percent return.

3 limp along but stay in business, 10 percent return.

2 meet their targets, 40 percent return.

1 is a superstar, 125 percent return.

Assuming the dollar amount invested in each deal is equal, the weighted average return in this portfolio is 25 percent.

The angel, let's say, only makes four investments in his or her venture portfolio.

1 write-off, 0 percent.

1 limps along, 15 percent.

1 meets its target, 40 percent.

1 is a superstar, 125 percent.

Our weighted average return here is a very impressive 45 percent. Let's eliminate the superstar, and say the angel experiences two write-offs, 1 limps along, and 1 meets target. The return for all of the angel's effort and risk is 13.75 percent. Stick to your mutual funds.

The successful angel, in order to match the venture capitalists' rate of return, must be able to find a superstar as well, out of a much smaller universe of presented opportunities, and must be careful to not absorb too many write-offs, because angels do not purchase as many chances to win in this game as venture capitalists do.

ADVICE FROM A VENTURE CAPITALIST

Eric Janszen, Managing Director, Osborn Capital LLC., www.osborncapital.com

How do angel investors differ from VC investors?

"They invest their own money.

"They are speculators more often than they are investors.

"They are active and numerous during stock market booms when investment risk appears lowest and disappear when market booms end.

"They often are not committed to their investments long term (i.e., do not follow up).

"They often have operational experience that venture capitalists do not have but lack financial experience that venture capitalists do have."

Differing Amounts of Investment

Angels invest a much lower amount per deal on average than venture capitalists. The amount venture capitalists invest has been rising steadily, with some estimates now putting the average investment per company as high as $10 million or more. Angels may put as little as $20,000 in an individual investment, but many, depending on their financial capability, can go much higher, in the $250,000 range or more. When angels invest as a group or through an organized angel group, the total investment in the company can exceed $1.5 million. This flexibility on the lower end of capital is another reason why angels are much more likely sources of capital for companies than VC firms.

ADVICE FROM AN ANGEL

Craig Johnson, Chairman, Venture Law Group, www.vlg.com

What would be the major difference between a venture capitalist and an angel? "I think a venture capitalist should be, at least in theory, a professional who does this for a living. An angel typically has another day job, and does this as an investment strategy and often as an avocation. The major difference is simply the degree of professionalism.

"Angels rarely do the amount of due diligence or have the degree of industry knowledge that a venture capitalist will have in a given area. Angels often have much more limited operating background. Sometimes angels have something that venture capitalists don't, and that is insight into a particular industry or a particular opportunity that a venture capitalist might miss."

Differing Approaches to Management

Venture capital firms are extremely concerned with building the best possible management team structure for their portfolio companies, even if it means telling the founder(s) they cannot be the CEO, or senior vice president of marketing, or whatever other position the founder might want to hold, and bringing in their own people. Angels are typically more willing to work within the structure the founders have put together, perhaps filling some gaps with the angel's own participation and expertise. Venture capitalists do not have the time to fill these gaps with their own participation, but they maintain an active network of managerial talent they can call upon to join up with their portfolio companies.

WHICH ONES ARE BETTER TO WORK WITH?

We tend to think of angels as being older, in general, than the average age of partners in venture capital firms. Venture capitalists position themselves, and rightly so, as having a great deal of market savvy and technical expertise, but the typical angel has something tremendously important that only a small portion of VCs do: the practical, hands-on experience of building their own company into a success that created wealth, the detailed operational experience of being on the firing line every day, not just sitting on a board of directors.

There is no substitute for that practical experience. What a tremendous benefit to a young entrepreneur to have an experienced angel with an understanding of how to run a business in good times and bad, in exuberant growth phases and painful contractions.

This is why angels tend to get more involved in companies they have invested in: Operations are what they know best. It is the area where they can make the greatest contribution. Having your personal financial well-being at stake each day, as CEO of your own company, is a much more high-pressure situation than being a fund manager, as a venture capitalist is. When a VC-backed company fails, it is a write-off for the accountants to deal with. If a wealthy individual's company fails, it is a personal and devastating loss.

Angels often take this same personal interest in companies they choose to back.

Specific differences between angel investors and venture capitalists will be addressed in the appropriate chapters.

Chapter Summary

- Venture capitalists advertise their location; angels tend to hide.
- Venture capitalists have a definite focus on technology investments; angels are attracted to technology investments but look at many other types of companies as well.
- Venture capitalists have more financial, due diligence, and valuation skill, and are more formalized in their approach to each of these areas.
- Successful angels, who stay in the game for long periods of time, may even have more success picking winning investments than many venture capitalists.
- Angels invest much smaller amounts in an average deal than venture capitalists do.
- Angels' flexibility in the size of their investments makes them likelier sources of capital for early-stage businesses.
- Venture capitalists like to think of themselves as the professional round, as though it were something the company graduates to after having worked with the presumably amateur angel investors.
- Angels and venture capitalists do not necessarily view each other in a positive light, but each of them offers entrepreneurs badly needed money that is the same shade of green.

CHAPTER

7

What Do Angels Want?

Investment Preferences

Entrepreneurs often are rejected by investors, particularly VC firms, not because there is anything wrong with their venture, but simply because it does not fit with the investor's criteria, in other words, the investment preferences they use to screen opportunities. Really, the entrepreneur is not rejected at all, but is simply never given any consideration. Preferences can include the industry the company is in, the stage of development of the company, the amount of capital needed, and geographic limitations. With angels, you needn't worry about approaching them looking for seed capital or very-early-stage support: Angels love early-stage companies. Regarding other preferences, an entrepreneur can save himself a lot of time and aggravation by simply doing some research and finding out which angels or angel groups match up well with his company.

INDUSTRY

ADVICE FROM AN ANGEL

Tom Horgan, AZTEC Venture Networks and Acorn Technologies, San Diego, CA

How broadly do you define technology companies? Do you look at a broad range of companies, or do you have specific niches you are most interested in? "We are very broad. One of our companies is a service-oriented business. The only criterion is that the company operates in a sizable space, a market of $1 billion or more.

"In screening, we look at the 'three M's': management, market size, and money (the financial projections; are they believable or not). In terms of what excites us, I think it is fair to say we have all been individually excited at various points of the process."

ADVICE FROM A VENTURE CAPITALIST WHO IS ALSO AN ANGEL

Frank A. McGrew IV, Managing Director, Paradigm Capital Partners, Memphis, TN, www.memphisangels.com

Do you concentrate on certain industries, or look at a broad range? "We are stage focused, we tend to do early-stage opportunities. And we try to leverage core areas of expertise within the venture group and the angel group. Those would include agriculture, logistics, as well as telecommunications. Outside of those three primary focus areas, we look at business-to-business infrastructure, fiber-optics networks, software, we have several investments in the e-learning space, and another investment in the education area."

ADVICE FROM AN ANGEL

Scott Woodard

From your perspective, how can entrepreneurs go about locating angels with an interest in their specific industry or market? "There are several investor forums available that the entrepreneur can locate in the technology associations (e.g., in Chicago it is the Chicago Software Association and the Prairie Angels, etc.). They can attempt to present to these groups and may get contacts for investment or people who would be willing to help them locate financing within the group."

GEOGRAPHY

Angels usually prefer to invest in companies near where they live. This could be within the same metropolitan area, or just within a reasonable driving distance. Angels invest locally for several reasons. The first is that they want to be able to periodically meet with the management of the company, even visit the company and see how it is progressing. Staying involved with a company you invest in is more difficult on a long-distance basis. The second reason most angels invest locally has to do with how angels source deals. They rely on other angels, business associates, or service providers such as their attorney or accountant. Most of these people would be in their home vicinity as well.

SIZE OF INVESTMENT

There really is no firm lower limit of capital requirement below which angels would not be interested. As a practical matter, however, angels are more interested in building small start-ups into medium-sized or large valuable enterprises that can be exited from with a high ROI for the investors. These kinds of start-ups often require $500,000 to $1 million or more of angel capital to get started, with subsequent rounds of investment that may total several millions of dollars.

In this example, a $500,000 total investment could be made by five angels each putting in $100,000, or 20 angels each putting in $25,000.

What Excites Angel Investors about a Deal?

This is a fascinating question, and gets to the heart of the investment process. What can an entrepreneur do to move the angel(s) toward saying "yes"? We wondered if it were possible to find several things for entrepreneurs to emphasize in their presentations, almost as though the investors have a checklist in their heads of favorable elements that need to be present for them to move forward. Once an entrepreneur locates angels whose investment preferences match up well with the company, the entrepeneur's attention turns to convincing the investor that this particular deal has a lot going for it, in specific areas:

The management team is strong, balanced, and experienced.

The market/industry the company serves is already large and has great growth potential.

The technology/product/service meets a compelling need in the marketplace.

The company will be able to establish a defensible competitive advantage.

The management team will be able to execute the strategies shown in the business plan.

The potential rate of return is exciting.

MANAGEMENT TEAM

The management team is strong, balanced, and experienced.

ADVICE FROM AN ANGEL

Brent Townshend

When you review a business plan or see a company's presentation, what makes you go, "wow, this sounds good"? What factors make you give it the green light to investigate further? "I look for intelligent people. People are the most important thing. Do they have a good idea of what they are going to do, what their business model is, how they are going to make money, and is it realistic? And honesty. The worst thing to see in a business plan is stories they can't back up. They start throwing in a lot of conjectures and presenting them as facts. It sours the whole thing.

"It has to be a good idea. You can't take an okay idea and fluff it up and expect to get funding. If the people are good in the sense of having energy, and able to think on their feet, they can usually get the thing to work even if the original idea wasn't perfect. They have the ability to make adjustments as they go.

"If you have a great idea with mediocre people it doesn't work as well."

ADVICE FROM AN ANGEL

Steven P. Subar

How can entrepreneurs demonstrate to an investor's satisfaction that their product or service has a defensible competitive advantage? "It is pretty darn hard to make a case that is believable other than they have an ability to execute that surpasses other likely competitors. If it is a really good idea, there will be other players in the space, so it comes down to who can execute most effectively.

"You are betting jockeys, not horses."

How can a management team prove it has the ability to execute? "It gets down to making really obvious the successes you have had to date. Talk about the evolution of your business in stages, and make it clear that you are not at Stage 1, you are at Stage 2, or somewhere along the way. Then you can talk about what your objectives were originally, at the earlier stages, and how you succeeded in achieving those goals. You also advertise the pedigree of the management team, that they were successful previously, and they are successful today. Therefore you are not taking that much risk. You are betting that Stages 3, 4, and 5 will happen."

Management teams often come together when the company starts. They may not ever have worked together before. They may not even be located in the same cities, just are linked up through communications devices like videoconferencing. How do you prove to yourself that this team can execute together? "I think that if people are not physically together it puts them at a big disadvantage. When you are talking about building a company, the collaboration that takes place each day, informally, is paramount. You are usually trying things to get a sense of what works and what doesn't and the immediate feedback, being able to brainstorm whether to continue going in one direction or move in a new direction—those things don't happen as well when you have to have 'scheduled' communication. The other part of it is you have to create a culture and organization where people learn to trust one another. If a football team never practiced together, but just got together for games, you'd lose the advantage of knowing the subtleties of how you play together.

"If the group is together in one location but may not have worked together before this, this is less of an issue for me personally provided that I can get comfortable that they have been successful before. It helps if they have a following of individuals who have worked with them before who would want to come and work with them again. This helps when you need to pull out the Rolodex to grow the organization quickly to the next stage."

ADVICE FROM AN ANGEL

Scott Woodard

Investors talk about how it is important to find management teams with the "ability to execute." How can entrepreneurs demonstrate this to investors? "Unfortunately, this is a bit of a chicken and egg problem. The old fashioned way, that I and many of my peers had to do, was to build a profitable business and then successfully sell it. The next time around, investors are much more likely to be interested. A couple of years ago, this changed with the Internet revolution, but it has reverted back more to the old way. Probably the best thing is to get the business going with some revenue.

"Alternatively, if they come from an industry where they have a great deal of success and a strong position, they may be able to convince investors to invest in a like business that they start."

MARKET/INDUSTRY

The market/industry the company serves should already be large and have great growth potential. Angels look for this factor because it is easier to ride the wave of a growing market than try to wrestle market share away from entrenched competitors in a stagnant one. How does the entrepreneur prove the market is large and growing? It can be difficult to find credible data to back up your forecast of market growth. You can obtain forecasts from three different research organizations and find that they vary widely, and you may not be able to determine the assumptions they used to come up with the forecast. If you are in a new or emerging market, forecast data may not be available at all. An angel does not expect the entrepreneur to have ironclad forecasts that no one could argue with; such a forecast does not exist.

TECHNOLOGY/PRODUCT/SERVICE

The technology/product/service meets a compelling need in the marketplace. This is something that entrepreneurs are repeatedly told to emphasize to investors. Angels develop their own ways of evaluating how strong the market need is for the product or service. The best way to present this compelling advantage is at the grass-roots customer level. How will one individual or one company benefit? Walk the investor through the process of the customer actually making the purchase decision and using the product/service. With many complex technologies, this is the only way to have the investor get it.

The popular notion about technology is that it begins with a maniacally dedicated inventor tinkering in a garage or small lab. The inventor discovers something, then goes out to see if there's a market for it. Actually, some of the best technologies start with a market focus, not just an invention. Technical people within big corporations see interesting market niches that their companies have ignored, then leave the company and adapt a technology to fit that niche. These types of companies can be of great interest to angel investors because the customer base for the product is already proven: An identifiable customer need in fact gave rise to the idea to begin with.

COMPETITIVE ADVANTAGE

All investors, whether venture capitalists or angels, try to identify companies that are doing something, or have something, so different and special that customers will readily see the difference and gravitate toward the product or service.

In an ideal situation, the company enjoys a monopoly; it has by far the largest market share and customers are very satisfied with the product or service offering. For most companies, this enviable situation does not last very long, if it occurs at all.

Even within the window of a temporary monopoly, however, great profits can be earned and great value can be created. Technology companies are often able to establish the defensible competitive advantage from patents or other intellectual property they hold. However, an equally powerful advantage is to provide such a high degree of customer service that the customer stays with you even though a competitor enters the market with a lower-priced offering.

Entrepreneurs need to tell the angel why this specialness of the company gives the customers exactly the solution they are seeking.

POTENTIAL RATE OF RETURN

The potential rate of return must be exciting. Our survey of 50 angels shows that the average return on investment (ROI) expected by angels is 34%. The highest rate expected is 100% and the lowest 20%.

ADVICE FROM AN ANGEL

Steve Miller, Co-founder, Prairie Angels, www.prairieangels.org

Do angels have the same expectation as venture capitalists about return on investment? "I think it's hard to generalize. Different angels have different motivations. I think many of us are not in this just for the huge financial gain. Venture capitalists have their investors to answer to, their limited partners who are expecting certain returns. Angels have only themselves to answer to. We are doing it to continue to be involved in building businesses. I'm not looking for the multibillion dollar opportunities. I want to help build great companies, have fun, and to make some money doing that, but really leverage my experience and continue to learn and grow and be part of building the New Economy. That's my motivation."

ADVICE FROM AN ANGEL

Steve Harari

What types of investments appeal to you? "I have tended to be the very first angel investor in a company. I like to find an early management team—not even a team, really just the founders, one or two individuals. Typically I like to find that there is more than just one founder involved, because I think it takes a tremendous amount of bandwidth or skill sets to pull off a new venture. When I see just one individual, I am skeptical, but teams of two to three I would describe as optimal. My focus has been the Internet, and early, early stage—the first investor in. And then, through my other networks and angel groups, I typically can find eight to ten other angels to come in and co-invest with me. Because they know I am going to be actively involved—and typically I allocate one day per week to work with each of these companies—these other angel investors feel good because many times they are not going to be as involved."

You are the "guardian angel"? "Sort of. It works both ways. If the company isn't doing well, I can have a very difficult job."

ADVICE FROM A MENTOR CAPITALIST

Bill Krause

What are some of the characteristics of a deal that would make you want to take at least that first step of talking with them? "Foremost, the introduction has to come from someone I know. If the connection is through someone whose judgment I respect, that is the first filter. The second filter is whether the entrepreneur has sent me a written document that compellingly and clearly articulates their business concept. If they cannot communicate this in a persuasive enough way to engage my interest, then it presents a challenge for them to communicate it in building a business. If they pass those filters, an in-person meeting would take place.

"There are certain kinds of companies I just don't get involved in. What I focus on are areas where my background is of value, particularly networking, telecommunications, Internet infrastructure, enterprise software."

EXIT STRATEGIES

The exit strategy simply tells the investors when and how they can reap the rewards of their investment and that the entrepreneur recognizes that the investment won't be forever.

ADVICE FROM AN ENTREPRENEUR

Dave Westin, www.channelautomation.com

What factors about a given venture really seem to excite angels? "Market size, market opportunity. Absence of significant competition. How quickly they can get an ROI done. In other words, is there an exit strategy?"

Do they look at three years, five years? "A three-to-five-year exit. The investors we have, the exit they wanted was an IPO, not an acquisition of the company. So everyone was looking for a 50-times ROI. Venture capitalists are happy with a 15- or 20-times ROI. The angel is taking more risk, so they deserve a higher return.

"Some angels aren't really concerned about the valuation as much as they are about getting started and adding value to their investment. There are other angels who will try to nickel and dime you for a half million of valuation. In reality, if you make it, you are going to win big anyway. So if it's a difference between a 20-times return and 22-times, who cares?

"The angels we dealt with in Silicon Valley absolutely understood valuation. They understand comparables. Every angel there has venture capitalist friends and understands the market."

Why Do Angels Say No?

This is looking at the issues we have discussed in the previous chapter from another angle, the mistakes entrepreneurs need to avoid in order to make the first "cut" in the process and move toward actual negotiations with potential angel investors.

ADVICE FROM AN ANGEL

Ian Patrick Sobieski, Ph.D., Managing Member, Band of Angels, www.bandangels.com

What are some of the frequent reasons you turn down a deal? "There are a number of reasons why you might immediately say no. Incomprehensible presentation, so that you spend half an hour with someone and you have no idea what they are doing because they have so poorly communicated their business. Then you just won't spend any more time with them. A poor team. Often the former goes along with the latter. You don't need a perfect team, but a poor team will scare you away. A business that has low barriers to entry, a small market, enormous entrenched competitors, that has no apparent sustainable competitive advantage, requires too much capital—those are all reasons to worry about a deal."

ADVICE FROM AN ANGEL

Barry Moltz, Co-founder, Prairie Angels, www.prairieangels.org

What causes you to quickly decline a deal? "People who say 'I have no competition.' That's a turnoff. People who say, 'I need $2 million dollars' and they haven't even developed a product and they want to pay themselves $150 thousand salary out of the investors' $2 million. If they haven't invested any of their own personal wealth in the company—they should be willing to put whatever they have into it. I try to be very honest and open with the entrepreneur and not leave the meeting and say, 'I'll get back to you and this was nice.' I try to tell them, this deal is not fundable, it's not the right time, or this plan isn't going anywhere unless you accomplish A, B, and C."

ADVICE FROM AN ANGEL

Steven P. Subar

What are the most common reasons you decline an investment after you go through the process of meeting with the manage-

ment team and perhaps conducting preliminary due diligence? "First would be the initial filters I talked about: Is the problem to be solved pervasive? Is it a high priority for the customer? Is it a profitable business model?

"There are lots of really good ideas out there, but not that address problems that are really big enough or that people really care about enough to react immediately to the solution. In today's economy that is more true than ever. Even in a strong economy, they are so busy they can only pay attention to the most urgent matter.

"Assuming the company meets all three criteria, then it gets down to the expertise of the individuals themselves: How well do they know the space? What has been the track record personally of building early-stage ventures into something bigger?

"Then, I try to get a feeling of the likelihood they will be successful. You need to look at where they are at that particular point. If it is a venture that will require them to invest significantly ahead of revenue, and they are struggling to raise money, that's a red flag.

"It doesn't take a lot of time to get a high-level perspective and answer these questions pretty well."

ADVICE FROM AN ANGEL

Steve Harari

When you look at a company, what is the most common reason you decline to invest? "The individuals themselves, the feeling that I do not have confidence in them. I'm not looking for blue-chip track records and 20 years of relevant experience, but there are certain qualities of maturity and perseverance. And, given the role I play as a mentor and advisor—do they listen? Also, do I think I can impact their trajectory? So, the most common reasons I would decline would be I don't think they are prepared to listen, and I don't think I can impact their trajectory."

Strategies for Dealing with Rejection

Entrepreneurs can waste a lot of energy getting angry about an angel declining to invest in their project. We have experienced this a number of times: An entrepreneur asks us whether we think venture capitalists would be interested in their project. Sometimes, you have to be brutally honest and say no. If you do give them this honest answer, the result is often that you receive back an e-mail peppered with colorfully expressed profanity, questioning your intelligence, validity of your parentage, what species you are, and so forth. Of course, signs of immaturity like this in an entrepreneur are one of the key reasons investors wouldn't be interested in their project. Angels and venture capitalists both prefer to back grown-ups.

There are several healthier ways to cope with rejection, anyway:

1. Learn from it. Angel investors, in contrast to some venture capitalists, will usually take the time to explain why they are declining. They may have reasons that are perfectly logical when you hear them, and those reasons may help you shape the planning of your venture so it is more salable to future investors you contact. If you don't get any feedback, ask for it, even if it takes several phone calls.
2. Expect it. The days of investors chasing after start-ups and throwing bushels of cash at them appear to be over, at least for the next few years. Nearly all entrepreneurs who have raised funds from angels have experienced a number of declines before they found just the right investor.
3. Use it as a means to widen your network. We have seen how angels get involved with start-ups primarily because they enjoy helping entrepreneurs. So even if they decline your deal, they may be willing to steer you in the right direction to find additional potential investors.
4. Consider the source. This piece of advice came by way of a client of ours who experienced a number of rejections before he found an angel. He simply disregarded a lot of the free advice angels gave him about what was wrong with his venture, because he had the self-confidence to realize he knew more about his company and his industry than they did. He wasn't one of the entrepreneurs who went around saying that the angels who declined were stupid; he simply understood that there are very few start-ups that every investor would agree is a sure-fire winner.
5. Angels have personal reasons for saying no. We sometimes forget that angels are busy people who most likely do not make these investments as a full-time job. Angels may tell you there is something they do not like about your venture, but the real reason for the decline may be that all their money is already tied up in other things. They are probably not going to say, "You have a great deal, but we're broke."

6. Separate yourself from your venture. The investor who declines is not saying that you are incompetent, not a good person, or anything of the sort. The angel is simply saying that he does not think he can achieve his targeted rate of return with your venture.
7. Rejections sometimes stem from a failure to communicate. The entrepreneur may say, "The investor just didn't get it." But it is the responsibility of the person seeking the financing to get the message across effectively. In working with entrepreneurs who are out there looking for capital, we would say that a decline comes from a poorly expressed presentation, in person or via business plan, as much as it does from the venture having limited merit.

Perfection Is Unattainable, but Worth Striving For

Do entrepreneurs and their ventures need to have all the positive qualities mentioned in this chapter, and to avoid all the mistakes cited in order to obtain angel financing?

Of course not. The wonderful thing about experienced angels is that they have walked the same path the entrepreneur is on, and they recall the mistakes they made along the way, the fortunate turn of events that was necessary for them to succeed, the help they got at critical times. The questions they ask may be tough, but they are fair. They may make a note that this entrepreneur needs improvement, but they also recognize when the second presentation the entrepreneur makes is much better, after the entrepreneur gets some coaching or feedback from angels.

Investors aren't perfect either. Far from it. We've often seen entrepreneurs who develop a terrible case of stage fright when meeting with angels or venture capitalists, a feeling almost as though they don't deserve to be there with the mighty investors. And, we've also observed almost laughable egocentric behavior by investors. But their myth of superiority was debunked irrevocably in the 1999–2000 period, when they chased after so many deals that should never have seen the light of day—just plain goofy deals, deals that must have come out of Looney Tunes Investment Banking firm.

Next time you find yourself in a meeting in which an investor is getting a little huffy-puffy, a bit too full of himself, we recommend just sitting back in your chair, relaxing for a moment, and saying, "So, tell me about that pets.com deal."

Chapter Summary

- Angels have investment preferences including industry concentration and geographic location of the venture.
- A number of elements must be present in a venture in order to attract angel investors, but the relative importance of each depends on the individual angel.
- Angels and entrepreneurs agree that there are a number of factors that cause investors to decline a particular deal. These factors reflect the critical importance of having a quality management team and the fact that it is not easy to communicate the virtues of an early-stage company as a potential investment.
- All entrepreneurs seeking capital will face rejection by angels at some point along the way. It is possible to learn from the rejection and thus improve your chances of later success in obtaining capital.

CHAPTER

8

Entrepreneur Characteristics That Attract Angels

Profile of a Successful Entrepreneur

Entrepreneurs who fit this profile definitely have an advantage in obtaining capital from angels.

- Open-minded regarding valuation of early-stage companies, but enters into negotiations having done at least some homework on current marketplace valuations.
- Welcomes participation of the angel investor in the company, at least at the advisory level.
- Can concisely explain the unique, compelling value of the proposed venture in written terms and in oral presentations, recognizing that some investors rely more on one than the other.
- Makes full disclosures to investors regarding both positive and negative aspects of the proposed venture.
- Allows sufficient time to complete the process of finding capital, including due diligence time for investors.

- Has a venture, or an idea, that can create equity value, not just current cash flow for the owners; this implies a proprietary technology or other element that would be of value if acquired by another company.
- Has at least a partial network of contacts in place to assist with making introductions to angels or angel groups.

The third item sounds simple enough, but it is in fact very difficult to achieve for most of us. The person presenting the company needs to be able to generate that initial spark of interest. Without that, the cause is pretty much lost.

The investor, in order to eventually be successful, must spot not only winning technologies but winning people, and this is all very subjective. Each of us has a slightly different view of what a winner looks like. At the stage during which the angel is normally investing, the people on the management team may be all the angel has to go by to decide whether the deal is worth pursuing. The technology or product may be at an embryonic stage. There may not be any customers to talk to in order to evaluate the market need. Venture capitalists have told us that they look for qualities such as successful track record, honesty, dedication, vision, intelligence, and leadership. What do angels look for?

ADVICE FROM AN ANGEL

Craig Johnson, Chairman, Venture Law Group, www.vlg.com

What characteristics do you look for in entrepreneurs? "Fundamental bedrock characteristics, they have to be honest, they have to have high integrity. Then, they have to have a high degree of dedication, ambition, and a willingness to work hard. They have to be smart, they have to have a pattern of success in their prior lives that shows they will succeed yet again. Then you get to the point of looking seriously at the given opportunity. We look primarily at size of the market and degree of the market demand for their product or service, and how willing people are to pay for it. That's the process we go through.

"Entrepreneurs really need to have the ability to listen, to be coached, to assimilate information and to change behavior and plans. The world is changing so rapidly, and markets are changing so rapidly, that entrepreneurs have to be nimble enough to change course and strategies as market conditions change. There's so much information you have to process. By listening I don't mean that they should blindly follow any advice they are given. They have to seek out real-life market information and they have to be flexible.

"The entrepreneurs I like to work with are adaptability engines. They are capable of processing an enormous amount of information and without being too tied to prior mindsets. They are willing to listen to customers and give customers what they want. I have seen very few companies fail if they listen to their market."

ADVICE FROM AN ANGEL

Steve Harari

What is the most important characteristic an entrepreneur needs to have to be successful? "It is tough to distill it down to one or two. I would almost say 'breadth': the ability to have a multiplex across fifteen or more functional tasks, and move them all forward in parallel, is one of the greatest skill sets an entrepreneur must have. If they just focus on technology, or they just do sales, or if they just try to raise money, or just develop the demo—to the exclusion of the other things—they will never make it. The ability to push 20 balls forward in parallel is a necessity."

ADVICE FROM A MENTOR CAPITALIST

Bill Krause

What do you think are the major characteristics of successful entrepreneurs? "The ability to communicate. The ability to persevere. If the entrepreneur cannot communicate, the entrepreneur cannot motivate others to join his or her cause."

ADVICE FROM A VENTURE CAPITALIST WHO IS ALSO AN ANGEL

Patrick Soheili, Barrington Partners, Silicon Valley

What are the most important characteristics entrepreneurs must have to be successful? "All of these I am going to mention are important;

there is no particular order: being aggressive, a go-getter, being a very committed individual, having an undying conviction that you are going to conquer this thing. I have been an entrepreneur myself; there are peaks and valleys that are very huge. You have to have incredible conviction that you can overcome the negatives and stay grounded when things are just so wonderful, and not get ahead of yourself. You have to be bright and be able to find the pain you are trying to solve. You have to know exactly what your customers want. You could call it empathy, marketeership, brightness, being a visionary. I would say having a soulmate is something we always look for, that there is more than just the one founder of the company involved. To some extent, the more the merrier. Soulmates are critical. To keep the other person grounded, to just have someone to bounce ideas off.

"Operational experience is now proving to be much more important than youth. Having been there before, knowing what ditches to avoid. Having industry contacts is key as well."

ADVICE FROM A CORPORATE VENTURE CAPITALIST

Matthew I. Growney, Managing Director, Motorola Ventures

What qualities do you feel an entrepreneur must have in order to be successful? "Flexibility and execution. A start-up company's management team may change its business plan 20 times over the course of a year. The key is to change and grow the company with agility and execute the new plan in a manner that is opportunistic for the market at that particular time and react on the way to assessing the next step. Mistakes are expected, but they cannot be regretted for any reason. Entrepreneurs must learn from them and move on. Meeting deadlines of prospective customers during beta testing or initial product sample roll-out is a rare thing, but being able to execute goals or activities on time proves that an entrepreneur is an individual with integrity who can deliver."

ADVICE FROM AN ANGEL

David Burwen

What are the most important characteristics of an entrepreneur to be successful? "Focus. An entrepreneur has to be extremely focused on what is needed to be done to realize the company's mission.

"Flexibility. When they are going down a path, and find out that the path is not quite right, they have to be capable of seeing this problem.

They also have to be willing and able to change strategy and readjust the course of the company accordingly.

"High energy, drive, and determination to be successful. The determination might stem from the fact they are simply greedy. I prefer entrepreneurs who have a burning desire to build a great company that will provide significant technology solutions and be a lasting monument to themselves. I think this is a more sustaining long-term driver than just wanting to have a high net worth.

"High intelligence. Starting a company involves a whole bunch of difficult puzzles and problems.

"Integrity. People who when they tell you something, you can count on it. You don't have to question whether you are being manipulated or told things that aren't quite right."

ADVICE FROM AN ANGEL

Ken Deemer, Tech Coast Angels, www.techcoastangels.com

Are there any qualities that successful entrepreneurs have in common? "Persistence is probably the most fundamental quality, and passion for what they are doing. Being a successful entrepreneur is an arduous, lonely task. The ones who succeed are the ones who come back after hearing 'no' over and over and over again."

ADVICE FROM AN ANGEL

Barry Moltz, Co-founder, Prairie Angels, www.prairieangels.org

How can entrepreneurs increase their chances of success in obtaining angel capital? "Who introduces you to whom is critical. If I get a referral from someone I know and respect I am more likely to listen than something that comes over the transom. In their presentation, if people just lay out simply, this is what we do, this is how we are going to make money, here's our competitive advantage, rather than a lot of New Economy jargon, that helps a lot as well.

"You also want to know who else is in the deal, who else the deal has been presented to. If you can get one person interested, others follow. Much of angel investing is done locally, so if I know Joe is in the deal, he is more likely to get Harry and Fred in the deal, because they trust each other. You also need a critical mass in the amount of money. There are many potential angels around Chicago."

Angel investors look to invest in entrepreneurs that have almost superhuman passion and dedication to making the venture succeed. They try to find out if the company founders have that single-mindedness, that man-on-a-mission attitude. The reason is simple: You can't build a successful company from the start-up stage without it. Unfortunately, some entrepreneurs believe you can start several companies at once, or start a company while working on another full-time career. The results can be disappointing.

Deal tales are stories from our experience with entrepreneurs looking for capital. All of the anecdotes about entrepreneurs we present in this book really happened, proving once again truth is stranger than fiction.

DEAL TALES: HOW MUCH STARCH DO YOU WANT ON THAT PLAN?

A wealthy stockbroker contacted us to help her finish her business plan. She was one of those gadabout entrepreneurs we were talking about earlier. She be-bopped around Los Angeles in her Mercedes, had power lunches, power dinners, even the occasional power high tea, but also had an idea for an Internet venture she wanted to bring to fruition.

We quickly saw that she didn't simply want us to help her with her business plan, she wanted to delegate the task completely to us. The planning of her venture was just something to check off the to-do list, not really that important to her. We tried to ask her basic questions about the business model and the proprietary aspects of the technology, but she was always too busy to talk to us about any of these little details. Finally, we told her that it was critical that the company founder be an integral part of writing the business plan.

She agreed to have a phone consultation to discuss her venture's technology, but said she was going to have to do her *ironing(!)* while she talked to us because she was running late for a meeting with a prospective new client, and this was the only opening in her schedule all day.

It's not easy to handle steam, starch, and proprietary technology all at the same time. She ended up giving us a rambling, incoherent monologue that couldn't be converted into paragraphs that any investor could follow. We're not completely sure they were in English. When the project was further along, she began to fuss at us that she was having to spend too much time on the business plan. Somehow, we don't associate fussing with successful CEOs. She actually spent more time fussing at us than she did on writing the plan. If you were an angel investor, would you want to put money behind a fussy founder like this woman? Entrepreneurship isn't like knitting: You can't put the venture away in the closet for a few weeks and then take it out and work on it while you're watching TV. It's more like a child that needs constant supervision and diligent effort to raise.

Angel Survey Results

In our Profit Dynamics, Inc. surveys, here are comments from angels regarding the most important characteristics an entrepreneur must have in order to be successful:

"Passion, Persistence, Pragmatism."

"The ability to develop and execute a realistic business plan."

"Knowledge of product potential."

"Got to be sharp and exceptional in their particular field, most of the rest is persistence and hard work with a willingness to learn."

"Competency."

"Experience, experience, experience."

"History of success."

"Honesty and integrity."

"Persistence and drive, as well as the ability to stay focused."

"Tenacity."

"Vision, drive, and discipline."

"Fire in the belly. An absolute belief that the company will be successful and a total commitment to making it successful."

"A really good team around them."

"Ability to attract strong management."

"Honesty and the intellectual power to adapt and change course as they get more involved in their company."

"Foresight."

"Adaptability."

Chapter Summary

- Angels and entrepreneurs understand that building a successful company requires a complex set of skills, experiences, and personal traits. Foremost among these are the drive to succeed, integrity, and vision.

TYPES OF ANGELS

CHAPTER

9

The Many, Many Types of Angels

During periods of extremely bullish stock market conditions, when wealth is being created, the ranks of angel investors are swelled by people who have recently made a large percentage of their accumulated assets. New money, in other words. Because literally trillions of dollars of wealth were created in the last great stock market run-up that ended in 2000, the numbers of angel investors correspondingly soared.

Because the stock market also goes down (as many investors seem to learn for the first time during each contraction phase in the market), as levels of paper wealth decline, so does the appetite many investors have toward placing money in high-risk early-stage companies.

But even in times of severe drought in the stock market, angel capital does not dry up because there is a group of corc angels whose net worth has weathered many short-term downward blips in the public equity markets. They continue their angel investing activity even when the new money folks disappear from the angel investing arena. In fact, many core angels look favorably at the downturns because it means less competition for good deals and also significantly lower valuations for early-stage companies (the angel can purchase more of the company for less money).

In this most recent cycle, because there were incredible fortunes made in high-tech stocks, many of the new money angels were people who had been among the founders or earliest employees of tech companies before they went public. Even a tiny percentage ownership in a company that had an exponential run-up in its stock value, such as Cisco Systems, ended up being worth many millions of dollars.

These new angels came into the game with perhaps less gray hair, and less experience operating companies than the core angels, but they brought a great deal of technical knowledge concerning what the next big thing was going to be, and they also had the same kind of entrepreneurial enthusiasm that the management teams of companies courting them did.

After the NASDAQ market lost more than half of its value between mid-2000 and early 2001, a number of these new-money angels felt the pinch of seriously eroded wealth and folded their wings as far as making new angel investments.

But a new segment of angel investors arose in the last 10 years as well. These are would-be wealthy individuals from all different backgrounds, including attorneys and investment professionals as well as business owners or executives, who see angel investing as a means of increasing the overall performance of their investment portfolio. They, too, may have experienced great increases in personal wealth in the 1990s. Because venture capital in particular and entrepreneurship in general have been covered much more closely by the press in the last 10 years, more and more people became aware of the terrific returns on investment that could be earned from angel investing. These new angels do not have quite the same enthusiasm for the process of building companies that core angels or high-tech angels might, but their money is just as green. They, too, however, can tend to become skittish when deals start to go south, or when valuations of companies fall significantly. Because many stockmarket investors focus too much on short-term gains, they may not have the nervous system to endure periods of illiquidity—which is all part of investing in young enterprises.

Here are ways we might classify angels:

Three Basic Types

Core angels are experienced business people whose wealth had been accumulated over a relatively long period of time. They stay with angel investing in good times and bad. Their wealth is diversified in public and private equity and real estate. They invest in just about all industries, not limiting themselves to high-tech or Internet-related companies. They can become valuable mentors to their invested companies.

Top guns of high-tech may have fewer number of years operating or owning companies, but they do have a significant willingness to take risks and have very up-to-date knowledge of trends in technology. Their ability to make these investments depends substantially on the value of their other high-tech holdings, which can fluctuate wildly. Some top guns invest because they like the excitement of bringing a new technology to market but don't want the day-to-day headaches of running a business.

ROI angels are in the game for the potential of a great financial reward. Their willingness to invest depends on their perception of what other angels are earning. They can disappear to some extent when times are tough. Many of the ROI angels look at an investment as a diversification in their portfolio and don't want to get particularly involved with that company.

Another Way of Looking

Lead dogs serve as lead investors or advocates to bring other angels into the deal. They want to be first in a deal and lead the pack of other investors. They pride themselves on the ability to sell the deal.

Guardian angels serve as advocates or mentors to their companies. They look at their mentoring contribution as at least as important, if not more important, than the money they contribute.

Silver spoons with silver wings are the second generation of angels; they are offspring of successful families. Although they may be younger than typical angels, they often have a lot of business experience from working at an executive level in the family business.

Dark angels' sole objective is to find a great company and invest with the intent of eventually taking over and booting the founders out.

Arch angels have established themselves as the definitive angel. When you think about angel investors, they immediately come to mind. You know who these people are so we don't have to tell you. They could be the leaders of the most influential angel groups, for example.

Cherubs are baby angels who haven't quite got the hang of using their investment wings yet. They invest in flocks rather than independently. Many grow up to become full-fledged angels. Others hang up their halos at the first sign of adversity.

Women Angels, and We Don't Mean the Victoria's Secret Kind

Although women always have been welcome to join angel networks, it has been only recently that women have been forming their own networks. These women-angel networks focus on the educational aspect of investing as well as promoting deal flow. While in most cases you have to be a woman to join, they do not necessarily focus on investing in companies managed or owned by women.

Seraph Capital Forum, www.seraphforum.com, is located in Seattle and prefers companies located in the Pacific Northwest. Business plans are screened and accepted entrepreneurs pay a $150.00 fee to have the opportunity to present at a luncheon meeting of the membership. Members invest independently and not as a group. A primary objective of Seraph Capital Forum is to educate its members to become more knowledgeable in the area of investing and to become more active. Members must be accredited to join.

WomenAngels.net is located in the Washington D.C. area and will invest as a limited partnership. Each member, who must be accredited, commits to a minimum investment of $75,000 over a three-year period. Each member makes the decision individually whether to invest in any one company, but the money is invested jointly.

Venture Capitalists Who Moonlight as Angels

Although some VC firms prohibit their partners from investing independently, many do not. Sometimes a company will be an attractive investment opportunity but not quite meet the investment parameters of the VC fund, so the VC partner invests on his or her own. Or the partners may invest their own funds alongside the funds of the VC firm. A third alternative is that the venture capitalist may invest independently when the company is in an early stage and the venture capital firm invests later on. And finally the venture capitalist may find opportunities that aren't appropriate for the venture capital firm but offer tremendous opportunity to the venture capitalist as an angel investor.

Will-Work-for-Equity Angels

Also known as sweat-equity investors, there are service providers who will exchange their services for shares of ownership. It seems like a good idea. The young company is able to utilize the services of an attorney, accountant, or consultant without expending any precious cash. There are also marketing firms, public relation firms, technology, and Web design and hosting firms that will do the same thing.

The problem with the will-work-for-equity situation is that the entrepreneur may not realize how important each portion of the equity is, and may not take into consideration the dilution that may occur. This argument that service providers should be willing to work for equity in lieu of cash overlooks an important fact: They are service providers, not risk takers. They have already started and funded and taken the risk with their own service company. Why should they be willing to take a risk on yours? And it is so tempting to give away stock shares in lieu of payment, because it seems like Monopoly money that is passed out at the beginning of the game. However, the entrepreneur can end up paying far more for the service in the long run than if they just went ahead and wrote a check when the service was provided.

DEAL TALES: DESPERATELY SEEKING SUCTION

An entrepreneur we were acquainted with started a venture to produce and market a consumer product he had patented. The product's utility was based on its ability to stick on the kitchen wall using suction cups. He was funding the venture himself, and selected a number of excellent service providers—accountant, lawyer, package designer, injection mold designer—offering some of them equity in the company as an incentive to work a little harder and defer part of their fees. This seemed to work well until problems arose that required group decision making. The service providers, who had no practical clout to affect key decisions, were usually overruled by the headstrong entrepreneur.

The most serious problem was that there were flaws in the design of the suction cups themselves. On certain types of kitchen surfaces, the product slid slowly and forlornly down the wall rather than holding its position. What the entrepreneur needed was an angel investor/partner who could say, "Wait. This isn't working. We really need to try another way." An investor who had put $150,000 or so of his money in the deal would have certainly spoken up. The service providers, if they had done that, would have of course been replaced.

For this entrepreneur, having total control was too much control. He needed an angel, experienced in building a company, to bounce ideas off and question some of the decisions being made. Someone who could have helped him avoid mistakes. A group of service providers, who were strangers to one another, could not offer the coordinated and firm advice that was needed. The entrepreneur kept going, but it was more expensive than necessary to start the company, and the product did not meet with the market acceptance he had hoped for.

Resources

Advise4stock.com introduces emerging companies to professionals willing to work for stock. Through the Advise4Stock Program, early-stage companies obtain services such as legal, marketing, financial, business plan development, and interim management teams, from advisors who have agreed to work for stock.

DigitalBridge.com's Venture Technology subsidiary will provide accepted companies with Internet strategy consulting, interactive agency, and technology development in exchange for equity.

stealthmode.com is a network of people and companies working together to help stealthmode.com portfolio ventures grow bigger, better, faster. Ventures that are accepted into the stealthmode.com portfolio receive coaching, consulting, and connections to the people and resources they need to reach success. Their Web site says that they and their network will consider working for equity.

SV Internet Accelerator, www.avce.com, matches service providers who will work for equity with entrepreneurs who require those services. SV Internet Accelerator then also takes a percentage of equity for the matching service.

Angels Who Build a Technology, Not a Company

Normally, we think of angel investors as individuals who put money into a corporate entity in order to build a business, sometimes around a new technology. The funding is used to build the infrastructure—facilities, staff, equipment—and to complete development of the technology and hopefully bring it to market.

Here is another approach: investing in just the development of a technology and then assisting the entrepreneur to license it to another, probably larger, corporation. The goal is to create a royalty stream from technical inventions, not build a portfolio of small companies that may grow into large ones.

ADVICE FROM AN ANGEL

Tom Horgan, Acorn Technologies, San Diego, CA

Tell us about your involvement with Acorn Technologies. "It is an intellectual property development and licensing company. We develop technologies to the point of licensing. We have a group of senior technologists and a network of business people. We acquire individual inventors' inventions. We license inventions from academia for purposes of developing it further and licensing to industry.

"For many large corporations, such as IBM, revenue from licensing technology is becoming more and more important. There has been a patent boom going on for quite some time. The six-millionth patent was issued in the United States in late 1999. One million of those have been issued in the last 10 years, and the patent office has been around since the nineteenth century."

How is this different from the incubator model? "Incubators work on the premise that the operator of the incubator will find a suitable technology and people to invest in it, and then bring their own expertise to help that company mature in the marketplace. We operate on the basis that there are great inventors out there, and that's all they should be doing. We will operate as a haven for the inventor, by applying our own expertise to bring the technology to the point where it is ready to be demonstrated to prospective customers, and then license it from there.

"We are able to operate with low overhead because we do not build companies. We work on getting inventions to market. In that sense, we are not placing our bet on building a company, which obviously is harder to tear down if you are wrong. We are betting that our technologies are substantially differentiated, have enough of a value proposition to be able to license them to industry.

"Since we are working on inventions, we are able to take mature markets and license technologies into those markets. The incubator model is always focused on the next wave of technology.

"We hope to be able to attract top-class inventors. We have developed 19 inventions already and are actively involved in pursuing two from a licensing standpoint. We were formed in 1998."

That's a lot of activity for just three years. Who is involved with this group? "We are funded by very high net worth individuals, well known in the technology world. The cream of the crop.

"We invest in the technology and add value to it."

Corporations as Angels

A corporation as an angel? It's not as odd as it might sound at first. Corporations fit the definition of angels in that they invest their own money.

THE UPSIDE

It is certainly true that having an industry giant as part owner can enable that company to take advantage of the technical skill within the larger company, which should enhance the value of the smaller company. In subsequent rounds of financing, the fact the larger company has already invested capital—and effort—in the smaller firm can make it easier to attract investors for that round, and even possibly increase the valuation the small company receives for its shares. In today's business world, where strategic alliances are so important to success, what better type of alliance can there be than to show investors that a major corporation has endorsed its technology to the point of being willing to put dollars behind it, and assign executives within the organization to help guide the company.

Corporate angels are not limited to the high-tech, communications, and Internet industries. They can be found in the pharmaceutical, publishing, insurance, finance, sports, recreation, mining, and many other industries as well.

The amount of capital invested by corporate angels is difficult to estimate. Venture One and PriceWaterhouseCoopers conduct quarterly surveys of venture capital invested and attempt to include corporate investments as well as traditional VC investments. They report that from 20 percent to 30 percent of the $30 billion a year of VC investment is invested by corporate angels. The problem is that there is no requirement for the corporate angels to report. The incentive for venture capitalists to report is to demonstrate how viable and active the firm is, and that same incentive isn't necessarily applicable for corporate angels.

Some large corporations use these internal venture investments as a way of retaining top technical talent who want to work on something more interesting or cutting-edge that may not be available through the company's basic business. Some of these individuals would forgo all the perks of being in a large profitable enterprise in order to get greater brain stimulation. These internal ventures prevent the people from wanting to leave.

Some companies, including Dell, Intel, and Motorola, actually set up a venture fund with its own management team. This can become necessary when the number of ventures they fund each year becomes appreciable. IBM, interestingly, has not set up a separate fund.

ADVICE FROM A CORPORATE VENTURE CAPITALIST

Richard Birney, Vice President, IBM

What is IBM's approach to venture investing? "Our approach to investing in emerging companies has its own unique fingerprint and is matched to our business-development strategy. IBM is very interested in start-up companies, is actively investing in start-ups around the world, and will continue, in fact will probably expand, its activities with these companies.

"IBM has traditionally been quiet about its investing precisely because we view investing as an important strategic activity. Think of us as the strong, silent type of investor. We don't do deals for show.

"We don't do deals just for dough. Financial returns are among our goals, but when we embarked on a more aggressive program of venture investing, we came to the conclusion that although equity returns would be nice, they would not be the primary driver or decision-making point for our investments."

So what are the decision-making points, as you call it, for your investment program? "As a company, IBM wanted access to small companies with smart people and new emerging technologies. Given the incredible pace of change and innovation, we ranked technology headlights at the top of the list of benefits we wanted through our start-up company outreach and investment.

"Second, we wanted to expand our business relationships. We view start-up company activities as a way to find companies who could OEM [original equipment manufacturer] their technology to us, or who wanted to license our technologies for use in their products.

"Third, we wanted new customers. We want tomorrow's *Fortune* 1000 to view IBM as relevant and as trustworthy as the current *Fortune* 1000 does. We want start-up companies to include IBM on their short lists when it's time to buy hardware, software, and services."

Why hasn't IBM set up its VC investing arm like many other companies have? "Setting up our own fund would provide benefits but only with a limited number of companies. It would also involve us in aspects of venture investing we're not as interested in, such as working on other companies' business plans or sitting on the boards. To build a broad range of relationships, we decided that our strategy would be to invest in start-up companies through top-tier VC firms. We're a technology company, not a VC company. We desire to partner with, not compete with, the VC community."

Would you ever consider a direct investment in a start-up company? "Although the core of our strategy is building relationships with venture capitalists and their portfolio companies, we also make a few direct minority investments. These investments must support the growth strategies of our various business units and have a clear, strategic, business rationale. For instance, we invested directly in Red Hat as part of our commitment to Linux. We invested directly in Data Channel, an XML portal provider, as part of our commitment to open standards. In several cases, we found it made sense to exchange goods and services for equity rather than cash. We have used this approach in working with fabless semiconductor companies that would like access to our leading-edge semiconductor foundry. We look for opportunities where IBM can create a business relationship that creates significant new revenue growth for IBM and the partner company."

Do you feel your strategy of investing in VC firms who invest in start-up companies has been successful? "Yes, our strategy is demonstrating success. The strategy is still young and is being tested by a turbulent economic environment in the VC industry but it is weathering well and continuing to create real value for IBM. By working with the best venture capitalists in geographical regions, we have gained excellent insights into innovation in those regions, we have protected ourselves from many bad deals, and we have developed important business relationships with new companies that we anticipate will grow into significant future revenues for IBM. We gain significant leverage, both intellectual and economic, by focusing on building relationships with high-quality VC firms."

Large corporations are not as unfamiliar with the ups and downs of investing in start-ups as we might imagine. Many of them have participated in this market by becoming limited partners in large VC funds.

Many of these investments done by corporate angels are in areas related to the core business of the large company. The theory is that both entities, the large and the start-up company, can benefit from utilizing each other's intellectual property. A large enterprise with a huge library of intellectual property can find a market for some of this property by funding small companies that may be able to use a component of the big company's technology in its products.

Investing in early-stage companies also helps the large corporation keep its ear to the ground regarding major technological shifts, or directions their markets may be taking. Small companies, in unsettled, emerging, frothy markets, have a more hands-on perspective sometimes than a large corporation that has dominated its market for some time.

Venture capital firms periodically must go out and raise more money from institutions. Some of these mammoth corporate angels have enormous internally generated financial resources that dwarf most of the venture funds' available cash. But, as with all angels, the corporate angels do not have to make these investments, and they may decide to devote less capital and management resources to making these investments at any time.

ADVICE FROM A CORPORATE VENTURE CAPITALIST

Matthew I. Growney, Managing Director, Motorola Ventures

From the entrepreneur's viewpoint, what are the advantages of corporate venture capital versus traditional venture capital? "Corporate venture capital allows an entrepreneur the opportunity to access over thousands of engineers, marketing and distribution channels, technology portfolios, and quality leadership. Whereas traditional venture capital provides capital and instrumental networking, it seldom provides actual real-time operating expertise centered on production volumes, margins, or complex technology planning. Corporate venture capitalists are sensitive to CAPEX issues and can be instrumental in assessing a start-up's time to macro markets. A leading multinational corporation gives a start-up future markets and real-time global exposure without having to wait decades to grow into those economies. Corporate venture capitalists can facilitate a promising start-up company's introductions into a large corporation thus acting as a true champion for entrepreneurs. Operating and strategic partnerships of the strongest kind will survive this economy regardless of whether you have traditional VC funding."

Why does Motorola invest in start-up companies? "Motorola Ventures (MV) actively invests at early stages in developing companies of strategic value to Motorola in order to accelerate access to new technologies, new markets, and new talent. The number of cutting-edge technologies being developed by young talented start-up companies compels Motorola Ventures to always envision Motorola's future and bring about valuable long-term partnerships with these rising newcos. In mere introductions between entrepreneurs and Motorola business group managers, Motorola and start-up companies share enthusiasm, vision, and qualitative speculation about the future of high technology. By solidifying new relationships with an equity investment, both parties begin the realization of building new and sometimes revolutionary businesses. Motorola Ventures makes those relationships a reality for both parties and ensures future value to Motorola businesses and shareholders."

Can you describe the selection process from the initial contact by the entrepreneur to the investment by Motorola Ventures? "Motorola Ventures makes the acquaintance of entrepreneurs through any number of avenues. University entrepreneurship and business school programs, traditional VC firms, corporate partners, and other entrepreneurs all have provided investment opportunities to the MV office. Upon receiving an electronic executive summary on a new opportunity, MV reviews the start-up company's market and technology offering. If both prove to be strategic to Motorola's core of emerging business platforms, MV brings the company in for an introductory face-to-face meeting and requests the full business plan and other helpful documented resources. Motorola Ventures then makes proper introductions between the start-up company's technology team and Motorola's pertinent engineering teams to assess the compatibility and quality of the start-up company's proposition. If several Motorola business groups believe that the start-up company has a technology or market opportunity extremely valuable to Motorola, then MV will commence due diligence on the start-up company, its investors, management, and internal Motorola technology groups that will receive the benefit or burden of working with the new company. All viable venture opportunities are brought before an investment advisory board where four officers of Motorola determine whether the opportunity is strategic to the visions of Motorola. Immediately upon their approval, the investment opportunity is then negotiated on terms relative to the relationship sought between both parties. The managing directors of MV make the final decision about whether to invest, and then the transaction occurs. MV has its own finance, legal, and press components so the process is usually streamlined. All companies invested in are managed 100 percent by MV and not the Motorola business group(s) that has development opportunities underway. This ensures a more holistic and healthier Motorola relationship with a delicate young start-up company."

THE DOWNSIDE

Dealing with the bureaucracy inside a large corporation can be a problem for the smaller company, and they may lose flexibility as a result or the ability to react quickly to changes in their market spaces.

Some of the corporate venture divisions are huge. As of early 2001, Intel has 280 people involved in their corporate investing activities. The company has invested in more than 600 companies and has invested $1.2 billion capital in 2000 alone. The conflict within the organization is the need to help the early-stage company they have invested in while still meeting the objectives of the larger parent company. The small company may have one executive within the organization who was instrumental in getting the deal done. If that person changes positions or leaves the company, the small company can be left without that champion of their cause, and they may not receive the attention or even the additional capital they may need.

The corporate venture capitalist can also be slower to make decisions on issues before the small company's board, because the issues have to travel through several layers of the large organization. At a speech given by a member of the venture team of one large technology company, the speaker was asked this point and countered that he was given wide latitude by the person he reported to, to make decisions regarding the companies in their portfolio. A man seated next to us leaned over and whispered, "Yeah, right. I've dealt with them, and he has to get permission from his boss's boss to get any investment approved."

If the technology has some synergy with the parent company's technology, the question arises whether the resources will be deployed to maximize the returns to the small company's shareholders, as they certainly would be with a VC firm as an investor, or will the benefits of the technology for the parent firm be emphasized.

Another issue to consider is whether the corporate venture capitalists will reduce their commitment to their investment division in times when the public market capitalization of the company is on the decline, or when the valuations of early-stage companies take a nosedive as they did in 2001. Early-stage companies typically require several rounds of follow-up funding to continue to reach important milestones. A reduction in financial commitment by their corporate partner can drastically slow down the company's growth.

Critics of large corporations as suppliers of start-up capital contend that you have to have a strong level of commitment to this type of investment activity in order to make a success of it—for both the large corporation and the start-ups they fund. They point to the fact that many companies become active in early-stage investing, then suspend or eliminate their investment division altogether, as evidence that large corporations do not make ideal angels.

Chapter Summary

- The total number of active angel investors rises and falls with the wealth created or lost in the public equity markets.
- Angels differ according to age, background, experience, and motivation for investing.
- Several specialized types of angels have sprung up, including women angel networks, angels who trade work for equity, and angels who license technology rather than build companies.

- Corporate angel investing is a significant slice of the total venture investment pie.
- Having a corporate angel as a partner can give the start-up company access to tremendous talent, technology, financing, and marketing resources.
- Corporations make venture investments in order to motivate and retain top technical talent who are seeking entrepreneurial challenges, to help monetize the company's library of intellectual property, and for strategic reasons.

CHAPTER

10

When Angels and Venture Capitalists Are on the Same Team

The time and effort angels expend in finding companies, reviewing business plans, analyzing companies, checking out the management, and verifying new technologies can be daunting. Some angels would rather pool their money and let someone else do all that work.

Several models have been developed that allow just that.

MANY NEW WAYS TO PARTICIPATE

In recent years new angel investment vehicles have been created to try to free pools of capital that have not been available to entrepreneurs. An example is a kind of high-risk mutual fund in which an angel might invest $50,000 to $250,000 and the fund's managers select the early-stage companies to invest in and conduct the due diligence. In this way angels who do not want to contribute a lot of time to this activity can still participate, and they get the benefit of a venture finance professional's experience in selecting companies.

Investment advisors that work with wealthy individuals are beginning to view investments in early-stage companies in a favorable light, seeing them as a good way to deploy a small percentage of one's portfolio and reach the upper end of the risk/reward spectrum. Prudent investors keep this percentage in the 5 percent to 10 percent range, however. The need for sleep at night precludes them from putting half their assets in deals that could very possibly be worth nothing.

Sport of Champions

We have all heard stories of wealthy athletes blowing large amounts of money on ill-advised venture investments—restaurant chains that went Chapter 7, real estate deals that go sour, dry-hole oil and gas partnerships. Ex-football stars Ronnie Lott and Harris Barton saw a need for an organized approach to helping athletes invest their money wisely and still take advantage of the tremendous returns available from backing early-stage companies. Their answer? Be angels who invest in the venture capitalists.

They put together Champion Ventures, a group that includes several hundred celebrity athletes from all the major sports. Approximately 250 individuals have invested in Champion Ventures as of mid-2001. Champion invests the athletes' money in some of the largest and best-known venture capital funds. The athletes' celebrity status opens the doors to these funds that would be closed for even extremely wealthy angels who don't have a similar claim to fame. The athletes get to take advantage of the skill and wisdom of the venture capitalists rather than having to make the investment decisions themselves. And because Champion has nearly $200 million in committed capital, it can place money in a number of different venture funds and thus achieve a further degree of portfolio diversification.

A VC Fund That Welcomes Little Guys

Another interesting approach was spawned with the backing of one of the nation's most respected VC firms, Draper Fisher Jurvetson. Called MeVC/Draper Fisher Jurvetson Fund, this new public venture fund welcomes small investments in what will be a $500 million fund. The professionals of Draper Fisher Jurvetson will make the decisions about what companies to invest in, just as they do for their private funds capitalized by large institutional investors and extremely wealthy individuals.

ADVICE FROM AN EXPERT

Peter S. Freudenthal, Chairman, President, CEO, meVC, Inc.

What was the motivation to start MeVC? "Traditionally, venture capital has been the exclusive domain of large institutions and ultrawealthy individuals. We believe that there is a need to democratize venture capital and private equity as an asset class, and allow any individual investor to invest a small amount of their investable assets (2% to 5%) in professionally managed and fully diversified venture funds."

What are the advantages to a private investor to invest in MeVC versus joining an angel network or investing directly into a start-up? "First, anyone can invest in our funds at any time by buying shares of our first fund (the meVC Draper Fisher Jurvetson Fund 1) on the NYSE (MVC). We intend to launch other funds in other sectors of venture capital and in other geographies so that, eventually, we will provide investors with the ability to choose from a number of different professionally managed VC fund vehicles. Most angel investors are not professional venture capitalists and do not have the technical background to make sound VC investments—particularly in individual companies that often require a fairly large minimum investment on the order of \$10,000 to \$25,000. Our investors can buy as little as one share. We think it is better left to professionals to pick the investments, and give the investor diversification over 30 to 50 different companies that each fund will invest in. Our funds also give daily trading liquidity, which is important to many individual investors."

Do you see more traditional VC companies starting public investment funds? "If our funds perform well, I think other venture capitalists will see that there are several advantages to raising money as a public investment fund, such as diversifying their capital base. Publicly listed closed-end venture funds (meVC Draper Fisher Jurvetson Fund 1 being the first) can be evergreen (existing for several decades if they perform well), which allows the managing venture capitalists to take a longer investment horizon and not have to raise a new partnership fund every 2 to 3 years. This allows them to focus on helping their portfolio companies instead of spending considerable time marketing to their limited partners."

Because MeVC is a publically traded stock, are there any differences in the screening process of a potential investment candidate (the company to be invested in) from the private Draper

Fisher Jurvetson Fund? "Just to clarify, meVC, Inc. is the private venture capital mutual-fund company. However, meVC Draper Fisher Jurvetson Fund 1 (NYSE:MVC) is the stock of our first fund in what will eventually be a family of VC mutual funds. Our fund managers use the same rigorous due-diligence process. If anything, our portfolio companies are benefiting from having tens of thousands of interested individual investors all rooting for their success."

Stock Exchange for Private Placements

In early 2001, a group of former Bear Stearns officials launched an online exchange for private equity securities, in other words, a stock market where wealthy individuals could trade shares in private companies, many of which were funded by venture capitalists or angel investors. They called the exchange the NYPPE, or New York Private Placement Exchange, www.nyppe.com.

This group said they already had 4,000 wealthy individual and institutional investors ready to participate when they announced the opening of the exchange. Their goal was to "create a secondary market for venture capital that is the equivalent of the public stock exchanges."

The innovation here is that it could allow angels who invest in private companies to obtain liquidity (be able to sell the shares) prior to the typical exit event of the sale of the whole company or the company going public—events that can take five years or more from the time the angel first made the investment.

The exchange also hopes to offer newly issued private placements, allowing wealthy individuals easier access to VC-type investments.

The founders of the exchange estimate that the total market value of VC assets is more than $3 trillion.

This is a very intriguing concept. Does this mean you will be able to look up the value of your angel investment every day, just as you check the price of Cisco Systems or Intel? That will depend on how many investors participate. To have a truly liquid market you need a significant amount of trading volume. It also poses the same kinds of valuation dilemmas an investor faces when first negotiating to purchase shares in an early-stage company.

If this becomes an active exchange, it could provide a badly needed benchmark for angel investors to use in setting the valuation on new ventures they are considering for investment. If you could see on a posted exchange what other comparable companies are selling for—and whether the market is bullish or bearish at the present time—it could take some of the guesswork and risk of overpaying for private equities out of the process. We will have to wait and see.

Chapter Summary

- New entities and investment vehicles are continually being created to encourage or facilitate venture investment.

CHAPTER 11

Devil in a Blue Suit: Spotting Frauds and Cheats

SOME ANGELS HAVE ANGLES TO WATCH OUT FOR

Like a tropical aviary, the angel world has a lot of colorful birds. Some, unfortunately, are birds of prey. They just may come to the meetings with their talons retracted. For entrepreneurs who don't want to find themselves plucked after the deal closes, it helps to beware of these types.

Dumb Angels: How Do They Manage to Get Their Wings on Straight in the Morning?

Wealth is not synonymous with business savvy. When one of us worked for a lending institution that made second mortgages, it was quite a surprise to find out how many of the jumbo loans, $500,000 and above, ended up in default. How did these affluent people mess up their finances this badly? As investors in your company, these people pose a hazard because they will not be able to understand the inevitable ups and downs of entrepreneurship. When you tell them about things that have slowed the company's development down, they will react with more hostility than an experienced angel who has been through all this before. Dumb angels also are less likely to be able to provide any substantive advisory assistance to the company.

You can spot dumb angels by the questions they ask. If they ask superficial questions (or "duh" diligence, you might call it), then you are pretty sure you know who you have on your hands.

Fallen Angels

We see these every time the stock market/real estate market/general economy has a serious slowdown or correction. People who had a reputation as high-flyers in a community, people you would be referred to as potential angels for your start-up, suddenly have a serious liquidity problem. They are still at the country club every day, but now they are running up a tab. The problem is that they won't act or behave any differently. If you contact them, they may even agree to meet with you. They have no choice: They can't let word get out that they are no longer running with the big dogs. If word of their difficulties got out, they would lose important status in the community and no longer be invited to the A-list parties. You will be told they are good friends of (Ms. X) (Mr. Y), and other people you know who have tremendous wealth. You will be impressed with this. But you're out of luck because your potential angel now has less liquid capital than you do.

Angel Knows Best: And Don't You Forget It

A key characteristic of a successful entrepreneur is the ability to build a team and work in a team format, with levels of authority, but also to create an environment where the CEO seeks out input from, and really listens to, the other members of the team. Enter the angel. He is now in an advisory position, a board position, perhaps, and has significant input. A number of successful business people, some of whom become angels, develop the belief that they were destined for greatness because of their clear superiority over everyone else. They would have to suddenly gain a lot of humility to come down just to the level of raving ego-maniac. They can't wait to tell you how much better they are than you. These can be overbearing, negative people who are hypercritical of every decision the entrepreneur makes. Negative people can drain a tremendous amount of energy out of entrepreneurial situations, which have tremendous swings between joy and agony as it is. Entrepreneurs need all the BTUs they can muster.

These people are fairly easy to spot. In our interviews with angels, we could identify them 5 minutes into the phone conversation. For one thing, they told us they were better writers than we are.

The Sweat Equity Specialist

This person appears before you with all sorts of enthusiasm; often he even has a friendly name like Bob or Ray. He cannot wait to plunge in and invest. He actually begins working with you before the deal closes. He may even want to get to know some of your suppliers or customers. If you are having any difficulties, he offers his considerable skills as a negotiator. He shows up at your office more and more frequently, until he is a virtual fixture there. When you press him to put in the capital he has promised to, he hedges, hems, and haws. If you press further, he will tell you that he is actually going to put in a much lesser amount, but wants equity "credit" for all the work he has done already. And further credit for the work he will do after putting in the capital. If you balk, he says he will walk, and you are at the point you need some capital, any capital. And you will lose face because he has told your customers, suppliers, employees, that he is coming aboard. Why didn't good ol' Bob invest, they will all ask you, as if there must be something wrong with your company.

Brokers Posing as Investors: That Masked Man Is Zero, Not Zorro

These people are all over the place. From their brochures, the publicity they receive, what they tell you in meetings, they appear to be individuals or firms that invest money in companies. In reality, they have very little, if any, capital, and little intention to invest it in your company.

They will eventually solicit you to sign a fee agreement to pay them to introduce you to actual investors. When you ask them where their money comes from, they will respond with vague terms such as, "the money comes from close associates." Close associates can be people whose names appear in a directory of VC firms on their bookshelf. Many times an entrepreneur, weary of the process of looking for capital, will go ahead and sign the fee agreement. The broker in disguise knows that, if he just cold called you and said he wanted to perform this service for you, you likely would not meet with him. You might even tell him to get lost.

There is nothing wrong with hiring an intermediary to help you find investors, nothing wrong with paying the intermediary a retainer to do so. But they ought to disclose to you who they really are. If a business relationship begins under false pretences, it is not likely to get better as it proceeds.

DEAL TALES: SAVE THE EQUITY, LOSE THE COMPANY

Entrepreneurs sometimes look favorably on deal structures that involve debt instead of equity, or a combination of the two. They like the idea of not having to part with so much of the equity in their company, quite reasonably believing that they will be able to retain more control, and eventually have a greater share of the proceeds when the company is sold.

But the entrepreneur needs to be careful regarding what kind of terms the investor/lender is proposing, because generally early-stage or growing companies do not have a great deal of extra cash to service the debt, and in a worst case it can end up strangling the whole venture.

The worst example of this we ever saw involved a manufacturing company that was growing modestly but saw the opportunity to capture the lion's share of its market in the Western United States. The lender put in capital to purchase inventory for expanded production. The terms of the loan, a revolving line of credit, reflected the VC risk associated with the funding of this company, the lender said.

Anxious to expand, the company went ahead with the deal. It worked out well for the lender. The loan covenants included management fees to be paid to the lender for advising the company (even though the lender was a finance person, not a manufacturing expert), a high interest rate, penalties if the company was not able to periodically pay down the line or make the monthly interest payments, and several other ways of nicking the company here and there for money. This company was in a relatively low-margin business in the first place, and had highly variable cash flow because of the large size of many of its orders.

After six months, the company's accountant did an analysis that showed that, at the end of the day, when all the payments to the lender were factored in, the annualized cost of the money was 96 percent.

The result was that by going with a loan instead of an equity investment, the company's management team nearly managed to kill the company. The short-term cost of this type of financing was simply too high for a company that was trying grow rapidly. The lender, of course, knew this was happening, and made sure that nearly every available dollar was paid to him. Was this smart business, or simply a crooked financier taking advantage of a naïve entrepreneur?

Concierge of Heartbreak Hotel

Entrepreneurs are so optimistic about their businesses that they often mistake slight interest by an investor as meaning the check is about to be written. Investors, though, are not blameless, either. They often procrastinate in making a decision, string the entrepreneur along, and give the entrepreneur false hope. The reasons for this vary. Sometimes the due diligence process becomes a wonderful way for an investor who has no intention of actually funding the company to learn about a new industry or new technologies. They just want to drain information out of the entrepreneur. Some investors enjoy being courted by the entrepreneur; it gives them a feeling of importance. But for the entrepreneur, the eventual rejection can be devastating because the entrepreneur may have not kept looking for other investors, thinking they had the deal in the bag. They end up holding the empty bag instead.

Inexperienced angels may think they are hurting the entrepreneur's feelings by declining, so they say nothing and hope the entrepreneur will just go away.

The best investors are those who can make decisions with a certain degree of promptness. We met in the offices of a Boston venture capitalist who told us it almost gave him an uneasy feeling to have too many deals that were in limbo between a yes and a no. He promised our client that, one way or the other, he would get their business plan off his desk as soon as he could. Of course, he declined, but he did decline promptly.

DEAL TALES: WE ASKED FOR A WHITE KNIGHT AND YOU BROUGHT US A BANKER INSTEAD

Sometimes in the course of our management consulting careers, we have found ourselves in the corporate equivalent of a black hole working with a company that is hopeless, with no chance of making it profitable. In one case, two bright marketing whizzes decided to buy an ailing manufacturing firm. They had set amazing sales records at their last company, though, and thought the cure for this manufacturer was sell, sell, sell. They forgot another component, however: margins, margins, margins. They doubled sales in six months after they bought this company, but the balance sheet actually deteriorated. The cure: find an angel to buy a minority interest in the company. However, angels are not stupid. We invited some investors to take a look at the company. One very sharp guy flew out from New York, spent the day at the company, and told us as we drove him back to the airport, "This thing would take a million dollars to fix. I have a million dollars, but it's staying where it is, not coming here."

These two entrepreneurs, whom we began to refer to as "the boys," did not get discouraged; they just worked all the harder to find an angel. Finally they did. He swept in and performed his due diligence with remarkable speed. As the gruesome balance sheet details were revealed to him, he just calmly stated, "Don't worry, I can take care of the payables problem." "The supplier won't ship any more unless you settle the past due? I'll take care of that."

He settled in and started working there before even closing the deal to purchase 50 percent of the company. The boys began to worry: When is this guy going to put in the cash investment? He promised cash.

He never did. He wasn't about to use his funds to solve problems caused by the stupidity of others. You don't get rich by being stupid. Instead he set up a secured lending arrangement with the company whereby he would purchase the materials, take title to the orders, manage the factory operations to make sure the orders got filled on time, and then have the customers send the payments to him. He would pay himself back, with interest, and whatever was left over went to the company to cover payroll, office expenses, and, perhaps, something for the boys. The boys didn't like this arrangement, of course, and called and told us so. "We asked you for a white knight and you sent us some kind of banker."

The question remains, does the white knight they referred to actually exist?

Presenting the One and Only Vulture Capitalist

There are bad, bad people whose sole intention of getting involved in early-stage investing is to take advantage of what they believe is the entrepreneur's lack of financial and deal-making experience. Generally, the stench of these people's reputation precedes them, so all you have to do is take a good whiff. With a little investigation, you can find out that no one in the business community has much good to say about them. It is up to the entrepreneur to actively do this reverse due diligence and find out. Vultures only go after animals that appear to be motionless.

Chapter Summary

- Angel investors are not always good people, and entrepreneurs must take great care to get complete information about the character and reputation of any prospective investors. The entrepreneur's tendency to be in a huge hurry to obtain the funding can end up being disastrous and play into the hands of the less scrupulous investor.

PREPARING FOR A GLIMPSE OF HEAVEN

CHAPTER

12

Why an Attorney Is an Absolute Must

Rule number 1. Get an attorney.
Rule number 2. See rule 1.
Rule number 3. Always follow rule 2.

A Brief Tour of Securities Laws

REGULATION D AND RULE 504 PRIVATE OFFERINGS

It is illegal to sell stock unless you are licensed to do so or the stock offering qualifies for an exemption from the SEC and your state securities' commission rules. In 1982, the SEC adopted Regulation D, which set forth rules for exemptions from federal registration. Offerings exempt under rules 504, 505, and 506 are a common cost and time saving way to raise capital from private investors. Keep in mind that although rule 504 provides an exemption from federal restrictions of stock offerings it does not provide an exemption from the individual state rules and regulations concerning securities offerings.

Although there are no requirements by the SEC under rule 504 about disclosure, some sort of offering document, such as a private placement memorandum, should be prepared to protect the company and its officers from fraud and liability litigation at a later date. Take your business plan to your law firm and have their securities attorney prepare the offering document. Each potential investor then signs a statement that they have seen the offering document and are aware of the risk inherent in making such an investment at the time they invest.

REGULATION D ACCREDITED INVESTORS AND PRIVATE PLACEMENTS

Regulation D allows an issuer of securities to sell securities. The offers of securities must specify that sales will only be made to accredited investors and sales of securities must be made exclusively to accredited investors.

An individual to be considered accredited must have a net worth (that means all assets minus all liabilities, including home mortgages) which exceeds $1,000,000 or an annual income of $250,000 (or a joint income with their spouse of $350,000) for the prior two years and a reasonable expectation of at least that level of income in the fiscal year the securities purchase takes place.

An accredited investor also includes: a bank, insurance company, registered investment company, business development company, or small business investment company; an employee benefit plan, within the meaning of the Employee Retirement Income Security Act, if a bank, insurance company, or registered investment advisor makes the investment decisions, or if the plan has total assets in excess of $5 million; a charitable organization, corporation, or partnership with assets exceeding $5 million; a director, executive officer, or general partner of the company selling the securities; a business in which all the equity owners are accredited investors; or a trust with assets of at least $5 million, not formed to acquire the securities offered, and whose purchases are directed by a sophisticated person.

Does the entrepreneur who is looking for an accredited investor have to verify or document that the potential investor is accredited? No. If the investor says they are accredited, that is all that is necessary, but again go to your attorney and make sure that your business plan, offering memorandum, and stock subscription agreement have the necessary language.

ADVICE FROM AN EXPERT

Pennies from Heaven: Angel Investors and the Securities Laws

Christopher D. Johnson, Partner, Squire, Sanders, & Dempsey L.L.P. Law Firm, www.ssd.com

Many early stage entrepreneurs, especially those whose businesses may be premature for investment by professional venture capitalists, have been counseled to seek financing from angel investors. Generally, these angels are well-to-do individuals who, either alone or in loosely or more formally organized associations (bands of angels), invest in start-up and very-early-stage enterprises. Angel investors provide a valuable and relatively approachable source of capital. Indeed, the very term angel investors summons the image of caring and generous souls eager to provide encouragement, guidance, and, of course, financial support to struggling entrepreneurs. This benign impression may tend to obscure the fact that, as with any other investment, investments by angel investors are subject to federal and state securities laws.

A short course in securities law provides a helpful context. When an entrepreneur offers an equity interest in his business to an investor, whether common stock, a partnership interest, or an interest in a limited liability company, he or she is offering to sell a security. Most debt instruments used to raise early-stage risk capital are also likely to be considered securities under federal and state law. Securities must be registered for sale under federal and state securities laws, unless an exemption is available. The registration process is time-consuming, complex, and prohibitively expensive in connection with early-stage investments. The most commonly used exemption is for private placements, in which securities may be sold to an unlimited number of accredited investors, and to a limited number (not to exceed 35) of nonaccredited, but sophisticated investors. Accredited investors include certain high net worth ($1,000,000 or more) and high-income ($250,000 individual/$350,000 with spouse) individuals, as well as a variety of institutions and other qualified entities.

Most angel investors are also accredited investors. The distinction between accredited investors and nonaccredited investors is significant under federal and state private placement exemptions. If only accredited investors are involved, no specific information is required to be furnished as a condition to the private placement exemption. In such a situation, preparation of a formal private placement memorandum may be dispensed with, which results in substantial savings in time and expense, including legal fees. However, if any nonaccredited investors are involved, the private placement rules require delivery of written information of the same type that would be contained in a registration statement that would be filed with the SEC in connection with a nonexempt offering. In addition, the seller would be required to have a reasonable basis to conclude that any nonaccredited investor had what is usually called investment sophistication (i.e., the capability through education, employment, or other experience of evaluating the merits and risks of the investment).

Of course, even if an offering is exempt, the antifraud provisions of the federal and state securities laws still apply. These provisions prohibit the sale of securities by means of any misstatement or omission of facts material to the investment decision.

A qualified securities attorney can guide an entrepreneur about the application of the securities laws to the specific circumstances of any proposed angel investment. Although the issues associated with securities law compliance in the angel investment context are usually easily manageable, the consequences of noncompliance can be severe. If an offering is not registered and no exemption is available, the investor may have a variety of securities claims against the entrepreneur and his or her business, including a right to rescind the investment and demand return of the invested funds. Attention to the applicable securities laws from the outset can help ensure that an angel investment doesn't wind up as a devilish problem.

Keeping a Tight Grip on Your Intellectual Property

ADVICE FROM AN EXPERT

Intellectual Property Protection

Paul G. Burns, Gallagher & Kennedy, P.A., www.gknet.com

It is critically important for all companies, especially emerging companies, to protect their intellectual property. Intellectual property protection may be obtained under four distinct areas of law: patent law, trade secret law, copyright law, and trademark law.

The U.S. Constitution grants Congress the power "to promote the progress of science and useful arts, by securing for limited times to . . .

inventors the exclusive right to their . . . discoveries." Accordingly, Congress passed the Patent Act, which gives inventors the right to obtain patents for their inventions.

A patent grants the right to an inventor to preclude others from making, using, selling, or offering to sell the invention. For patents that issue from applications filed after June 8, 1995, the inventor's patent rights last for 20 years from the effective date of the application.

The invention must qualify as patentable subject matter (i.e., a process, a machine, an article of manufacture, or a composition of matter, or an improvement thereof). Moreover, it must satisfy three critical tests. First, it must be novel. Second it must not have been obvious to one of ordinary skill in the art. Third, it must satisfy the utility requirement; that is, it must be useful.

In the United States, inventors must file a patent application with the United States Patent and Trademark Office within one year of the invention being described in a printed publication, in public use, on sale or offered for sale, or else they lose the right to do so. In many foreign countries, no such grace period exists. Moreover, if a first inventor fails to act diligently in filing the patent application, one who was a subsequent inventor of the same invention may be able to obtain the patent rights to the invention, and thus preclude the first inventor from being able to profit from it!

A trade secret is information that derives independent economic value from not being generally known. As a condition precedent to obtaining patent rights, an inventor must fully describe the invention in sufficient detail to enable one of ordinary skill in the art to make and use the invention. In contrast, to take advantage of trade-secret protection, the trade-secret owner must take precautions to preserve the secrecy of the trade secret. For so long as such precautions are taken and the information does not otherwise become generally known, trade-secret protection continues. Trade-secret protection applies without the need to file any application or registration. State laws provide trade-secret owners with the right to obtain an injunction to stop any actual or threatened misappropriation of a trade secret as well as to obtain money damages from the misappropriation.

Copyright law protects original works of authorship. It is said that copyright law does not protect ideas, systems, or methods (as patent law does for patentable subject matter), but it may protect the expression of these things. Protectable works of authorship include writings, songs, artistic works, dramatic works, architecture, and computer software. Although copyright protection applies regardless of whether an application for registration has been filed with the United States Copyright Office, the filing and subsequent copyright registration approval gives the copyright owner certain additional rights if another person subsequently infringes upon the owner's copyright. These additional rights include the ability to recover statutory damages and attorneys' fees if the copyright owner has to commence a suit against an alleged infringer to stop the infringement.

Trademark law protects a word, phrase, color, design, symbol, smell, group of letters or numbers or any combination thereof that enables a consumer to recognize the source of a product or service. Although certain trademark rights will apply in the absence of any registration, maximum protection may only be obtained by seeking a federal trademark registration. Before adopting a trademark, a search should be conducted to determine whether another has previously obtained a federal registration or whether other evidence exists of another's prior use of the same or similar mark for the same or similar goods or services. Otherwise, the subsequent user of the mark could be liable for trademark infringement.

Nondisclosure or Confidentiality Agreements

Entrepreneurs often whip out a nondisclosure agreement (NDA) for investors to sign before they even reveal the name of their company. The belief is that these agreements protect them against theft of valuable intellectual property they may disclose over the course of meeting and presenting information to potential investors. Venture capital firms often absolutely refuse to sign these, because so many entrepreneurs come to them with similar ideas that they would be opening themselves up to litigation if they went ahead and signed. Angels, on the other hand are frequently willing to sign these if the entrepreneur insists.

ADVICE FROM AN ANGEL

Luis Villalobos, Founder and Director, Tech Coast Angels, www.techcoastangels.com

How do you address the sensitive issue of confidentiality with entrepreneurs and signing nondisclosure agreements (NDA)? "Our group has a policy that is very overt: We posted it on our Web site, and we tell the entrepreneurs in any meeting that they should give us only that part of their information that is not confidential. Only in exceptional circumstances, and partway along due diligence, would we entertain signing an NDA."

Do you encounter entrepreneurs who are very stubborn about wanting the NDA signed? "Not many. In the end, most recognize that if they want money they have to either present their idea and leave out the confidential part initially or realize that, as I tell them, they could probably publish their idea in the newspaper and no one would take it anyway. I have been both an inventor and an entrepreneur, and I know it is natural to worry that someone will steal your idea. In reality, it is hard to get people to pay attention to a new idea."

Aren't investors focused just as much on whether the management team can execute the idea as on whether the idea by itself is great? "I am basically a technologist at heart, but I've learned over the years that marketing beats technology 9 times out of 10."

An attorney should prepare this document for the entrepreneur. It is a balancing act to prepare an NDA that satisfies the entrepreneur's need for protection while not being too off-putting to the investor. We've been asked to sign documents that are so long, complex, and horribly worded that we needed to have our attorney review it before we felt comfortable signing.

ADVICE FROM AN ANGEL

Brent Townshend

What is your policy regarding signing entrepreneurs' nondisclosure agreements? "Some unsophisticated angels will sign anything, but angels should be sensitive about signing NDAs. Many angels invest in companies that are somewhat related to their own, so you have to be careful about the restrictive language in the agreement.

"I would have to be pretty interested in the public disclosures the company is making before I would sign an NDA. But I will sign them if they are not too restrictive.

"A lot of times if entrepreneurs are overly sensitive, it is a bad sign. You see companies that are overprotective of their ideas. They are so worried about the idea being stolen that they actually never sell anything. The most important thing they need to do is network for business development. They need to be out there getting strategic alliances, getting things going. If they are oversecretive with the angel, they are probably not going to be able to get the idea out there and develop the business."

Chapter Summary

- Anyone seeking capital must have the counsel of an attorney experienced in financial transactions.
- Competence can be expensive, but invariably it is worth the expense.

CHAPTER

13

Putting Together Your Advisory Board

In recent years it has become very popular for early-stage companies to recruit experienced business people to serve on what has come to be called an advisory board. This board is very different from the board of directors, which is established when the corporation is formed and the by-laws are drawn up. The board of directors thus has a formal legal status that implies a certain amount of liability for the board members. There are even requirements for corporations to file an annual disclosure statement that lists the names and addresses of board members. The board of directors of a corporation meets at regular intervals, and votes on matters of importance to the corporation.

The advisory board is a much looser association. It may not have any meetings at all. It could just be a few individuals who have agreed to provide the company with a few hours a month of consulting assistance.

The question comes up as to whether having an advisory board with heavyweights, such as well-known executives in your industry, helps in obtaining angel investors. Does the fact you were able to recruit these people lend credability to your business model and your potential for success? Does it make the potential investor say, "These are the kind of people I want to get involved with"? Furthermore, does having this advisory talent on board have a practical benefit of helping the company with its strategic planning? Some people who work with early-stage companies believe that the advisory board can help fill in some of the gaps in the management team that inevitably exist with start-ups.

ADVICE FROM AN ANGEL

Lore Harp McGovern

Do you recommend they put together a strong advisory board, and does that help them in their search for an angel? "I think an advisory board always puts a degree of maturity onto what they are trying to do. Especially advisors who are complementary, out of the technology side, the financial side, out of marketing. It makes the deal look much, much richer."

Opening Doors to Important Strategic Relationships

It has become almost cliché to talk about the business world moving faster and faster all the time. In this case the cliché is instructive, though, because it points up one of the major benefits of an advisory board. In this fast-moving world, the ability to quickly solidify strategic partnerships with other more established companies can be a make or break factor for an early-stage company. Many entrepreneurs use their advisory board as a means to build these relationships, even going so far as inviting executives of the larger companies to serve on the advisory board.

These strategic relationships can be as vital to the company as the investment capital provided by an angel. They add tremendous value to a young enterprise. Having the relationships in place are important milestones that can induce angels to invest in an early-stage company in the first place.

Why would these busy executives want to take on the added responsibility of advising a start-up? Some of them look at it as a valuable opportunity to learn from the experience of watching a young company grow, and to learn from working with other members of the board. It is flattering to the ego to be sought after by dozens of young technology entrepreneurs, as some of the high-profile executives of companies such as Cisco Systems are.

When the IPO market was flourishing in 1999–2000, there was also the potential of a financial windfall. Advisory board members are often compensated through stock options in the start-up at low striking prices (low purchase price to activate the options). If one of the start-ups you were assisting went public at $10 per share and then shot up to $100 per share or more, as many of them did for a while, the advisory board members could reap terrific profits.

Since this frenetic IPO activity cooled off, advisory board members had to look to the traditional reasons for wanting to get involved; many executives simply love the problem-solving tasks involved in guiding a young enterprise or a team of young entrepreneurs.

There is no doubt that having influential business people on the board can help open doors to potential large customers or strategic partners. In fact, this has been so prevalent that it has led some people to question the ethics of the whole relationship. When an advisory board member puts in a good word with his company on behalf of the start-up, is there an inherent conflict of interest between his duties to the company he works for and the small company he owns stock options in?

Some large companies have gone so far as writing policy guidelines about when an employee can and cannot serve on advisory boards. Other companies don't seem to care; perhaps they feel that serving on the advisory board keeps their executives out of mischief.

Even if the start-up does not do any kind of business with the board member's company, the board member can use industry contacts to put the entrepreneur in front of decision makers at other companies. In many business plans, you see a statement to the effect that, once we get the first large customer for our technology, others will immediately follow. Many technology entrepreneurs use the advisory board members to facilitate attracting the attention of that first large customer. The technology may be unproven, but the advisory board member, by virtue of his career success, is proven in the minds of the potential customer. Instead of the entrepreneur knocking on the door of the large corporation for an extended period of time, the whole process is expedited.

Designing an Advisory Board

Many entrepreneurs have a conscious strategy behind how they select advisory board members. They may be looking months down the road, trying to figure out what kinds of contacts they may need to develop important customer relationships. They may also look at precisely what kinds of advice they need, such as financial guidance from an executive who has worked in a rapidly growing technology company. The board could include someone who is an expert in marketing or public relations strategy. Or the board members could just be good, solid, experienced business people who have traveled the entrepreneurial road themselves. Nonoperations people such as management consultants, attorneys, CPAs, and even members of the press are asked to serve on boards as well. They may be able to contribute an important perspective on the future direction of an industry or market space and help an entrepreneur take advantage of developing trends. Board members can provide any or all of the following:

- Contacts you may need
- Specific competencies
- General business success
- Industry knowledge

ADVICE FROM AN EXPERT

Adapted from *The Board Book* (Amacom)

Susan F. Shultz, SSA Executive Search International, Ltd.
www.ssaexec.com

We win by outthinking our competition, by thinking into tomorrow. That is the purpose—and the promise—of boards of directors, statutory and advisory.

Essentially, the role of the board is to address the big issues—and avoid the big mistakes, the fatal mistakes. The board is a powerful multiplier—for example, providing credibility and access to partners, the financial community, and expertise available in no other way.

It is ironic that the one group with the power to decide the fate of an organization—the board—is the one group that is often randomly selected, rarely evaluated, and almost never held accountable.

If you don't have a strategic board you are already in trouble and you don't even know it.

If a board is riddled with the 10 mistakes in *The Board Book*, watch out. Analysts know this and are willing to pay a 20 percent premium for good boards.

Boards are a pivotal success factor for all companies, especially start-ups, companies without the resources of the Fortune 500s.

We know that 95 of every 100 start-ups fail. Why not leverage every possible resource to help lock in success?

Here are the 10 most common mistakes:

1. **Failure to recruit strategically.** Proactively recruit to your future—to your strategic plan.
2. **Too many insiders.** The best number of insiders is one.
3. **Too many paid consultants.** This includes your venture capitalist partners, your commercial banker, your lawyer, your accountant, your management consultant, and anyone else who stands to have his or her income compromised. You already have their commitment and expertise.

If a conflict does exist, it is most likely to surface during the very crises the director is there to help resolve. For example, as a founder, you want a high valuation and as much money for as little stock as possible. The venture capitalist wants the opposite. With a high-growth, start-up company, there is built-in conflict.

The first challenge, then, becomes selecting the best investors possible and resisting the temptation to go with the first offer.

The second key is creating a small independent board prior to funding to obtain the governance balance so critical to strategic boards.

4. **Too many cronies.** What could be wrong with inviting your friends and colleagues to sit on your board? First, you are severely limiting your universe. Second, cronyism tends to beget favors and compromise objectivity.
5. **Too much family.**
6. **Getting the money wrong.** Too many boards reward mediocrity and failure instead of achievement.
7. **Fear of diversity.** Diversity means that you have access to the best.
8. **Information block.** Too often management parcels out information to their board. Strategic governance means entrusting your directors with full information, good and bad, and trusting directors to do the right thing.
9. **Passive boards.** Boards that exist solely to stamp their approval on management's decisions are failed boards. Entrenched directors are another symptom of a failed board.
10. **Failed leadership.** It's the CEO who imprints and empowers the board.

Strategic Board Continuum
Captive Board ------------------------------Strategic Board
0 ---10

Ultimately, you get what you ask for. Do you want a captive board or a strategic board? Avoid the 10 mistakes and score a 10 on the continuum.

Too Many Cooks? Or Angels in the Making

The types of assistance advisory board members can provide may sound awfully similar to what angel investors themselves can provide. There may be situations in which the entrepreneur finds himself with too many people chiming in with opinions about what to do. It is important to note that advisors are just that—providers of opinions—and entrepreneurs are free to call upon the advisors as much or as little as they want. One other positive benefit of having the advisory board involved with a company is that often one of the advisors can actually end up being part of the group of angels that invests in the company. They have already performed a certain amount of due diligence by virtue of their participation on the board and learning the inside story about the company, and many have already developed a working rapport with the entrepreneur.

ADVICE FROM AN ANGEL

David Burwen

Does an advisory board make a company more attractive to private investors? "I tend to discount them to a large degree. This is because entrepreneurs often put a group of advisory board names on a piece of paper to try to impress investors. You do not know whether this is an effective board that is going to help the company. How much time are the various individuals going to spend with the company? How is the company going to use the advisory board? Under what circumstances will the management team follow the recommendations of the advisory board? All that stuff is usually not really very well defined. People often just try to come up with prestigious names, so the investors are supposed to say, 'so and so is involved, it must be a good deal.'

"There were times during the dot.com mania a year or so ago, when I used to see the same names popping up on many advisory boards. They were prominent people who just wanted to get a little bit of stock in a large number of companies. They would get 5,000, or so, shares for simply lending their name to the company and then only talking to the CEO once in a while.

"A good advisory board can be helpful in a number of ways. At the beginning a company needs advice to determine strategic direction, business models, product development strategies, resource allocations, organizational issues, sales, and marketing. The company needs to get advice and feedback from experienced people. If members of the advisory board actually have experience in these areas and are willing to spend time with the company, then I think they can help management chart a successful course."

Does the entrepreneur invite the board member to be an investor, or does he wait for the board member to suggest that he might be interested? That's more a question of dating philosophy than financial strategy. It is entirely up to the entrepreneur.

A New Kind of Status Symbol

Several things about the popularity of advisory boards are surprising. The first is how so many people with high-level positions in large corporations take on the time-consuming task of serving on many boards. An answer may be that their participation on the boards enables them to build up their contact base and cement new relationships as well. Suppose an individual serves on six boards that each have five other influential people on them. That person now has the opportunity to network with 30 new people who could do business with that person or his or her company in the future.

It is also interesting that these advisory boards contain former politicians, athletes, and entertainment celebrities, not people we normally associate with business-operations experience.

What do you get with a glittering celebrity on your board? You get access to all the other influential business people these individuals have met over the years. And they, of course, get to attend the Academy Awards dinner or the ESPY Awards and remark to the celebrity next to them, "Oh, yes, the wireless company I'm an advisor to just went public at $43 a share. I own 15,000 options, you know."

By putting thought and effort into selecting advisory board members, an entrepreneur may find it far easier to reach important milestones in the company's development than it would have been without the involvement of these individuals.

ADVICE FROM AN EXPERT

How Can an Advisory Team Be an Asset When Looking for Investors?

John Sizer, Deloitte & Touche LLP Accountants, www.deloitte&touche.com

If a metal detector would help finding a needle in a haystack, a professional services firm might serve a similar purpose when a start-up is looking for investors. Finding the proverbial needle is key—but which haystack, which farm? Which farmer? As an entrepreneur filling out your management team, what qualities will you consider when hiring professional services? Here are some considerations:

Understanding Your Business

Your business advisory/accounting firm should have depth of experience in all areas key to your business—whether that be education, real estate, hospitality, or high technology. The depth needs to be a yard wide and a mile deep versus a mile wide and a yard deep. Know the experience your business advisory team brings to the table and let them do what they do best.

Share Your Business Plan . . . Share Your Marketing Plan

Make certain you feel comfortable sharing knowledge with your professional advisors. You need shoulder-to-shoulder business planning advice with sweat equity and a global view of your business goals, objectives, and future plans. You must require nothing short of professionals to provide the utmost in service, exceeding your needs from a technical and business perspective. Each of the professionals selected as part of the engagement team must have significant experience in the types of transactions you have completed or are contemplating, including financing, business growth, capitalizing on technology, e-business/.com background, and growth strategies. Additionally, has the team served both traditional business models and emerging technology companies? No dinosaurs, but no folks so proficient at surfing that they're a fish-out-of-water when it comes to writing a business or marketing plan. This is your business—don't risk the final stage of financing to a fly-by-night cowboy, nor to an antiquated firm so bogged down in history they don't muster up the energy and enthusiasm it will take to get your venture funded.

Ask Smart Questions . . . Ask Stupid Questions . . . Ask Questions

Does your potential advisory team have experience with:

- Financing transactions—from seed investing to bridge financing to an initial public offering? Find business advisors with local experience with IPOs and other public filings and private placements, who are knowledgeable and experienced with SEC regulations, and coordination with underwriters and attorneys.
- Information technology consulting, e-commerce and .com background, including the special nuances of next-step financing?
- Extensive services focused on e-commerce and .com business models, strategies, and implementation resources?
- From seed financing to IPO, the wisest way to navigate growing rapidly with steady income growth?
- Mergers and acquisitions, including due diligence, structuring, and integration?
- Multistate and international strategic tax planning specifically tailored to your industry, be that an e-business model, an m-business or wireless model, or a traditional one.
- Executive compensation strategies, including stock option plans?

Get resources. Ask for a list of recent publications specific to your industry. Visit their Web sites to review these publications or to get samples of their knowledge sharing on-line. Deloitte & Touche, for example, was the first to publish a comprehensive federal and multistate guide to the current state of e-commerce taxation, Taxation of Cyberspace, and monitors, on a daily basis, the evolving taxation structure for these types of transactions.

Service to Your Industry

Perhaps the best indication of a firm's expertise in and commitment to your industry lies in its clients. A large and diverse client base enables the firm to share best practices, identify advisory opportunities, stay abreast of trends, and understand the special issues of the industries. You and your venture benefit from the history and experience of other clients before you. Think of the firm you hire as a network—they must be well-connected, understand the industry, be a player with angel investors and venture capitalists.

Where Are They in Your Community?

Make sure your professional service advisors talk the talk and walk the walk. Have you seen representatives from the firm at your industry meetings? Sponsoring your industry breakfasts? Speaking on or writing about how to obtain and raise capital through an initial public offering? How many have significant experience negotiating their way through private offerings and IPOs? Find out.

Your venture no doubt offers an exciting vision. Often lack of planning is the entrepreneur's greatest stumbling block to succeed financially. Your product—your existing and growing intellectual property—carefully and thoughtfully melded with your business plan, and strategically executed with the proper business partners may have all of the makings of a successful, lucrative, long-term venture.

New ideas from a variety of sources can be brought to bear on any problems you may encounter.

Chapter Summary

- An advisory board can be valuable to an early-stage company, providing strategic direction and contacts to build strategic alliances that will help develop the business.
- Advisory boards must be selected thoughtfully, not just on the basis of marquee value but on how the individuals will help fill the gaps that exist in the management team.

CHAPTER

14

The Poor, Misunderstood Business Plan

Pity the poor business plan. Think of all the stress it is under. It has to fly across the country and land on an investor's desk, along with dozens or even hundreds of competing plans. It has to speak for a management team that is not there; it has to work all by itself. It has to convince a stranger to part with hundreds of thousands, even millions of dollars, all by itself. And it is expected to do this in a matter of weeks. Perhaps faster. "Hurry up and get me the money," says the entrepreneur to the plan. So much is demanded out of 40 pages, a nice cover, and a 75-cent plastic binder.

The plan is also a convenient whipping boy when the investment is not forthcoming. We have had many conversations with entrepreneurs that went this way:

Us: "How did it go with the investor?"

Entrepreneur: "Lousy. He said he didn't like the business plan."

It's all the document's fault! The entrepreneur would have the money by now if it weren't for that slacker, the business plan.

Entrepreneurs Say the Cutest Things

A man operating a company with his wife and his brother said, after being turned down by an angel, that this rejection was due to his business plan sounding too mom-and-popish. What should it have sounded like, mom, pop, and bro, we wondered?

The founder of a start-up medical-technology company, with a niche product that had at most 1000 potential customers worldwide, lamented after a rough presentation to an angel group that his business plan "made the market seem too small."

Perhaps it is time to lower expectations for the business plan. The problem is not in our plans, but in ourselves. When people called us for assistance with writing their plan, they often asked this question: "What's your success rate, how frequently have plans you've written gotten capital?" (These same people ask their doctor, "How many of your patients live?")

Tired of answering this, we started to just say, "None," followed by stunned silence.

But that is the truth. A business plan does not raise money for an early-stage venture. It merely opens the door to discussion. From that point, it is still a long, torturous road to getting the check, the success of which mainly depends on the perceived and demonstrated competence of the management team. There is an old expression that a great team and an okay idea get funded more often than a superior idea and an average management team. We could extend that to say a superior idea, a superior business plan, and an average team will probably not obtain capital.

We follow up our answer of "None" by explaining that the business plan is still critical because a poorly prepared plan can cause investors to be turned off from even a good deal. The plan is the first "brochure" the customer receives about your deal. This first impression can be the difference in whether the discussion moves forward or not. Thus, the time and expense you put into preparing your plan is clearly worth it, but your plan is just a member of the team you need to win at the game of attracting angel capital. The other team members, including yourself, need to be at the top of their game as well.

A client told us a story about interviewing two companies to provide receivables factoring services for his company. One firm sent over a guy wearing a cheap suit with high-water pants and an unconvincing comb-over hairdo. The other sent over a typical banker-looking person. Even though the first guy's terms were slightly better, our client went with the second firm's services. "The first one disqualified himself when he walked in the door," our client said. The professional-looking business plan prevents this from happening to your deal.

What Should Be Included in Your Business Plan?

STEP ONE: SIMPLIFY THE PROCESS

The best way to approach any lengthy writing project, including a business plan, is to begin with an outline. We recommend that entrepreneurs view the creation of a plan as a matter of answering a series of questions. Start with short, bullet-point answers and then build the bullet points into fluid paragraphs.

It is easy to make the process of writing the plan needlessly complex. We recently met with a consultant who writes plans for technology companies. He charges quite a bit of money for his services, $25,000 to $50,000 per plan. He began describing how he goes about analyzing the company's market, its competition, and all the different complicated methods he used to come up with the financial projections. Although we have written over 100 business plans ourselves, we had no idea what he was talking about. Some individuals need to make things overly complicated in order to justify themselves.

An outline follows of each segment of a business plan developed for presentation to potential investors. The length of a business plan varies from 20 to 40 pages, not including the financial projections or the appendix.

STEP TWO: CONSTRUCT AN OUTLINE SUCH AS THE ONE THAT FOLLOWS

Executive summary of two to three pages—The executive summary is not a miniversion of the entire business plan. Keep it brief. The purpose of the executive summary is to entice the reader to review, or request to review, the entire business plan. It should be viewed as a marketing tool, a very important marketing tool. Although the executive summary is presented first, it is written after the entire plan has been completed. It should not contain any information that cannot be found elsewhere in the business plan. Do not write the executive summary first, thinking you can expand it later into a full-blown business plan; that just does not work.

Keys: This summary is extracted from the other parts of the plan when completed, with these themes:

The opportunity is large

The market is not being served adequately by existing competitors

Your unique capabilities to serve this market

The compelling competitive advantage that will result

Business Description—This should state the following:

Business Purpose: Why did you start this company?

Company History and Current Status: When did you begin and what have you accomplished?

Company Mission: What is your vision for the company?

Summary of Objectives: How large do you want to grow and how fast?

Business Model: Where do the revenues come from?

Keys:

Be extremely clear about what you will be doing.

Express your vision for the company with great enthusiasm.

Products and Services—Itemize the following clearly and specifically:

Specific Products/Services: What are they and how do they serve the customer?

Features and User Benefits: What pain or problem are you solving for the customer?

Proprietary Aspects: What have you created that cannot be duplicated by competitors?

System Design Challenges: What needs to be done to get ready to market the product/service?

Next Generation of Products/Services or Upgrades: Show you are constantly looking ahead.

Keys:

Make certain the angel understands how your technology works to solve the customer's problem.

Keep the terminology simple.

Industry and Market Analysis—Give the reader these points of information:

History of the Industry: How has your industry evolved?

Market Description: How large is it? How fast is it projected to grow?

Keys:

Make sure you can defend the sources of information you used to estimate market size.

Competitive Profile—Give your reader a fair picture of what you will be up against.

Description of Most Significant Competitors: Who are they, and what are their strengths and weaknesses?

Key Success Factors: What makes a business succeed in your market?

Barriers to Entry: How can you keep competitors out once you are established?

Unique Capabilities/Competitive Advantage: What will make your company an effective competitor?

Keys:

Do not underestimate the number or strengths of competitors.

Do not think you have no competitors.

Customer Profile—Provide a customer profile: Who are your potential customers? How many are there?

Keys:

Be realistic in your description of how broad your customer base might be.

Marketing Plan—Detailed discussion of marketing plans follows in the next chapter.

Strategic Alliances Undertaken or Proposed, Hopefully with Well-Known Successful Entities

Keys:

Angel investors view these alliances as potentially adding great value to the venture.

Management Team—Briefly describe the following:

Key Individuals

Accomplishments and Strengths of Team

Current Ownership of Company

Key Personnel to Be Added In Order to Build a Successful Team

Organization Structure: Chart showing staff levels by category, by quarter

Keys:

Focus on relating the experience and capabilities of the management team and how they relate specifically to succeeding in the proposed venture.

Operations and Facilities: Where will they be located, size of space required?

Key Vendors/Suppliers: Who have you chosen and why?

Licensing and Regulatory Issues: How will these impact your venture?

Risk Factors: What might cause your company's results to vary significantly from plan?

Keys:

> Considering these factors shows that you have the ability to make contingency plans to deal with the inevitable changes in market forces that will affect your venture.

Capital Requirements and Proposed Transaction Structure—How much capital do you need and in what stages? Also be sure to include information about how soon and by what method the angel investors will be able to earn their return on invested capital.

Keys:

> Provide sufficient detail about what the major categories of expenditure are and when the next round of funding will be needed.

Financial Plan—This section will be reviewed carefully. Be sure to include:

> Profit and Loss Statement Forecasts (3 to 5 Years)
> Monthly Year 1
> Monthly or Quarterly Year 2
> Annually Years 3 to 5
> Cash Flow Forecasts (3 to 5 Years)

Keys:

> It is not important to have 50 pages of financial projections in finite detail; it is important that every number you present is backed up by logical assumptions.

Appendix—Letters of intent regarding customer agreements and strategic alliances.

Keys:

> These help show the angel that you have a "real" business.

Who Should Write the Plan?

It is a good idea for everyone in the management team to contribute ideas and information for the business plan. The different perspectives of the various people involved can make for a more complete end product. It is interesting to watch these team efforts unfold and to see what the plan looks like when they are finished. Sometimes, you can tell which person in the team wrote most of the plan, based on how the plan turns out. Basically, it goes like this:

> Technical person rules: Lots of confusing schematic drawings of the product. Five acronyms per sentence. Management section emphasizes how many college degrees everyone has earned, and technical accreditation and certifications. You see the name Microsoft over and over.
>
> Marketing person rules: Five superlatives per sentence: "This is the best-of-class solution," "We have first-to-market advantage wrapped up." Great detail about the aggressive scope of the marketing plan, but no estimate of how much this is all going to cost. Management section has one paragraph on everyone else, five on himself, showing that he increased revenues 500 percent at each job he has held.
>
> Finance person rules: Very sober language, bordering on boring. Ten pages of cash flow forecasts, but only one on why the consumer needs or wants the product. Risk factors are fairly frightening. Management section just lists prior positions everyone has held, in standard resume format.

DEAL TALES: YOU GOT TO ACCENTUATE THE POSITIVE, COMPLETELY IGNORE THE NEGATIVE

A company that was struggling with their business plan, using the committee method, asked us to help referee the final rewrite. It became clear that the marketing guy was primarily in charge. He was convinced that a good plan was just a series of bullet points, what a marketing guy would deliver in an in-person presentation. "Gotta keep it brief," he advised us. "People are busy these days, don't like to read." Authors particularly like to hear that. We took his bullet points and expanded them into real live English sentences. We also noticed they had a "Strengths, Weaknesses, Opportunities, Risks" section that had no weaknesses and no risks listed. "I hate it when I see negative things in a plan; really turns people off," he told us. Then he added that he welcomed our input.

It was fairly easy for us to come up with a page or so of risks about this deal. We also wrote a four-page executive summary for them because, in our view, the complexity of the technology and the market required that much detail in order to not confuse the angels who would be reading it. We sent the plan back to the client (the marketing guy) for his review.

The plan came back. The executive summary was now two pages, the bullet points were back. The risk factors were deleted.

"Thanks for your help," he said. "The plan's really coming together."

"It's always rewarding to see entrepreneurs implement our advice," we said.

For many of us it is difficult to see the big picture, to recognize that all the sections of the plan are important. We should not make a weak effort at writing the marketing sections just because our background is finance, for example.

How Do You Know Your Plan Is Ready?

A good way to test your plan for doneness is to give it to trusted business associates to read and ask for their comments. There are also many consultants who will review your plan from the standpoint of a potential angel investor and advise you of any gaps of inconsistencies. By the time you finish the process of writing the plan, you are so close to it that maintaining objectivity is difficult. One or more additional pairs of eyes can be of great value.

Chapter Summary

- Be realistic: the business plan does not raise money for a venture. Angel investors will evaluate the competence of the management team as well as the quality of the ideas in the plan.
- Using an outline and question-and-answer approach can simplify the process of writing a plan.
- Input from all the members of the management team can help make the plan better. A solid effort should go into all the sections of the plan, and not just the areas the entrepreneurs are strongest in.
- Outside review of the plan prior to presenting to angel investors can help put the final polish on the document.

CHAPTER 15

The All-Important Marketing Plan

Why It Must Be Carefully Thought Out

The marketing plan is absolutely critical to an early-stage company's eventual success, and it is also very important to potential angel investors who are considering putting money into the company. However, in today's technology-focused world, many entrepreneurs spend just enough time on the marketing plan to be able to come up with a short write-up on it to insert in the business plan. The marketing plan ends up sounding generic and does not inspire confidence in the ability of the management team to execute the plan.

Marketing planning is a process, not just a part of the business plan document. The marketing plan emerges out of an intensive, iterative effort involving all the key individuals in the company.

We have seen even very large corporations do a sloppy, halfhearted job on their marketing plan, again viewing it as just a chore they are forced to get through each year. Sooner or later, this shows up in the company's performance, when competitors with better-focused plans go sprinting past.

Our contributing expert, Beth Gallob, points out that the marketing plan must be very carefully thought out and very detailed. A wonderful technology is not of great value to potential investors if they are not convinced that the management team has the strategy and tactics in place to take the technology in the marketplace. How are you going to do this? In what stages? How much will each stage cost? These difficult questions must be addressed.

Structure

ADVICE FROM AN EXPERT ON MARKETING PLANS

Ready, Fire, Aim Is for Amateurs: Or Why You Need a Marketing Plan

Beth Gallob, Gallob Communication, www.gallobcomm.com, Phoenix, Arizona

"It takes real courage to reach out and stake your claim."
Tom Peters and Nancy Austin

Optimism is something a successful entrepreneur has to have a lot of. But the idea that you'll get funding—or sell your product, for that matter—just because you're a great bunch of folks and you have a really cool product or service is simply unrealistic. If you build, will they come? The real question is: So what?

Frankly, angel investors are looking for companies that know what they're doing and can prove it. Your company must be able to rise above all the noise out there to reach the attention of those who, to be blunt, have heard it all before. One of the best ways is to have a kick-ass marketing plan.

The Marketing Plan: It's Your Big Gun

"They didn't want it good. They wanted it Wednesday."
Robert Heinlein

It's a common fallacy that because things move at such a rapid pace these days you must start marketing your company, product, or service immediately—the ready-fire-aim philosophy. However, taking action without a clear view is a good way to shoot yourself in the foot!

You'll be so much more successful if you have a target in your sights when you pull the trigger, and it doesn't have to take a long time. Although it is true that in today's highly competitive marketplace you have to do it fast, that does not mean you cannot take the time do it right. The truth is that one chance is often all you get, so it better be good.

It's a Long and Winding Road

"Sustaining advantage requires continuous improvement and change, not a static solution in which strategy can be set and forgotten."
Michael Porter

The more information you have articulated, the better you reach your business and marketing objectives. Remember that your marketing plan is a work in progress—because as your vision for your company changes, so does this document.

It is also critical that your marketing plan is a group effort. Representatives from throughout the corporation should take part in developing your plan. If your company is a small one, find outside advisors with expertise in the appropriate areas.

- Development
- Consulting/professional services
- Finance and legal
- IT and customer support
- Training
- Operations

Company Description

Describe the company using as few words as possible. Identify who you are, what you do, and why customers should use your company. Think about how you want the company to grow and what you want to happen in the future. Ask yourself:

- What is the most important statement you can make about the company?
- Why use this company?
- How much do you want the company to grow?
- What are your goals for the company?

Products and/or Services

Describe clearly and succinctly what the product is and/or what services you provide. What are the benefits to the customer and why? If you cannot state this clearly, how can you expect the world to understand?

- The product/service is . . .
- The product/service enables . . .
- The product/service provides . . .

Marketing Objectives

What are the desired outcomes?

- Attract investors?
- Reposition company?
- Introduce new company focus and strategy?
- Introduce new product?
- Increase company awareness?
- Generate leads?

Target Market

It's critical that you be able to identify your market, and that means research, research, research.

- Who are they?
- What is their pain?
- What are the important market trends?
- What are the industry analysts and media saying?

Positioning/Messaging

If you can't explain who you are and what you do so that your mother can understand it, it's too complicated to bring to the marketplace. Focus on business solution, rather than just cool technology. Keep in mind that it's rare to create a new category of business or solution. The tendency will be to pigeonhole you somewhere.

- How do industry analysts categorize your company?
- How are your competitors categorized?
- Develop an elevator pitch.
- Make sure everyone in your company agrees with and understands your positioning.

Competition

Of course you have competition—real and perceived—even if your product is unique. Even the first automobile competed with the horse and buggy.

- Who is your competition?
- What are their strengths and weaknesses?

- How do you differentiate yourself?
- What are your competitive advantages?

Partners/Business Relationships

One of the best ways to be successful is to find complementary partners and build mutually beneficial relationships. Results could include beta plan, OEM/VAR agreement, and joint marketing plan. Partners can include:

- Beta candidates
- Indirect channels
- Technology partners
- Marketing partners
- Industry-analyst sponsor/champion

Marketing Programs

How do you get the word out and how much is it going to cost? How do you combine traditional and new media? The marketing communication plan will result from this section. Areas of marketing activity include:

- Budget (10 to 15 percent of projected revenue, and sometimes significantly more)
- Target industry and business publications
- Target industry analysts
- Public relations
- Direct mail/advertising
- Trade shows
- Collateral
- Web site
- Internal/external launch
- Process/tools to track results

Sales and Distribution

What are your short and long-term sales goals? How will you sell and distribute the product? Will it differ for existing and new customers?

- Sales goals
- New/existing customers
- Direct channels
- Indirect channels
- Telemarketing
- Sales training, targeted customers, compensation plan

Risks and Assumptions

Determine what your challenges and issues are, and be realistic about what can go wrong. Gather information from different points of view, and develop a plan to address issues.

- Develop a SWOT Analysis (strengths, weaknesses, opportunities, threats).
- Involve all areas of the company as well as outside advisors.
- Ask yourself: What if?
- Think about the worst-case scenario.
- Consider Plan B and beyond.

Schedule/Milestones

Decide who will do what when and write it down. Determine whether there are any key events, such as a trade show, that drive marketing. Remember, planning is only half the battle. You also have to implement well.

- Priorities
- Resources and responsibilities
- Time lines
- Key events

Getting Started: It's the Only Way You'll Ever Get It Done

> *"I think I did pretty well, considering I started out with nothing but a bunch of blank paper."* Steve Martin

---

Chapter Summary (from Beth Gallob)

- At times, your task may seem a bit overwhelming. The best way to start is to do just that—start. Use the above information presented as a template and simply start answering the questions.
- Developing a marketing plan is just plain hard work—a long, painful process, but a very necessary one. Your marketing plan will be your road map for marketing your company to investors, promoting your product or service, and ensuring your internal and external company teams are all on the same page.
- Most people don't do their own dental work. The same is true for a marketing plan. A marketing consultant can help by providing an important outside perspective and keeping the project on track. Consider using one—it's what they do.

CHAPTER

16

Do Angels Put Any Credence in Business Plans?

We received an e-mail that said, "I need a business plan that will attract angels. Can you help?"

We get the mental image of a business plan having some kind of fragrance or pheromone that wealthy people find irresistible. They drop whatever they are doing and grab the nearest copy.

We can see the commercial—a beautiful but tragically underfed entrepreneur sitting on the seashore in the Hamptons, with her laptop computer, printing out her plan as the yachts sail lazily by in the background. Some of the pages blow away, but no matter. She takes her sunglasses off and looks provocatively into the camera. "Venture, the new fragrance from Calvin Klein."

If it were possible to concoct these remarkable additives, writing your business plan would be fairly simple. You just have to decide, What do we put on the plan and how thick do we spread it?

ADVICE FROM AN ENTREPRENEUR

Dave Westin, CEO, www.channelautomation.com

How much did the angels rely on the business plan? "They took a pretty hard look at the business plan and the financials. They did a complete SWOT (strengths, weaknesses, opportunities, threats) analysis."

Did you spend a lot of time putting your plan together? "Absolutely. It is worthwhile, because you are going to need it somewhere down the line. I think you should start building the product right away, but also begin planning everything else out. Whether you are going into a virgin market or one that is mature with five fully funded competitors, you have to out-execute the other guy, because there's no guarantee the competitors are running their businesses correctly or that more competition won't be moving into the space."

What Do Angels Think?

Many veteran angels have read hundreds of business plans, and they know a professional, comprehensive plan when they see one. The degree of importance attached to plans and how skeptical angels are regarding what they read in plans depend on the individual angel.

ADVICE FROM AN ANGEL

Craig Johnson, Chairman, Venture Law Group, www.vlg.com

When an entrepreneur comes to you, do you rely on the business plan to make your investment decision? "Remember, I'm a lawyer. I'm an angel, too. But usually when I am meeting with people it is to decide whether to take them on as a client. The investment part comes with it.

"I put whatever they are trying to do through the filter of my own mind, my own experience, and my own common sense. I try to figure it out. I'm very patient with entrepreneurs. I will often meet with teams three or four times. My general test is whether I get it or not. I mostly ask questions. I am trying to understand how the company can grow into a multi-hundred-million-dollar revenue company, how it can protect against competitors, what the margins will be, how big the market will be.

"If I go through three or four meetings and I still have questions I can't quite figure out, then no matter how interesting the company might be, I just pass. I'm not going to be an effective advocate for a company whose business strategy I haven't totally bought into. Then, if I do have a company whose strategy I have bought into, I can be evangelical. In fact many companies have gotten funding because, as one venture capitalist described me, I'm somewhat like a rabid dog. If I truly understand why a company is going to be a significant success, I will be very persistent in explaining in every way I can think of to a venture capitalist why that company will in fact succeed. I have a pretty good track record of companies that I have taken on in that manner ultimately succeeding, so venture capitalists listen to me. If the venture capitalist doesn't understand it immediately, I just explain it another way. For me to be able to do that effectively, I have to fully understand the company's business strategy.

"Business plans for early-stage companies are quite malleable. They are soft clay. I start probing and asking questions and what starts to happen is the business plan starts to change in front of my eyes, because the entrepreneurial team starts to adapt it to meet my objections. Sometimes they adapt it to the point that it is a completely different business.

"Just the act of observing the plan changes it."

When looking for angel capital, the rapport you develop with the individual writing the check is much more important to your success than how brilliant, how professional, how complete your business plan is. So it is a mistake to assume all you have to do is prepare a plan and funding follows. There are many more steps to the process.

ADVICE FROM AN ANGEL

Tom Horgan, AZTEC Venture Networks and Acorn Technologies, San Diego, CA

What do you think of the quality of business plans you receive? "We find that a lot of business plans are too superficial in their analysis of the market, the market size, and how they are going to participate in it. What you tend to find is a lot of focus on the value proposition, which is fair; a lot of focus on the competition, which is also fair; but the mechanism of how they are going to win in the marketplace is always the weakest."

The "how you're going to do it," not just "what you are going to do." "You get the standard Excel spreadsheet assumptions. If the market is this big, we can assume a market penetration rate of X going to

Y in Z number of years. After a while it becomes rote. What's really missing is an understanding of what it takes to win in business, and how to grow and leverage that.

"Typically what I've found in a lot of business plans is that their rationale for their percentage share of the market is weak and flawed. That is important because the selling, general, and administrative expense assumed in the plan is not high enough."

And the time assumed to reach the revenue milestones is too short? "Yes. With early-stage companies, angels are still going to ask the questions you might ask of later-stage companies.

"Many times the ideas are just not strong enough, though. In essence, the differentiation or the intellectual property advantages are minimal, and the business is really just a race for market share. And I think that has been spawned by the Internet era."

ADVICE FROM AN ANGEL

Barry Moltz, Co-founder, Prairie Angels, www.prairieangels.org

How much do you rely on the business-plan document from the company in making a decision? "I think pretty little. I look at the executive summary, and if that is interesting, then I will try to meet with the company. If their presentation goes well, then after that I will try to read the whole plan. Business-plan documents are necessary evils, but they are a lot of fluff. And the financials you can pretty much throw out altogether, because every set of financials from every business plan looks interchangeable. First year revenues are projected at $1 million, then second year it's $7 million, then it goes to $25 million, then it goes to $53 million, then it goes to $75 million in year five. Every one is the same.

"In the financial section, what is important to look at is whether the assumptions make sense. Do the numbers relate to each other? What kind of gross margin do they have? Do they have the correct cost structure there to produce the revenues they are talking about?

"My goal is basically to insure we can hit enough milestones for the company to become self-sustaining."

ADVICE FROM AN ANGEL

Lore Harp McGovern

What is the most critical part of the business plan? "I look at the size of the market. Is there enough growth potential? What is their competitive advantage over time and can it lead to profitability? Then, I look at if the company does not do an IPO in the future, who would be a likely buy-out candidate? Then I look at the team, the founders, their vision, their enthusiasm, and whether they are willing to surround themselves with complementary strong people, or are they people who are not willing to delegate. The last thing I look at is how much money they need. If all the other criteria have been met, then raising the money is something that is doable, especially if you have a very good angel supporting the initial deal and bringing other partners to the party."

An Expression of Success

When we are assisting our clients with writing their business plans, we encourage them to ask this question when they get to the management section of the plan: What have you and your team accomplished in the past that will lead to success in this venture?

Another way to look at this is: What are the keys to success in this type of venture and why does your team have them? For some reason, working with several hundred entrepreneurs over the course of 15 years, only a fraction of them could answer this question. Most miss the mark completely when they try to answer it.

The reason? They cannot progress from the "I have a wonderful idea!" stage to the stage of understanding how they are going to execute their wonderful idea, and the relationship of the combined experience of the team to the probability of being able to execute the idea. We even go so far as to tell them to not try so hard to write brilliant essays on each person involved, but to think of the management team as pooled talent and experiences. When you look at this pool, what do you see? How deep is it?

It is much easier to just write, "Joe was VP of Marketing for a technology company, where he increased sales from $1 million to $18 million in six months." This idea of relating past experience to the task at hand with the new venture is very difficult for entrepreneurs to grasp.

Entrepreneurs and angels have significantly different points of view of why an enterprise succeeds.

How do each of these factors contribute to the success of an enterprise? Table 16.1, Differences in Success Factors, shows how the relative weights might look.

Table 16.1 Differences in Success Factors

Factor	*Entrepreneurs*	*Angels*
The great idea (business concept, business model)	45%	20%
Management's team background	10%	20%
Ability to execute (carry out the business plan)	10%	25%
Availability of capital	30%	15%
External factors (economy, competition, and so on)	5%	20%

Entrepreneurs tend to have the notion that a venture is their great idea combined with capital, a kind of simple plant-seeds-add-fertilizer process. Investors worry about what other crops you have grown and how big a garden you managed in the past. Entrepreneurs also give very little consideration to risks from external factors. They tend to minimize the strength of competitors and seldom look at the general state of the economy at all. Weeds? Bugs? That won't happen in my garden. The great idea is impervious to attack by any and all pests.

The angels, the people who have the money, and have made money before, do not think that capital by itself leads to success. Money is part of the answer, but not the most important part.

These differences in how each group filters information partially explains why so many presentations entrepreneurs make to investors don't really hit the target. A super sales job of the great idea can actually end up turning investors off if it isn't combined with these other elements and presented with the relative weight the angels give to each one. It is easy for investors to tune out the great idea when they don't hear these other things that give them a comfort level about the deal.

Should You Tailor a Business Plan Specifically for Angels?

Are there really significant differences in what angels need to see in a business plan compared to venture capitalists? Venture capitalists believe management is of critical importance; so do angels. So the plan must include a thorough discussion of the management team's experience and competence. A statement of what skill areas the company needs to add, and welcoming the angel to participate in the company and supply some of those skills, is a good way to assure the angel that the entrepreneur views this as a true partnership, not a give-me-the-money-and-go-away attitude. Entrepreneurs tend to overestimate how much knowledge all investors, including angels, have about their particular industry or technology. They make the assumption that a detailed discussion of the technology, in simple terms, is not necessary. This is a sometimes fatal error, because it is human nature to put aside a business plan that goes over our head or is incomprehensible.

Explain the problem, and then explain how your product/service is the solution—that is something to always keep in mind when writing a business plan. Other people call this the what-is-the-pain-in-the-marketplace?-and-how-do-you-solve-the-pain? method. We usually go so far as to show a real-life example of the consumer of the product or service, actually using it in practice and showing the resulting time, money, or trouble saved by using the product/service. Bringing complex technologies down to the individual user perspective is a great way to avoid investors getting lost by page 3 of the plan. Remember in grade school how hard it was to raise your hand and tell the teacher, "I don't get it." Later in life we don't always raise our hand, either. We just go on to the next deal.

ADVICE FROM AN ANGEL

Luis Villalobos, Founder and Director, Tech Coast Angels, www.techcoastangels.com

How much do you rely on the entrepreneur's forecast of the size of their market or how fast the company will grow? "It is certainly the starting point. We have entrepreneurs come in who project they will reach only $11 million in sales after five years—that is already a huge danger sign, even if we believe they might exceed it. We have one at the other extreme who will project $2 billion in two years. Most of them have figured out that venture capitalists and many angels are looking for a projection of between $50 million and $150 million in revenues somewhere between the third and fifth year. The plans tend to look the same, but that's when you need to look at the data behind the projections. The key things to me are whether they have identified a niche that they can dominate and they have identified a way to reach the specific customers that make up that niche.

"The biggest flaw is when they say, 'We have a $2 billion market, or a $12 billion market, or a $30 billion market.' I tell them, that's awful—you're never going to be a player in that size market. It tells me you have not clearly segmented the market to identify what part of the market you can really go after. If you really go after that big market, you are probably going to fail.

"It is positive if they can defend the numbers by saying, 'These are five customers I would call on the first week.' I look at whether they have thought things through on that basis rather than pulling out statistical numbers about an industry.

"The large, $10 billion market can actually be a turnoff: The costs of reaching that market in terms of promotion or advertising can be prohibitive."

Entrepreneurs tend to want to impress investor/readers with the degree of detail they have in the financial section of the business plan. It is true that venture capitalists view a plan with scanty financial projections as being incomplete, but page after page of detailed financials do not a better plan make. A good technique is to bring a summary of the financial projections forward in the plan, into the very first pages. This gives the reader a high-impact statement of how attractive the financial opportunity is; that is the point you want to get across, anyway, not that you enjoy your spreadsheet software. Because angels are not in the full-time business of reading business plans and making investment decisions, they have even less patience with being inundated with confusing numbers than venture capitalists do. The best approach is to have brief, well-documented numbers and schedules that clearly illustrate the assumptions you used to come up with the projections of the key items: revenues, cost of goods sold, marketing expense, research and development.

The numbers in the business plan boil down to these considerations:

- What kind of margins can you achieve?
- How long will it take (how much overhead must be financed) before revenues rise enough to cover all expenses?
- How large a marketing budget do you need to build the brand name and launch the products/services?

As long as you answer these questions reasonably with the financial projections and your assumptions, the investors can then turn their attention to the critical issues: Why will the marketplace readily embrace this product/service? What leads us to believe your team can actually go out and sell the product/service? Answering these questions satisfactorily is really much more important to investors than the degree of curve in the hockey-stick graph of projected revenues.

ADVICE FROM AN ANGEL

Steve Miller, Co-founder, Prairie Angels, www.prairieangels.org

How much do you rely on a company's business plan in evaluating an investment? "Not a lot. It should be complete and well-written and it should cover the important points about the vision of the business—it should state that very early on and very succinctly; it should have a complete discussion of the competition and potential competitive threats and also the barriers to entry. I don't spend a lot of time looking at the financials, because they are pie-in-the-sky stuff anyway, especially at the very early stage opportunities I look at. It is much more important to have the killer executive summary, rather than the perfect business plan. The business plan should be a living, breathing document, that changes as the business changes and grows, as the competitive environment changes, as the economy changes, as the entrepreneurs learn things going forward as they build the company and realize that, although they thought this was going to happen, somehting else happened, and that changes the whole outlook of the business.

"I rely more heavily on my discussions with entrepreneurs on how effectively I think the management team is going to deal with change than I do on the business plan document itself."

Critical Mistakes You Don't Want to Make

What do angels think are the critical mistakes? Results of our Profit Dynamics, Inc. survey are reflected in Table 16.2.

UNREALISTIC FINANCIAL PROJECTIONS

Financial projections are a challenge for entrepreneurs: too conservative and it is difficult to interest an investor; too optimistic and the projections are seen as unobtainable. The hockey-stick scenario, where revenues start out the first year on a slight upward track and then go nearly

Table 16.2 Most Critical Mistakes from Angel Investors' Perspective

Unrealistic financial projections	32%
Weak analysis of market and competition	32%
Not realistic about challenges ahead	24%
Incorrect valuation and exit strategy	12%

straight up in the second and third years is almost considered a joke among angel investors and venture capitalists.

Entrepreneurs fail to recognize that it will almost always take longer than anticipated to develop their product and get it to market, and it will almost always cost more than is projected.

Unrealistic financial projections are tied for first place among angels and venture capitalists as the most critical mistake in business plans. Their opinions are shown in Tables 16.2 and 16.3. Entrepreneurs give it a much lower ranking—sixth place—as shown in Table 16.4.

Angel investors told us:

"Overly optimistic revenue projections and too low expense projections."

"Unrealistic revenue model."

"Way too aggressive about projected revenues."

Table 16.3 Most Critical Mistakes from Venture Capital Firms' Perspective

Unrealistic financial projections	21%
Weak analysis of market and competition	18%
Lacking in clarity	17%
Mistakes and errors	10%
Incomplete	8%
Discussion of management weak	8%
Other	18%

Table 16.4 Most Critical Mistakes from Entrepreneurs' Perspective

Unrealistic about challenges ahead	27%
Lacking in clarity	16%
Weak analysis of market and competition	16%
Incomplete	15%
Incorrect valuation and exit strategy	10%
Unrealistic financial projections	8%
Discussion of management weak	4%
Other	4%

"Too short a revenue ramp up."

"Not watching their cash flow."

"Projections unrealistic with no clear revenue model defined."

"Overly optimistic."

MARKET AND COMPETITION

Defining your market, developing the marketing strategies, and analyzing your competition are critical. The business plan must clearly designate who your customers are and how you are going to reach them. It must also define who else is in your market space competing for your customers.

Angels ranked market and weak analysis of competition as equal to unrealistic financial projections at 32 percent. Although it rates a second-class ranking by both entrepreneurs and venture capitalists, that percentage is only half of the angels' 32 percent.

Angel investors said:

"They have the solution, but they don't know what the problem is."

"Do not understand their customer, competition, and ability to deliver."

"Underestimate and misunderstand the sales and marketing challenge."

"Ignore competition—no unique product or service."

"Unrealistic understanding of market expectation/financial projections."

"Lack of realistic market penetration."

BEING REALISTIC ABOUT THE CHALLENGES OF BUILDING A BUSINESS

It seems angels felt obligated to not only specify that the financial projections were unrealistic but that the business plans as a whole were unrealistic in showing how the management team could achieve benchmarks, control expenses, and finish product research and development. Entrepreneurs also mentioned unrealistic as being the most critical mistake. Curiously venture capitalists didn't feel it necessary to specify it as a mistake. However, they did go on to include several more categories that angels didn't mention at all. That could be a result of the average venture capitalist seeing many more business plans than the average angel investor, or it could be that the venture capitalists are just harsher critics of the business plans they receive.

Angel investors remarked:

"They are usually unrealistic. It seems that the time it takes to accomplish the stated goals is always underestimated, as is the cost. I want to see a product that at least a few customers are delighted with and a market that is open to accept such a new product."

"Too optimistic about timing of benchmarks."

"Unrealistic capital requirement."

"Unrealistic pace of adoption."

VALUATION

Valuation is an area of contention between angels and entrepreneurs and they give it about the same ranking, fourth or fifth. It doesn't show up at all on the venture capitalists' list of mistakes.

Angel investors said:

"Overvaluing their company."

"Too greedy a valuation."

Angels seem to be more general about the mistakes they consider as critical, whereas venture capitalists are specific; entrepreneurs fall in the middle. Lack of clarity isn't mentioned by angels, bur it is put in second and third place by venture capitalists and entrepreneurs, respectively. Perhaps lack of clarity was lumped into the unrealistic category by angels, or perhaps they did not bother to finish to reading the business plans that are unclear.

Interesting Comments by Angel Investors

"They are afraid to put in enough details to allow a person to fully appreciate what they have. If they can protect it, they should describe it; if they cannot protect it, then I have no interest in it. Consequently, I assume that the incomplete disclosure is due to the fact that the technology cannot be defended or protected legally."

"So much optimism and arrogance in their own vision and skills that they don't prepare realistic contingency plans and multiple routes to success if plan A doesn't work."

Most critical mistakes as seen by angels, venture capitalists, and entrepreneurs in our survey can be compared in Tables 16.2, 16.3, and 16.4.

Chapter Summary

- Angel investors certainly read the company's business plan carefully, but the plans often contain a number of flaws that cause angels to view the plans with considerable skepticism.
- Angels concur with venture capitalists that entrepreneurs' plans are too unrealistic and have too little substantive discussion about the market and the competition.
- Entrepreneurs are prone to stressing how wonderful their business idea might be; investors are equally concerned about the management team's ability to carry out the plan successfully and profitably.
- When writing a business plan, entrepreneurs should concentrate on making them realistic, clear, and complete.

CHAPTER

17

Polishing Your Pitch

The Really Great Presentation

The first thing to do when crafting a pitch to make at a gathering of angels is to give your audience simple conclusions that are easy to remember. Don't overload the audience with details. Too much detail can lead to confusion; confusion leads to tuning out the presenter and thinking about important matters—such as where to go to lunch that day. One good presentation we saw was as simple as this:

What we do.

Market need for our product.

Why our competition is vulnerable.

How much capital we need and how much we project we can earn with the capital.

The great things we have accomplished already.

Note that the presenter finished up with accomplishments, not projections. Companies that have reached milestones prior to getting the angel round of financing are very much in vogue today. Angels like to see that an entrepreneur has been able to get somewhere already, on their own, with their own funding.

Another good presentation had this format and focus:

The specific market need: the pain we are solving for the customer.

How we solve the problem at the individual customer level—we save money, time.

Our accomplishments in arranging key strategic partners.

Our target customers and how we will sell to them.

Our funding needs.

Why we will succeed (expressed with considerable excitement).

In this case, the presenter brought the venture down to the individual customer level: Here is a person using our product and here is why it will be of great benefit to them. It was also impressive that the company was talking with or had lined up important players in their industry as strategic partners. Again, this is emphasizing accomplishments, showing the investors this is a real company that is moving forward with or without them. The closing why-we-will-succeed section was particularly effective. It left us with the clear impression that this was a highly committed management team, and management is critically important to investors.

ADVICE FROM AN ANGEL

Luis Villalobos, Founder, Director, Tech Coast Angels, www.techcoastangels.com

Entrepreneurs seem to get nervous about presenting to an angel group. "I don't know about that. It's almost like being a rock star—there may be some nervousness before they get onstage, then they love it. Entrepreneurs get to talk about their vision for their venture, with people who may really be interested. It is more of a rush than a nerve-racking experience.

"And we work with entrepreneurs all the way along the process to help improve their plans, their business models, and their presentations. When I started the angel group, I never imagined the value of getting all

> these high-powered people in a room evaluating an entrepreneur's company and asking questions—the points of view, the experience, the expertise the angels bring are just fabulous. We have received feedback from entrepreneurs that even if we didn't fund them, they believe they have received tremendous value from the presentation sessions themselves; the angels really make them think."

Passion Combined with Rigorous Analysis

Angels respond very favorably to entrepreneurs who can combine these two aspects in their presentations. By way of example, let's compare two consecutive presentations we saw at a venture capital conference. In the first one, the presenter was a very articulate young woman with a software deal. She was obviously well mentored about all the elements of a good presentation to investors. She covered all the bases, almost giving us a minibusiness plan in 15 minutes. Her delivery was crisp, very professional. But at the end, the audience seemed to go, "Ho, hum. Another software venture aimed at a large, lucrative niche." This wasn't fair: Her deal probably had a lot of merit. She supported every point she made. Her assertions were, for the most part, bullet proof. However, she didn't deliver it with much passion, and if she didn't provide the spark, where were we going to get it?

Next up was a fellow with a biotech venture. He started out by exclaiming, "We're going to save lives with this, maybe yours!" Now, we might have reacted to that as just being overheated rhetoric, except he quickly followed up with a chart that showed he was selling into a $5 billion market, and other statistics followed indicating there was a great financial opportunity here. Then he went right back into showing how the technology worked, with tremendous enthusiasm. Then he showed us the projected profits, which were huge. He used this passion/analysis punch/counterpunch very effectively. When he finished, we were sold on the idea of at least asking for more information, which is the chief goal of any presentation, to stimulate further interest and discussion.

HELPFUL TIPS

Rehearse the presentation several times with individuals whose business acumen you have respect for. Obtain their individual critique of your presentation and try to improve it. Check out the venue. Some of the apprehension of putting on a presentation can be lessened by seeing where you will be giving the presentation, what style of meeting it is, how many people in attendance. If you are expecting a friendly, low-key meeting and you walk into a large banquet room with bright lights and 250 people in attendance, your first challenge will be overcoming a natural nervous reaction. By becoming comfortable with the venue, you can turn an away game into a home game.

Attend other venture forums and make mental critiques of those presentations. What did the presenters do to capture the attention of the audience? Did they conclude the presentation on a high note, or did they just trail off?

Critical Mistakes in Your Presentation

ADVICE FROM AN ANGEL

Tom Horgan, AZTEC Venture Networks and Acorn Technologies, San Diego, CA

What mistakes do you see entrepreneurs making when presenting to angel investors? "They forget who they are dealing with. The type of entrepreneurs we're seeing haven't had enough life experiences. They are coming at it with rose-colored glasses. In terms of how they present themselves, they have to be acutely sensitive whom they are pitching to. We are going to be testing them. There is a tendency for them to be off their guard, to be a little less shrewd and a little more sales-y. They need to change the style of their pitch."

Too sales oriented and not enough substance? "Yes."

We've seen so many of these presentations, and entrepreneurs seem to have such a hard time getting to the heart of the matter—what is really extraordinary about the company's solution. "They are too wrapped up in what they have. You have to study the target audience, the angels. There are some basic assumptions you can make about angels. Angels aren't rich because they have struck it lucky. They are good business people, and good business people are likely to ask tough questions. The entrepreneur should be ready for that.

"Entrepreneurs should really be careful when bringing in a team of two or three, that the team members aren't at odds with each other. There should be one person taking the lead, and everyone else plays their role.

"Also, we always look at how the team members relate to each other and whether ego is at play here. Starting from scratch, in essence, we like to know the personalities and how they interact, and see a lack of ego. We want to see that there truly is interaction and energy within the team, and they can be honest about their abilities and their prospects."

Do entrepreneurs listen to the advice you give? Or are they just focused on getting the money? "The good ones will listen. They will recognize they are sitting across the table from people who have done this before.

"It is always useful to follow up and just get feedback about your pitch. Only a few entrepreneurs have done that in all the companies that have presented to us."

That seems like fundamental marketing. Follow up with the prospective customer. "That's what's missing a lot of times. Fundamental marketing."

ADVICE FROM AN ANGEL WHO ALSO IS A VENTURE CAPITALIST

Patrick Soheili, Barrington Partners, Silicon Valley

When entrepreneurs come in and make a presentation to you, what is the most critical mistake they make? "They lie. The worst thing to happen is to hear the first lie, then I just do not focus on the presentation and the technology and keep looking for yet another lie to come out so I can throw them out of the room."

Of course, it's not just the information, but how you deliver it. One impressive presentation focused on how the founder had generated wealth for investors in prior technology companies. This presentation also took a complex technology and broke it down into simple terms. He had great passion for the technology and for his customers, and passion for helping others, making it a better world. A technical innovation only becomes a potential company after the compelling benefits of it to a large number of consumers can be shown.

The problem with most technologies is that the best you can say after you see the presentation is, "Oh, that was a neat innovation." There is no WOW factor, nothing about how the technology is going to change the world for the better.

ADVICE FROM AN ANGEL

Steve Miller, Co-founder, Prairie Angels, www.prairieangels.org

The process of presenting to a formal angel group is a mystery to entrepreneurs. Could you take us behind the scenes? "We get pitches all the time, so what we are looking for is a 10-minute presentation that tells us four things: (1) what the problem is, the pain in the marketplace that this idea is going to solve; (2) what the solution is, what the aspirin is; (3) how the entrepreneurs are going to make money and how much money they are going to make doing this; (4) why this is the management team to execute this thing successfully.

"Any 10-minute presentation should be able to do that. Now, I've seen hundreds of these things, and very few of them do."

What are the common errors entrepreneurs make in their presentation? "Trying to say too much is a common error, packing too much information in 10 minutes, and, therefore, the presentation as a whole is ineffective. Assuming too much about what the audience knows about the business is another common error. Entrepreneurs are so close to their ideas, to their businesses, that they don't realize that nobody else in the room is spending 23½ hours a day thinking about this business. So another common error is not explaining what the business is, what the vision of the company is, what the thing is going to do, clearly and succinctly. They just go into a big long story about their potential major customer or something.

"And they often say 'Oh, these financial projections are conservative,' which they never are. What I want them to say is, 'This is really my best informed guess of what I think the financials are going to be.' Don't tell me this hockey stick is conservative and this company is really going to be worth $10 billion in the third year."

ADVICE FROM AN ANGEL

Steven P. Subar

What are the common mistakes entrepreneurs make when presenting to angels? "The problems fit into two categories, style and substance. Most professional investors can overlook style, but not altogether, because it does say something about the experience and maturity of the individual. It is the easiest one to address if you are working with an early-stage company. These are sort of the obvious things like not knocking the drink over on the person next to you. Because they have an abbreviated period of time to make their presentations and generally they are a little bit nervous, they tend to make these kinds of obvious mistakes. They may forget to make sure that the audiovisual and demonstration materials are up and running rather than trying to futz with that while you have the audience's attention. You sort of feel bad for the presenters because you see they are struggling. These things are easy to correct, but they do affect your impression. For example, you may watch five presentations and all the deals look fundable, but only one of the presentations goes flawlessly. The content and the business idea may not be better in a material way than the others, but the management team may appear to have a better chance of success.

"Too frequently entrepreneurs will assume that their enthusiasm for their idea makes it as obvious to others why they have a solution to a problem that is both a high priority for the target market to address and pervasive in the market they are selling to. It is very often not the case. Frequently they can make a case that it is a pervasive problem, but it is not always clear the problem is something people need to address today. There is a big difference in the momentum a company may have if it has to convince people they need to solve a problem rather than walking in the door with a solution to a problem that everyone acknowledges is needed right now."

Chapter Summary

- A presentation to angels needs to be carefully crafted to emphasize a few key points, and should not be a recitation of the full business plan.
- Entrepreneurs should know the audience they will be presenting to and should even have a feel for the venue where the presentation will take place.

FINDING AN ANGEL

CHAPTER

18

How Do Angels Find the Deals?

AN INEFFICIENT MARKET— THAT OFTEN WORKS

Angels, even more so than VC firms, find potential early-stage investments through recommendations from others. For the entrepreneur, then, successfully reaching an angel investor depends primarily on knowing someone the angel also knows and trusts. If we drew a chart of how a company found investment from angels, it might look like the drawing of a family tree, with a few branches becoming many. The entrepreneur starting on this road may end up in a different place than he expected, when he finally meets the right angel.

Referrals and Groups

A referral is everything in the world of angel investing. It is almost as though nothing would get done unless someone makes an introduction on behalf of an entrepreneur to an angel. And more importantly, the tacit endorsement that occurs. If your trusted investment advisor tells you to take a look at an interesting private placement memorandum—or better yet a long-time friend at the country club says that he is seriously considering investing in a company—this gives the venture immediate credibility.

One entrepreneur who has started multiple technology companies told us about the terrible struggle he had to raise start-up capital from angels for a venture that ultimately was extremely successful. On his next venture, in which he was also an investor, he called upon the same angels, and received commitments from them almost immediately with much less due diligence being conducted on the new venture by the angel investors. They were eager to join in with an angel they had won with before.

ADVICE FROM AN ANGEL

Lore Harp McGovern

How do you find the companies? "Two ways. I belong to the Band of Angels, listen to the presentations and get involved with some of those companies. Secondly, I get many business plans sent to me because people refer other people to me."

Do you ever attend venture capital conferences to find companies? "I have done that off and on. Given the huge supply of business plans that come directly my way and the plans that come through Band of Angels, I have more on my plate than I can handle."

How would you suggest an entrepreneur go about finding an angel? "Have what they are trying to do thought through very well before they approach any investors. People invest in people, then they invest in the idea. If the person is not able to articulate the vision properly, they are not going to get results."

ADVICE FROM AN ANGEL

David Burwen

How do you find companies? "I started angel investing by joining two angel groups, the Band of Angels and Tenex. In doing this I met many other angels and quickly gained visibility as an angel investor. These groups often have subgroups, people who respect each other, have common investment interests, and share deals among themselves. Through these people, your friends, and other business contacts, word spreads that you are an angel investor and people start contacting you. Individuals in the angel group are often contacted by entrepreneurs starting companies. Often you bring these companies to the group to help evaluate the business potential and to raise enough seed capital.

"Angels usually invest from $25,000 up to a hundred thousand dollars, or so, in a deal. The average investment is probably $50,000 to $75,000. To get a company started in a high-tech area, a company typically needs about $1 million for a first round of financing. Most angels do not have the capability to finance a complete deal by themselves. Therefore they have to pool their money with other angels or venture capitalists. Of course an angel might be able to fund one or two start-ups alone. However, they probably wouldn't be able to finance a whole portfolio without group funding participation.

"It is important to have a number of investments if you expect to get a return on your angel investment. This is because venture capital investing is, to some degree, a matter of numbers. You need to have a dozen or so investments. At least 50 percent of start-ups fail, another 40 percent or so become little companies that never go anywhere, and maybe 5 percent or less really become substantial companies. You are playing a game with these statistics. To do better you have to make better decisions than the average VC. These odds are low enough that when I first became an angel, I wondered if I was investing or just spending money."

On-line Matching Services: Do They Work?

In the last several years, many Internet-based services were launched with the purpose of matching entrepreneurs with angel investors. The general method used by these Web sites is to post information about companies looking for capital in a password-protected area where only accredited investors can view them. The investor then makes the decision about whether to proceed with further discussions with the company and negotiate terms of a potential deal. The on-line service generally receives a success fee, or commission, when a transaction is consummated through the site. Several of the sites charge a placement fee only, and several charge a placement fee and a success fee.

These services started with excellent business concepts: Use the speed of the Internet to disseminate information about companies looking for capital. Let entrepreneurs be introduced to angel investors in all regions around the country instead of prospecting in just their local area. Allow new angels to enter this market and quickly find potential companies to invest in without having to do a lot of time-consuming networking on their own.

ADVICE FROM AN ANGEL

Craig Johnson, Chairman, Venture Law Group, www.vlg.com

It seems that the number of Internet matching services has dwindled. Why is that? "I think that one reason is simply that we are going through a difficult patch and it could be quite a bit worse than it is right now as the future develops for private investors with the massive decline in NASDAQ valuations and the many trillions of dollars of wealth that have evaporated. People are not quite as willing to risk capital as they were a year or two ago. Angels are simply drawing in their wings. That always happens in this kind of cycle.

"I also think that very few people would be willing to trust a significant amount of money to an early-stage entrepreneurial team on the basis of information they can learn on a Web site. Garage.com realized early on that its Web site was simply an adjunct to its eyeball-to-eyeball business, and that's why you see them having showcase events where entrepreneurs can present in person to selected angels. They have follow-up lunches. They have boot-camp conferences. You need to mix the real world and the world of the Internet to end up with a successful business model."

The on-line matching sites hoped to usher in a new era of greatly increased angel investments. Although on-line deals have been done, the volume has not been quite as great as some of the more optimistic sites had projected. One problem has been subsiding interest of many angels, after the "dot.com" bubble burst in the public stock markets, and valuations of early-stage companies returned to more normal levels. There simply were not as many angels getting into the market, on-line or off-line, as the operators of the investment matching sites had hoped. Also it turned out that there are certain flaws in this model for both the entrepreneur and the angel investor. For the angel, it is difficult to evaluate the merits of a company by just reading an executive summary or a business plan posted on a Web site. So much of the decision hinges on an individual angel's evaluation of the management team, and this cannot be done easily from a long distance, or done impersonally through the World Wide Web.

ADVICE FROM AN ANGEL

Barry Moltz, Co-founder, Prairie Angels, www.prairieangels.org

Do you ever use Internet matching services to find deals? "Never. There are too many people in the local community willing to pass along good quality deals to you. I don't think those things really work, especially right now. You need to go out in the community and meet people. There are so many risks associated with these investments—market risk, technology risks—you have to evaluate each of these individually."

It has been widely observed that e-commerce does not work well for products that consumers are accustomed to using their senses to evaluate, particularly the senses of touch and smell. Many angels prefer to "sniff out" good investments through in-person meetings with the entrepreneurs rather than through the admittedly faster and streamlined process of an Internet investment matching service.

ADVICE FROM AN ANGEL

Bob Bozeman, General Partner, Angel Investors LP, www.svangels.com

On-line matching networks were springing up everywhere, then all of a sudden a lot of them decided to cut back or close. Why? "It doesn't work. To decide to invest in a company you have to have the white of the entrepreneur's eyes in front of your face. It is a consuming task. We would get as many as 150 opportunities a week coming in and have to narrow that down tremendously to find the very best deals to invest in. If we couldn't really see the team and see how they handle the challenges, we didn't want to invest. To go through that as an angel on the Net, you don't get the full experience of being able to know whether that's a smart investment or not.

"You're only as good as how you can roll up your sleeves and embrace all the concepts and challenges that are involved with that business, and it's just a lot of work. You can't do that through the present on-line approaches. I wish it would work, because the demand for entrepreneurism funding is huge and it would be nice to open it up. But effectively, it doesn't work that way."

Investment Banking Networks

Angelstreet.com, Offroadcapital.com, Earlybirdcapital.com, University-Angels.com, garage.com are examples of investment banking networks. They screen the companies and accept only those they feel will be successful in attracting investment from their own memberships. The company's business plan is put on-line in a password-protected area for the membership to review. Depending on the network, there may be scheduled chats, Web casts, or virtual road shows, where the investor/member can interact with the presenting company's management. Several of the networks rely on a bidding or auction method to determine the price of the shares, in other words, the more investors that want to invest, the higher the per-share price. Other networks will negotiate ahead of time with the company to establish a firm price per share.

Offroadcapital.com based in San Francisco says that their on-line private securities marketplace has resulted in investments of more than $155 million in 14 transactions, as of mid-2001.

Garage.com announced that it has arranged 74 financing transactions, raising over $260 million in equity financing for its client companies.

EarlyBirdCapital.com located in New York has completed 7 transactions that resulted in $40 million of investment.

VSource1.com based in Atlanta has closed four transactions for $11 million total.

How Do Entrepreneurs Think Angels Find the Deals?

We asked entrepreneurs through our survey:

What do you think is the most common way angel investors find the companies they have actually invested in?

It is clear, as shown in Table 18.1, that the entrepreneurs who responded to the survey understood that angels rely on a number of differ-

Table 18.1 How Entrepreneurs Think Angels Find the Deals

Referral from another angel	24%
Direct contact by the entrepreneur	20%
From a finder or intermediary	19%
Through an angel network	17%
Referral from an attorney	8%
Referral from an accountant	5%
Venture capital conference	3%
Referral from a vc firm	2%
Matchmaking services	2%

ent sources for deals. The first four sources were ranked fairly closely. They correctly saw that angels give a lot of credence to deals referred to them by their angel colleagues. The second choice, direct contact by the entrepreneur, was ranked higher by the entrepreneurs than by many angels we interviewed, some of whom stated that they much prefer to have a deal referred to them by someone they know and trust. It was interesting that entrepreneurs ranked intermediaries as more important sources of deals than attorneys or accountants. Again, if the attorney or accountant knows the angel well, the angel investor is likely to give the deal more attention. The most professional intermediaries make an effort to gain the trust of angel investors as well.

Angel networks was the next most popular choice. Many angels do not yet belong to formal networks, and in some metro areas angel networks are nonexistent or not very active. Angels who do participate in networks tend to use them as preferred sources of deals rather than deals sent directly to the individual investor. Many angels will invest both as individuals or as part of a group, however.

Chapter Summary

- Most deals with angels are initiated through referrals.
- On-line matching services have not yet fulfilled their promise of creating a large new wave of angel investing.
- Entrepreneurs understand that it is necessary to try a number of different methods to reach angel investors.

CHAPTER

19

Why Do Angels Band Together?

A favorable development for entrepreneurs seeking capital in recent years has been the increase in the number of formal groups of angels, sometimes called angel networks, around the country. Some are loosely organized, the main purpose being to introduce investors to entrepreneurs in a social setting. Others are almost as tightly organized as VC firms, with highly structured procedures for analyzing companies and performing due diligence, and ongoing monitoring of portfolio companies.

Some angel groups go so far as to not include investors without a background in specific areas related to the types of investments that will be made, such as technology companies, or prior experience with early-stage companies. The combined available capital isn't the whole key to having a successful angel group; the combined expertise of the members is as important to the eventual investment success they will have.

Types of Angel Networks

With some groups, the purpose of the meetings is mainly networking, allowing potential investors and entrepreneurs to meet, and then it is up to the individual angel to decide whether to pursue an investment in that venture. After making presentations, the entrepreneurs sit at individual tables and wait for the investors to seek them out, almost like waiting to be chosen for the baseball or basketball team in school. On the other side of the spectrum, there are groups that bring entrepreneurs, after the deals have been carefully scrutinized, to present before a formal gathering of the group members, and then actually vote right there on whether to fund that deal, as a group.

Some angel groups are fairly open about who can attend the presentations. Others restrict admittance only to group members. Many groups limit their total membership to what they consider to be a manageable number, such as 50 or 75.

Because scores of these groups have formed just within the last few years, it may be too early to tell what is the most efficient way to organize an angel network. These are very much works in progress. With some groups:

YOU'RE ON YOUR OWN

There may be an annual fee to join and/or a monthly fee to cover the meeting costs. Selected entrepreneurs can present at the meetings, or an entrepreneur's business plan is posted at the angel network's password-protected Web site. Angels then review the business plans or hear the entrepreneur's presentation and make the decision to invest independently. Each investor contacts the entrepreneur, negotiates, conducts his or her own due diligence independently. The network acts as a conduit to increase deal flow but takes no active part in any other function.

DEMOCRACY RULES

There is usually a managing partner for the angel network who is responsible for the administration of the network; there can also be paid employees. The partner and the staff screen the deals and select those that merit further consideration; often the angels themselves may bring deals to the group. Those selected go through a due-diligence process and can also go through a mentoring session before they present to the members. The members review the business plan and ask questions of the entrepreneur. Each member then decides whether he or she would like to invest, and a limited partnership of those investing members is established.

ONE FOR ALL—ALL FOR ONE

Several angel networks are actually more like venture capital firms, with professional and experienced money managers. The manager or sometimes a committee of members screens the business plans and selects a few companies for further review and analysis. The selected companies go through a due-diligence process. Some networks allow the entrepreneurs to present to the membership, and the membership then votes on whether to invest as a whole in the company. If the membership votes to invest, every member has to contribute his or her fair share of funds, whether they personally voted to invest or not. The pooled money is then invested in the company and one angel or the manager sits on the board.

A REASONABLE QUESTION TO ASK

One of the mystifying things about angel meetings, as well as other types of venture forums, is why more of them don't have an exhibition area where more entrepreneurs could be introduced to more investors. If angels only have the time or attention span to hear three presentations in a dinner meeting, why not invite seven other companies to at least have an exhibit table and a networking opportunity? The chance to meet or begin a dialogue with an actual angel is extremely beneficial for the entrepreneur, whether he or she receives capital from those angels or not.

INFORMAL ANGEL GROUPS

Angels do not just band together in large, visible groups that have structured meetings. Angels often come together in groups of a half dozen or less and meet informally to look at deals. One of these we knew involved rich poker buddies who got together every few months and, in between hands, discussed interesting investments that had come their way. These smaller groups provide the angels with some of the same benefits as belonging to larger ones: They can share the due diligence chores, they get the benefit of multiple viewpoints about a deal, and they diversify the risk to some extent. The poker group also had quite a bit of fun along the way. And of course they made money at their angel investments.

ADVICE FROM AN ANGEL

Brent Townshend

Some angel groups are very informal, others are almost as structured as venture capital firms. Does it matter to the entrepreneur? "I think they should understand how the group works and whether it fits with their own company's culture. If it is a group that has thousands of angels that each put in $1,000, that isn't as good as finding a group where five angels will put in several hundred thousand dollars each, a more concentrated investment."

Do you invest as a group, or individually? "Both. Primarily through Band of Angels, 75 percent, and then 25 percent on my own."

ADVICE FROM AN ANGEL

Barry Moltz, Co-founder, Prairie Angels, www.prairieangels.org

Why did you start a network, rather than looking for deals on your own? "I was really new to the game. I started to get interested in angel investing about a year ago, and didn't know anything about it. I've been an entrepreneur for the last 10 years, so I knew about operating a company, but didn't know about advising one. I wanted to get involved with people who had been doing this a lot longer than I have, and I wanted to invest alongside them. As a good entrepreneur, you have to be aware of what you don't know. I hooked up with several other people in the area who had been doing this awhile. We were looking in Chicago to do something a little more professional. We have a professional administration staff, and corporate sponsors for the dinner event."

ADVICE FROM AN ANGEL

Ian Patrick Sobieski, Ph.D., Managing Member, Band of Angels, www.bandangels.com

From an entrepreneur's standpoint, why approach an organized group of angels rather than just networking one on one? "The question is, what kind of organized group are you going to approach? Is it just a group of guys brought together by a coordinator who charges a transaction fee on money that is raised? In that case, the only advantage is being able to do one presentation and having many eyeballs look at it. A group like ours does a rigorous diligence up front, negotiates professional terms that are industry standard, can provide a board member that has founded a successful company before, has served on other boards, and knows how to grow a big company and to mentor your company. Then there are many value adds for an entrepreneur beyond the money, such as organizing your company in such a way that it will be successful in the business arena, and successful in future financing, opening doors for both business development and further capital development, forcing your company to step through a diligence process. The greater degree of intelligent process that investors bring to bear on the investment, the greater good that is done for the company."

Why do angels decide to join groups? "You get to meet other angels. There is a big social aspect to angel networks, and joining does broaden deal flow horizons. Perhaps angels may have made their money in software and are now getting interested in biotech. They have expertise that is applicable to business areas, but they are conscious of their lack of technical knowledge in evaluating many of these deals. Perhaps they would like to invest and be involved in biotech. By hooking up with groups that have biotech experts in them, they are able to make those investments.

"The entrepreneur's point of view is that you can raise $1 million in one sitting if you're hot. But it can still be frustrating because it doesn't make it any easier to get in front of this group, considering we turn down 50 deals a month."

There seem to be more and more organized angel groups. "There will be less and less, a huge fallout. They've been investing in me-too deals with no sustainable competitive advantage, and they are going to run out of cash. People are going to lose money. You will see articles about how venture capitalists are greedy exploiters. It's a risky space to be in anyway. Oliver Stone will make a movie about venture capitalists.

"Some angel groups were formed by people with cash but without any particular focus. They're looking at it for a quick financial reward, looking at one- to two-year flips, 100-times returns, which were ridiculous and abnormal. The notion of putting your money away for six years and actually working hard on the deal before you see returns is not what a lot of angels were motivated by. Some of these groups are just going to disappear."

To join an angel network, the investors register with the organization, and they typically provide information about their investment interests as well as their background, experience, and capabilities. Knowing the member angels' backgrounds allows the network to team up investors to analyze a technology they are familiar with. Not all the angels who end up investing may be equally involved in evaluating the investment. Although they rely to some extent on the information gathered by their colleagues, angels within the group do not really solicit or sell other members to join with them in an investment, because they would be opening themselves up to liability should the investment not work out (at the very least they would lose friends). Typically one angel expresses his or her interest in the deal, explains why, and others join in.

ADVICE FROM AN ANGEL

Ken Deemer, Tech Coast Angels, www.techcoastangels.com

Could you give us a profile of your group's membership? "It's hard to describe an average member of our group; they are all over the place. They are all accredited investors, all experienced in investing in early-stage private companies and in assisting them, mentoring them. They are in their 30s to 60s. They come from a variety of backgrounds. Many have been entrepreneurs, founders, CEOs. There are business professionals from all kinds of industries. Some members are very technical, others are generalists."

How many members are in your groups? "The total is about 200. Seventy-five to 80 in each of Los Angeles and Orange County, slightly fewer—50 or 60 in—San Diego."

Different Meeting Structures

COME ONE—COME ALL

Some angel groups use an open house format, primarily for networking within a loose organization, where anyone can attend. Usually there is only a minimal fee or no fee at all. Attendees wear badges to identify themselves as Have Capital, Need Capital, or Service Provider. Maybe these organizers should consider hats instead of badges. The investors wear the hat on their head, the entrepreneurs hold the hats out in their hands, and the service providers conceal their identity under the hat.

STEP RIGHT UP, SEE A DEAL

Here, the entrepreneur has an exhibit booth, or perhaps just a table, and waits to pounce on any investors who happen to stroll by. Entrepreneurs can be charged a fee from a few hundred dollars to a few thousand dollars to exhibit. Investors usually pay an attendance fee, but some shows have no attendance fee. Some shows are open to the public and the entrepreneur cannot tell who is a legitimate potential investor and who is just a passerby or worse—a competitor.

DINNER THEATRE FOR RICH GUYS

This does not have to be dinner. These events also take place at lunch and breakfast. For the women angel networks, it could be called the-ladies-who-lunch club. This is probably the most common format for angel network meetings. The entrepreneurs stage their dog- and-pony show for the entertainment benefit of the rich patrons in the audience, a few select questions are asked, and then the entrepreneurs join the patrons for a leisurely dinner and bond.

ADVICE FROM A VENTURE CAPITALIST WHO IS ALSO AN ANGEL

Frank A. McGrew IV, Managing Director, Paradigm Capital Partners, www.memphisangels.com

How did Memphis Angels get started? "We wanted to be more than a source of capital for entrepreneurs. We wanted people who not only had experience; we wanted people who had the reputation for changing the paradigm of their industries.

"The angels themselves have insight, they have relationships, more than they have just capital. We wanted to give them enough information about the companies they were investing in so they, too, could be helpful. This way, the entrepreneur gets more than money. We've also added McKinsey and Company to the relationship. McKinsey has been retained as a strategic advisor to Paradigm Capital and Memphis Angels. We can thus rely on their 6,000 consultants around the world to leverage their industry expertise, their strategic insights."

Why was there a need for a formal angel group in your region? What was the need it served? "There are a number of needs. The South, traditionally, outside of Atlanta and maybe Nashville, has not been known for its risk-seeking investor base. This is an underserved market for venture capital.

"Each of the angels will tell you that you can build a successful business whether you are in Memphis, Tennessee or in Palo Alto, California. Although it may not be the technology nucleus for software, servers, or optical infrastructure, Memphis has a number of strategic advantages for entrepreneurs and for building new businesses."

ADVICE FROM AN ANGEL

Tom Horgan, AZTEC Venture Networks and Acorn Technologies, San Diego, CA

Tell us about AZTEC Venture Networks. "The group is comprised of high net worth individuals who are very high profile. Most are grey hairs, 50 years old or more. Through that network we get a lot of business plans. We're a group of executives who can provide capital, coach the entrepreneurs, take a board seat, and help them with their next round of financing.

"AZTEC Venture Networks is partnered with San Diego State University to assist their entrepreneur-in-residence program. One of their professors of business sits in the AZTEC group, so it is linked to the university in that sense."

ADVICE FROM AN ANGEL

Ian Patrick Sobieski, Ph.D., Managing Partner, Band of Angels www.bandangels.com

Tell us about Band of Angels. "Band members have founded companies such as Cirrius Logic, Symantec, National SemiConductor, and Logitech, and have been executive officers at Sun Microsystems, Hewlett Packard, Intel, 3Com, and Intuit. Institutional support for portfolio companies, such as bridge financing and follow-on rounds, is provided by the Band of Angels Fund, L.P., a VC fund made up exclusively of institutional partners, and by the numerous venture capitalists with close ties to the Band. We typically put in $1 million per deal. We have put in $100 million in 125 companies since 1995. Five have gone public, 12 were acquired, and 10 went bankrupt."

ADVICE FROM AN ANGEL

Barry Moltz, Co-founder, Prairie Angels, www.prairieangels.org

Tell us about the angel group you've founded. "It's based in Chicago; it's called Prairie Angels. There are about 80 people in the group. We meet every other month. Each presenting company has a sponsoring angel to bring it to the group. Usually two or three companies present at each meeting. You have to be an accredited investor to attend the meeting. There are no members of the press, no service providers, nothing like that. We started November of 2000, and we will have made our first couple of investments by the end of 2001."

Organized angel groups can play a critical role in stimulating early-stage investing in areas of the country not traditionally considered hotbeds of venture capital; these can be both larger cities and smaller, even rural areas. The angel investment activity helps strengthen the economies of these areas and spur entrepreneurship. With great dedication and pride in their hometown or regions, these groups provide the ingredients needed to turn capital deserts into productive gardens, although sometimes they find the soil to be rockier than expected.

ADVICE FROM A VENTURE CAPITALIST WHO IS ALSO AN ANGEL

Frank A. McGrew IV, Managing Director, Paradigm Capital Partners, www.memphisangels.com

"One of the value propositions by forming the Memphis Angels, is how we can recirculate or recycle the capital. Angel groups in other parts of the country have been led or been formed by entrepreneurs who have been successful, sold their business, took their company public, then took part of that capital generated from the transaction and deployed it in a new entrepreneurial deal. In the South we haven't really had this recycling as much. The angels in our group are not forming tech companies, selling them, and then looking for the next deal. They are looking to diversify a portion of their wealth, as well as benefit from new opportunities and help the region grow. It's quasiphilanthropic, but at the end of the day, each of the investments we make must stand on its own financial merits."

ADVICE FROM AN EXPERT

Cliff J. Grant, President, LocalFund.com, Inc., Billings, MT, www.localfund.com

Mr. Grant's company provides infrastructure for Montana Private Capital Network, an on-line forum matching angels with Montana entrepreneurs.

What has been the interest level in angel investing by the wealthy individuals in Montana? Is there a lot of enthusiasm for angel investing right now? "What we've found is that there are significant numbers of high-net-worth individuals who have previously been or could potentially become angel investors. They have an interest in diversifying their investment portfolios (by investing in private companies) and in local economic development (job growth). The problem has been that they didn't know there was a way to combine these two interests. This is a great opportunity for innovative economic development organizations (such as TechRanch in Bozeman). TechRanch is implementing a statewide, Internet-based, private capital network. This is the catalyst that will stimulate private equity in Montana. The network provides entrepreneurs with a way to get their business plans in front of potential angel investors, and investors with a tool to review more investment opportunities. The network increases the enthusiasm since it increases access to investors and potential deal flow."

How do you address the (incorrect) perception that there are not a lot of high-quality early-stage companies outside the major metropolitan areas? "One reason this perception exists is because the mechanisms are not in place to give the early-stage companies the exposure they need to attract investors. Each major metro area has at least a few well-established angel networks, conferences, breakfasts, and so on where high-quality early-stage companies can go for potential funding. Entrepreneurs in nontraditional areas (rural and intercity) simply don't have the opportunities that the metro areas offer. The presence of significantly lower populations in rural areas does mean that there are going to be fewer early-stage companies, but that doesn't mean they don't exist. *Inc.* magazine reported (in its Sixth Annual State of Small Business issue, May 2001) that the top 10 states by average start-ups per 1,000 workers were: (1) Colorado, (2) Florida, (3) Montana, (4) Wyoming, (5) Nevada, (6) Idaho, (7) Oregon, (8) Washington, (9) Utah, and (10) Arizona. I've shared these numbers with many who are amazed that there are so many start-ups in the mountain and western states. One of our goals is to work with business incubators, primarily from rural and intercity areas, in order to increase the number of high-quality early-stage companies in our network. Then when we go to an investor or group of investors we can show them what's out there. It's a matter of education."

Are you working on finding capital for primarily technology companies, or a wider scope of companies? "The companies are as diverse as the investors. We have many investors who are content to invest in a local coffee shop or car wash. They don't necessarily want the risk associated with a high-tech venture, especially considering the recent disappointments in high-tech companies. Angel investors primarily invest in industries that they understand (at least somewhat), and many of the investors in nontraditional areas did well in low-tech industries, so that's what they're looking for. The scope of businesses and investors covers the entire spectrum."

Chapter Summary

- Angel networks can be organized in many different ways, with widely varying procedures for selecting, analyzing, and funding companies.
- Investors band together to gain access to more and better deals, and to take advantage of each other's expertise in analyzing potential investments.
- Part of the mission of angel networks outside the major high-tech hubs is to stimulate economic growth through investment in emerging enterprises.

CHAPTER

20

Behind Closed Doors

How Are Entrepreneurs Selected to Present?

The initial contact information an entrepreneur sends an angel network is very much like the information a VC firm asks for. Usually, an Executive Summary of the company's business plan is submitted. This can vary in length from two to four pages, and formats can vary as well. Some groups are very picky about how the summary is constructed; others merely provide general guidelines on the preparation of the summary. To get the relationship off on the right foot, entrepreneurs need to study the suggested format and conform as much as possible to it.

The proliferation of organized angel groups has been a boon for entrepreneurs seeking capital, because it saves considerable time. No longer do you have to talk to 50 people individually about your deal, you can reach them all at once in one forum. But then again, no system designed by humans is ever perfect.

DEAL TALES: SPECIAL ORDERS MIGHT UPSET US

A founder of a dot.com company we worked with decided to contact as many of these organizations as he could in both Northern and Southern California. The problem he encountered was that each angel network had slightly different requirements about the information they wanted you to submit. Our conversations with him ended up sounding like this:

Founder: "Okay, could you take the three-page executive summary and cut it to two? That's what angel group A wants."

Founder a few days later: "No, hold the executive summary, we need a PowerPoint for angel group B. No more than 15 slides, by the way."

Following week: "It turns out the three-page summary was fine for angel group C. I hope you didn't erase that file."

Next conversation: "Angel group D likes my concept, but says the plan's too long. We need to shrink it down to 10 pages max."

Then: "This new group wants us to shorten the market analysis section, but they want extra stuff in the competition section."

Last conversation: "These guys want us to take our plan and extract it into their on-line submission form. This is gonna take all week."

Eventually, the entrepreneur started to think he was in the business of business plan writing rather than trying to run his e-commerce company. In retrospect, his time might have been conserved had he chosen just one of the groups and concentrated on them rather than trying to hit everyone at once. But he thought, if reaching 50 angels is good, then reaching 500 is great.

ADVICE FROM AN ANGEL

Ken Deemer, Tech Coast Angels, www.techcoastangels.com

With your group, entrepreneurs are asked to submit an executive summary and you have an on-line format for them to use. Are all the submissions personally screened? "We have three networks, or you could call them chapters, and each of those has a designated person who filters through the initial postings on our Web site. All of them are paid staff people."

What happens next? "For the Los Angeles and Orange County networks, the companies that look to be a potential fit for us get assigned to a prescreening team. We have about 20 teams of three to four members each that will contact the company and meet with them face to face for an hour or two, to hear the company's pitch and ask questions to determine if it looks like they would be of interest to our larger membership. If so, then they get recommended to proceed to the next level.

"This is a more formal screening session. Each network has one or two screening sessions per month where they will invite four or five companies in to give a pitch to a larger group, usually 20 to 30 of our members. This session takes all morning. We give each company about a half hour to give a pitch and then we ask questions.

"Based on that, we ask people in our group to express interest based on that presentation, interest in being part of a group that would dig deeper into that company's business and see if it would be something they want to pursue."

SELECTION

What is the best way for angel networks to select which entrepreneurs are going to present to the group, out of the many dozens of business plans that are sent to them? One approach would be to gather all the entrepreneurs who are going to be presenting that night into one room spotlighted in a semicircle around an interrogator, then ask them the same questions. It goes something like this:

Mentor/interrogator: "Tell me about your competition."

Entrepreneur 1: "We have a highly fragmented market where no competitor has more than a 5 percent market share."

Entrepreneur 2: "Our market is dominated by two large companies, but we have already secured letters of interest from 10 significant customers, which validates our technology."

Entrepreneur 3: "Our technology is so much ahead of everyone else in the market that we don't really see any competitive threats."

Mentor/interrogator: "Entrepreneur 3, yours is the weakest plan. You won't be presenting at our group. Goodbye. No competition. Indeed. Tell me, Entrepreneur 3, how long have you lived in fantasy land?"

So now we're down to two candidates for presenting that night.

Mentor/interrogator: "What is your revenue projection for year 3 and what are your assumptions?

Entrepreneur 1: "Revenues will reach, we feel conservatively, $500 million, by that time. And that assumes we only get 7.5 percent of our total market!"

Entrepreneur 2: "We built our forecast by verifying how many customers we could actually reach given our assumed level of marketing resources, while being mindful of the need to maintain high margins. We came up with a forecast of $57 million for year 3."

Mentor/Interrogator: "Entrepreneur 1, yours is the weakest plan. No dinner for you either. And why don't we leave the hockey sticks to the Philadelphia Flyers. Goodbye."

Luckily, the real process is not quite that combative, but unfortunately it is extremely subjective. The reality is that there are only a few presentation slots open at each meeting, and active angel networks get many dozens or even hundreds of inquiries from entrepreneurs. Some good deals inevitably fall through the cracks. Entrepreneurs should never look at not being selected by one group as evidence their venture will not be of interest to other angels.

The Mentoring Process

Many angel groups tutor the entrepreneurs on their presentation and help them fine tune their business plan, before they are brought into the lion's den of the full angel group dinner meeting.

What goes on at these mentoring sessions? Typically, there is a panel of angels representing a range of backgrounds—technology, marketing, finance. The entrepreneurs then do the same presentation they intend to do before the whole group. The questioning by the mentor teams can be just as tough as those in the general session. That is the idea, to inoculate the entrepreneurs a little bit, and get them ready for anything they might encounter, and prevent those awkward, "I don't really know" answers in front of the group and the profuse perspiring that follows.

ADVICE FROM AN EXPERT

Bruce Borup, Assistant Professor of Entrepreneurship, Alaska Pacific University

Do most entrepreneurs need coaching? "I am on the board of Alaska Investnet, which is an angel network here in Alaska. I was the M/C of the venture forum at our last capital investment conference, and I was the person who did the coaching for two days before the presentations. Virtually all the presenting companies had to switch around their presentations (which all sounded like trade show technical presentations to start with) to communicate to investors how the presenting companies were going to fulfill the needs and desires of the investors. I coached them on describing who their customers were; how many there were; what there problems were, and how they were going to provide the solution at great margins. They were also coached to discuss whether the solution was temporary or long-term, aspirin or morphine (I'm trying so hard not to say the customer's pain!). I coached them to communicate not just their product but to convey their business model and value proposition. Furthermore they were coached on how to talk to investors at the trade-show portion of the event and how to encapsulate the presentation in their one-page executive summaries, which the angel network allowed to be kept at the show booths."

What Happens When You Meet with an Angel?

One angel who has been involved in dozens of these investments has a technique he employs when meeting with an entrepreneur and listening to the pitch. Because entrepreneurs are coached to use the in-person meeting to sell the deal to the investor, the entrepreneur will try to pick up on the reaction of the investor to various aspects of the deal. This investor avoids showing any reaction at all to the presentation, which he says causes the entrepreneur to blurt out revealing comments about the business that are not part of the rehearsed pitch. Some of what might be blurted out may be negatives that the investor really needs to know in order to negotiate from a position of strength.

This particular investor coaches his fellow angels to employ this technique, sort of a sit-there-and-watch-'em-sweat strategy.

Well, what could an entrepreneur do to counter this? The entrepreneurs might imagine themselves delivering the presentation not to this single individual in his cramped little office or conference room, but to a roomful of angels at a conference. They might focus on the ideas and their enthusiasm for their venture, rather than trying to please this one person and obtain immediate positive nonverbal feedback.

Or they might try a more direct approach. Stop the presentation halfway through and ask, "Excuse me, sir, just checking whether you're still alive before I continue."

ADVICE FROM A VENTURE CAPITALIST WHO IS ALSO AN ANGEL

Frank A. McGrew IV, Managing Director, Paradigm Capital Partners, www.memphisangels.com

When a company has passed the first screening, and you are ready to invite them in to present at the monthly Memphis Angel group meeting, what happens next? "We coach the management team. We make sure they are ready to present well and are prepared for the questions. Once we have validated the opportunity, we want to give them every chance to be successful. We give them a number of guidelines on how to present.

"We encourage them to use slides that allow you to streamline the amount of words you say. Demonstrations of products or services are helpful. Customer testimonials go a long way toward reassuring investors. A lot of great technologies come in, but you need to show that there are customers today that are looking for the solution."

ADVICE FROM AN ANGEL

Ian Patrick Sobieski, Ph.D., Managing Member, Band of Angels, www.bandangels.com

Could you briefly walk through the investment process in your organization? "Band of Angels does not take unsolicited deals. I turn away anyone who contacts me directly. Angels bring in the deals. Each month there are about 10 deals referred from the members. We invite them in and they give a small pitch to a subset of angels and make a decision about what three we should invite to the full Band of Angels dinner meeting. Three come each month, based on preliminary screening, and get 20 minutes to present at a dinner at which 70 people attend. The following week we have a lunch on three separate days, two hours for each company, at which time people can ask detailed questions, really dig into the company and try to understand it better. As a result of those two meetings, you get a sense of which of the three companies are really of interest to the group;

and typically someone from the group steps in to be a sort of lead, do additional work on the deal, help coordinate the interest of various members, sign off on terms that are negotiated, and ultimately coordinate the investment. We typically put in $1 million."

ADVICE FROM AN ANGEL

Tom Horgan, AZTEC Venture Networks and Acorn Technologies, San Diego, CA

How does the process work at AZTEC Ventures? "From a process standpoint, we hired a fellow from Lehman Brothers (investment banking firm) to basically be the initial contact point for receiving the business plans. We break down the 30 angels into teams of five. And each team owes the group one week of evaluating business plans every six weeks. We share the workload. Much of this is done via e-mail. We get an abstract of the business plan or an executive summary. The five-member team votes whether to invite that company in for a presentation.

"If that company is selected, a team out of our group is assembled with relative expertise in that particular business area. That team meets with the entrepreneur's team. A determination is then made whether this company will be invited to present to the complete AZTEC group, which meets on the first Tuesday of each month.

"We would decide if a presentation that is coming to the meeting is one we are going to vote on at that time. That would be decided beforehand. They would come in, do their pitch, then have a Q&A session. We would ask the team to leave, there would be an open discussion, and the votes would be cast."

This sounds as though it could go pretty fast. "It could. Clearly, there are three processes: Business plan comes in, gets screened, then there is a meeting with the committee, then a presentation to the group. So it may not be as fast as we want it to be."

So, between the time they are meeting with the committee and the presentation to the full group, there is a lot of due diligence that goes on. "Due diligence is done in anticipation of a vote."

If in the due diligence process you find some things you don't like, you can still decline to have them come in and present to the full group. "That's right. Or, at times the judgment has been to reveal those issues in the open discussion phase and determine whether they are significant. I think it is fair to say that out of the 185 companies that have contacted us, we have brought in 10 to 12 to the due-diligence phase."

DEAL (SAD) TALES: A GOOD DEAL GOES WANTING

Are there any situations in which a start-up venture never gets funding, despite doing everything right? Yes.

A group of young ex-Marines, all in their early thirties, decided to pool their technology background and start a venture that applied the flight simulation technology they had seen in the military to create a high-tech family entertainment center (FEC). This group was extraordinarily skilled at the organizational tasks of starting a company: They did their homework, listened carefully to good advice, and knew when to reject bad advice, and they moved forward with a relentless can-do spirit, and never saw setbacks as an opportunity for self-pity.

They had a great combination of technology experience, leadership skills, and prior experience running a retail operation.

They put together a terrific business plan. They negotiated favorable terms with the developer of the site they picked out. They met with a well-known entertainment angel who was impressed with them, but told them their concept needed more *shtick*.

So they went back home, looked up what *shtick* meant, and then revised their facility design, the menu of their restaurant, and even produced a video to demonstrate the concept. There was no shortage of *shtick* when they got through, we can assure you.

They built a solid advisory board of business leaders who could refer them to potential angels and fill in gaps they had in the management teams. They made dozens of presentations. They even obtained an audience with one of the largest VC firms in the world, one that seldom did entertainment deals, but liked the professionalism of this group and gave them good suggestions about how to refine their concept.

They came up with the idea of throwing an angel party and invited wealthy individuals to meet them in a social setting and even to see a live demonstration of the entertainment system they were proposing. The party was very well-received by the investors.

But the months went by, and no one ever pulled the trigger on the investment. These determined fellows kept at it. Persevered. But nothing ever happened. Eventually, the need to make a living caused the group members to get other jobs and they slowly drifted apart. Their wonderful concept now collects dust on a shelf.

They simply never had the good fortune to meet the right lead angel to get involved and then attract other angels to join in.

ADVICE FROM AN ENTREPRENEUR IN THE MIDWEST

Did anyone from the angel network help prepare you by coaching you as you rehearsed the presentation? Did you feel this coaching was helpful? "Yes, a guardian angel works through the presentation to fine tune it."

Who on your management team presented with you? "CEO."

How long did the presentation last? "Twenty minutes plus five minutes of questions."

Were you able to remain through any other entrepreneur's presentation? "Yes."

What were some of the questions the angel investors asked after your presentation? "Marketing plan details, sales cycle, more explanation of the selling process."

How did you feel? "Very high level of adrenaline before and during."

Was there anything you would do differently? "Clearer slides and more rehearsing."

Was the experience worthwhile? "Very. Good introductions to people at and after the meeting."

Did it result in any investment in your company? "Not directly from the network."

ADVICE FROM AN ENTREPRENEUR IN CALIFORNIA

How did you prepare for the meeting? "I created a presentation, rehearsed presenting the material, and presented in front of a very successful friend who grilled me exhaustively (and I had to buy him dinner afterwards)."

Did someone from the network coach you before the presentation? "No, no coaching."

Who on your team attended? "The Chairman and the CTO."

How long did your presentation last? "The presentation was designed for 15 minutes, and it took me precisely that."

How did you feel? "Anxious."

Was there anything you'd do differently? "Videotape myself, critique the presentation, and practice some more."

Do you feel presenting at an angel network was a worthwhile experience? "Yes."

ADVICE FROM AN ENTREPRENEUR FROM ALASKA

Can you tell us about your experience? "We did little preparation for the presentation. We did not understand concepts such as business model or value proposition, and we were focused on the benefits of our product. We used the if-only market-share argument (if we get only 1% of this huge market!). I attended as the chief marketing officer, as did the CEO of this start-up. The presentation was 30 minutes and we were extremely disappointed, although, as it turns out, we had no right to be disappointed since we talked about what we could do for us and never spoke to the investors about what we could do for them. We never talked about our customers: who they were, how many of them there were, and why they would fork over tons of money for us to solve their problem. In fact, I very much doubt we even knew what our customers' problem was. We had confused a good idea for a business model."

ADVICE FROM AN ENTREPRENEUR

William G. Teags, xPackage.Com, Inc., www.xpackage.com

How did you prepare for the meeting? "We basically did weekly meetings with the mentor team and my management team. We went over the PowerPoint presentation and shredded it top to bottom. We also had a few people specifically watch my presentation skills—voice, motion, presence, and so forth."

Did someone from the network coach you before the presentation, and if they did, was this coaching helpful? "Yes. I found it useful, helpful, and sometimes confusing. Key to a good presentation is to be yourself. Listen to your team for clues to build over your own weaknesses, but do not try to be what you are not."

How long did your presentation last? "About 10 minutes—not enough to go into depth."

How did you feel? "I had a few mentors who were very worried because I am usually quiet and reserved, but I have been on stage many times in the past. I loved it, felt very up and had no nervous feelings at all. A little awkward because the microphone was stationary and I had rehearsed with the idea of a lapel mike."

Do you feel presenting at an angel network was a worthwhile experience? "It was a good learning experience. A lot of pressure was on me to make everything happen, but the timing was absolutely the worst with respect to the marketplace (December 2000 and nobody was investing much)."

Chapter Summary

- Entrepreneurs must pass through a sometimes intensive screening process before being accepted as a presenter to an angel group.
- Groups often provide mentoring assistance to help get entrepreneurs ready to make an effective presentation.
- They key to the process is to find that one angel who will become enthusiastic about the venture and bring other angels in. Without that person, obtaining angel capital can be difficult.

CHAPTER

21

Tracking the Flight Path of Angels Is Difficult: They Don't Show Up on Radar

First Step: Construct a Perfect Angel

We worked with an entrepreneur several times over the last 10 years who was one of the most effective marketing people we have ever seen. One of his favorite axioms was, "First you construct your perfect customer: who he is, where he lives, what his attributes are. Then marketing is simply a matter of going out and finding more and more that look just like him."

Did his ideas work? He owns the big house on the golf course. So there you go.

We began wondering whether these concepts apply to the search for capital, particularly angels, because they have a much broader demographic than venture capitalists. It seems that this type of advance consideration of the ideal partner can help. Entrepreneurs need to take inventory of themselves, their aspirations for the company, the stage of the development the company is in, asking themselves such questions as:

- Would I be more comfortable with an investor who is older and more experienced than I am, or with someone who is more of a contemporary of mine?
- Is it important to me that the investor has a thorough knowledge of my industry, or will I be able to explain the strengths of my industry and technology to the investor? Do they need intimate knowledge of the industry to get it?
- Will it be easier to deal with just one or two investors who have a large chunk of equity, or 10 to 20 investors with smaller shares?
- Does the investor need to live near me in order to participate in guiding the company, or can we do this by phone, fax, and Internet?
- What are the gaps in my management team that the angel investor could help to fill?
- Can I cope with an angel who has a large ego, a strong-willed individual?

After you have constructed your perfect angel, now you have to go out there and find him or her. That's all.

ADVICE FROM AN ENTREPRENEUR

Alexandre Gonthier, CTO, iPIN—Interactive Transaction Services

What methods did you use to find angels? What worked well and what didn't? "Initially, we really went through business associates, friends, and family, mainly. Because we were five initial founders, our personal networks were quite extensive. Also, Silicon Valley is an amazing source of individuals who have experienced success first hand and were open to helping us. There were some venture capitalists who were interested, but not at our stage of development. However, they made initial introductions to seed funds and angels for us."

Why did you elect to seek capital from angels rather than from VC firms? "We were young and did not have the pedigree (founder resumes that showed that the founders had done it a couple times before, personal relationships with venture capitalists, etc.) and it was not a time when venture capitalists were pouring money into any Internet ventures. Venture capitalists were too hard to convince at our infant stage, so we sought funds through angel investors and seed funds."

ADVICE FROM AN ENTREPRENEUR

Dave Westin, CEO, www.channelautomation.com

How much capital did you raise through angels? "We raised $2 million with our Series A round, mainly driven by angels. We raised, in December 1999, $1.5 million, then $500,000 more six months later."

Why did you elect to use angels rather than VC firms? "There is a myth that should be dispelled: that angels don't have any idea of what's going on. A lot of the angels that we dealt with are mini-venture capitalists for all intents and purposes. They are not unsophisticated investors; in fact many angels are industry leaders or they have been in the high-tech arena investing for 20 years, so they have as much experience as many of the venture capitalists out there in the (Silicon) Valley.

"Unless you are doing something that requires a lot of money to get going, such as networking technology, where you need to raise tens of millions, angels are ideal investors."

How did you go about networking to find angels? Were there any surprises? "The thing that didn't meet our expectations is the time it took. What you have to network for is not necessarily the full $2 million, but you have to network for the first few guys who invest and that will help you find the rest of the $2 million. You develop relationships over the course of your business career, people who know other rich people. From there you can tap into the money. The time process was a little longer than I expected, because, at the very last minute, one of the lead investors decided to change the terms of the deal, literally two days before we were going to close the round. Since they represented 30 percent to 40 percent of the round, we had to waste another month or so getting everyone lined up again.

"I have had solid experiences with angels, but a lot of negative experiences as well. You have to understand why each angel is investing in your company. What is their objective? A return on investment? To provide mentorship, because it's an area they feel they can add value to an organization? On the negative side, do they have a conflict of interest so that they want to steer you into directions that may not be in the best interest of your venture, such as having you form an alliance with another technology partner or a development partner they may know?

"Some investors want to cut their own side deals; 'I brought in this much money along with mine, so I want a finder's fee,' which is fine. But above and beyond that, do they want to sit on the board, do they want additional stock to sit on the board, do they want a consulting agreement and fees?

"You have to scrutinize. It's better to take less money and deal with fewer headaches. The time you are putting into solving these issues takes away from your time running the business.

"As an entrepreneur, you have to be very cognizant of why people are investing, what their expectations are, basically what their agendas are. If you can meet them, great. If not, you shouldn't take the money."

ADVICE FROM AN ENTREPRENEUR

Dave Howard, CEO, 1Vision Software, Inc., www.1visionsoftware.com

What methods did you use to find angels? What worked well and what didn't? "We used the services of an investment banker that contacted potential angels. This method worked well for us. One of our early investors was actually a global capital markets and entrepreneurial business consulting firm. They, in turn, helped us identify and contact additional investors."

Why did you elect to seek capital from angels rather than from VC firms? "Capital needs at the time removed any choice."

ADVICE FROM AN ENTREPRENEUR

Ken Deemer, Tech Coast Angels, www.techcoastangels.com

What would you advise an entrepreneur who is starting to look for angel investors? "I would tell them to find somebody who doesn't necessarily have a business card that identifies them as angel or investor. Find someone with been-there, done-that experience, a role model or mentor, someone who has built a successful company either in their industry or in a similar industry, and go to them as much for advice and coaching as for money.

"If they can get this successful person interested in assisting their project, the money often will follow. So many entrepreneurs just kind of go after the phone book of whom they think are angel investors. Angel investors, more than any institutional investors, need to have some kind of connection or passion or interest in the project and in the people. It is more than just money.

"So, find someone who may not even think of himself as an angel investor, but is a successful business person, and has been an entrepreneur. If you get that person on your side, chances are either they'll invest or help you find an investor."

Will an Intermediary Really Help You Find Angel Capital?

Entrepreneurs tend to believe that the purpose of the intermediary is to go out and sell their deal to investors, much as a stock broker convinces a client to purchase shares of a hot new IPO. They also believe the intermediary is thick-skinned and used to getting no for an answer, and will persevere on behalf of the entrepreneur, almost indefinitely. People also tend to believe in the pay-only-on-performance idea when working with intermediaries, the concept that the hungry broker will do almost anything to collect the 2 percent or 5 percent success fee when the deal closes.

But what goes on inside an intermediary firm, whether it is a seedy guy working out of a shabby office suite, or a well-bred individual in the silk-stocking district? Intermediaries spend a lot of their time researching what the investors they know are interested in. The better ones put an exhaustive effort into this function. Often they have automated databases of investor preferences, the types of companies investors are most enthusiastic about. Then, they network in the business community to find companies that match the investor's criteria for the hottest deals they have collected. That is the true value the intermediary provides: He has taken the time to know and understand the needs of the investors. The selling aspect of this whole process is secondary, and highly overrated.

With intermediaries, you may be able to jump start them into action by paying them a retainer fee. Some intermediaries will not work for you without it. The fee could be a one-time payment of $5,000, for example, or it could be a certain amount per month for six months.

If the intermediary miscalculated what the investor appetite for your deal will be, the intermediary may lose interest after a period of time, even if you are paying a retainer. Rejection can exhaust an intermediary just as it can an entrepreneur, because the goal of the intermediary is to close as many deals as possible with the investors he or she knows, to bring them good deals and make them happy. An intermediary, too, needs the reinforcement of a positive reaction to a deal in order to continue working on it. If the reaction is uniformly negative, the effort will slack off. Again, the intermediary cannot sell the deal to a savvy investor. He can only present deals to investors who have the highest likelihood of buying.

DEAL TALES: JUST A SLIGHT CONFLICT OF INTEREST HERE

We were contacted by a real estate developer who wanted to expand his health spa concept into a national chain. He asked us to do a feasibility study for him, investigate the size of this market, existing competitors, and advise him whether his idea could be taken across the country. We quoted him a price of $10,000 for the study and waited to hear back.

He called and said, "I reviewed your proposal. Everything looks good. I called your references; you were highly recommended. But up-front fees of $10,000? Up-front fees are always a red flag for me. I'll tell you what I'll do. Do the study. We'll go raise the capital, and I'll pay you $25,000 at funding."

We politely remarked, "But if we're only going to get paid if we come back with a feasibility study that says your idea is great and you should move forward, how can it be a feasibility study? Generally, a feasibility study implies the possibility that infeasibility exists."

"No, no," he said, "I'm sure it will come out that the deal is feasible."

"Then why do you need us to do a study if you already know the answer?"

"Investors ask for that kind of stuff. Just covering all the bases."

"But just because we say the deal is feasible it doesn't mean the investors will put the money in."

"But once you see it's feasible, you'll be confident that I'll get the funding and when I do get the funding, you'll be paid for your work."

Angels and Incubators

Many start-up entrepreneurs consider the option of joining a business incubator in order to obtain the infrastructure and advisory resources the company needs to get started. How does this affect your options and chances of attracting angel investment?

ADVICE FROM AN EXPERT

The Angel Investor and Incubators

Woody Maggard, Director, Arizona Technology Incubator

With a history of only 50 years, incubators are a relatively recent business development phenomenon. In their simplest form, however, incubators simply mirror the de-risking process most angel investors would hope to see in a start-up or early-stage company. In fact, most incubators invest far more in a company than they receive in return and take on the role of a generous angel investor. An angel investor can find great value in working closely with an incubator, not simply for development of a deal stream but for a compatible partner as well.

A working definition of an incubator is a structured environment for mentoring or virtual settings, but all have in common a set of targeted services and networking designed to dramatically improve a company's chances for success. Research by the National Business Incubation Association (NBIA) has shown that 87 percent of companies developed within an incubator will be successful (still in business after five years). This compares, of course, to the generally accepted success rate of 20 percent for all companies.

For purposes of this discussion, the focus will be on technology incubators. Incubator services usually include common secretarial and administrative support functions, such as reception, shipping/receiving, access to copy, fax, and other equipment; meeting space, lunch and break-room facilities; T1 and other technical infrastructure, networking, and in appropriate markets, access to lab space. In addition, most incubators provide on-site mentoring by seasoned entrepreneurs and professionals; advisory teams comprised of top experts in the community in each area of business and technology; access to payroll administration, employee benefits, and insurance; links to a major research university; support in applying for research and development funding; counsel on intellectual property, licensing, and related areas; and connections with angel, venture, and lending financial sources. Most incubators are nonprofit entities focusing on expanding local economies through development of high-growth, wealth-generating companies.

The key to the success of an incubator and the client company is due diligence in the selection process. In many ways, this process is similar to the process an angel investor would use to screen a potential investment. Most incubators require at least a draft of a business plan to make certain that the business is at least considering all the major factors. This also provides a mechanism for future help in identifying strengths and weaknesses. The company is then presented to a committee comprised of professionals representing each key area for business (legal, accounting, technology, marketing, experienced entrepreneurs). Typically, about 1 in 10 applicants is selected. A written agreement is normally used to identify the expectations of each party, and the incubator often takes a royalty or equity position in the company. The client companies normally pay a market rent plus a small amount per month for mentoring. Most incubators expect a company to graduate within two to three years.

Although the average applicant will initially state that the only ingredient missing for their success is money, incubators take the approach that the money will find its way to the company if the company is properly prepared. Consequently, the key factor for a successful incubator company is the willingness and capacity of the company to be mentored. The incubator should respect the private ownership and investment of the company, but it also should expect to have its services valued. Along these lines, each applicant is carefully questioned about whether they value control over wealth creation. If they value control more than wealth creation, they are a poor candidate for the incubator, just as they would be for the angel investor.

Most incubators also develop strong relationships with key large corporations as a mechanism for creating pathways to market for their client companies. This matrix of services, supplied by seasoned professionals and a cadre of volunteers, is impossible to duplicate by either the angel investor or the client companies.

Because most angel investors invest on the first or second round, an incubator relationship is very beneficial. Incubators typically have relationships with two types of angel investors. First, there is the prototypical angel investor who invests either on their own or with only a few others. Second, there are the angel groups who prefer to invest smaller individual amounts but benefit from group due diligence. Rounding out these contacts, incubators work closely with venture capitalists who can move the company to another level, and with banks and private equity sources for alternative sources of capital.

Most incubators focus on high-growth and wealth-creating companies. Typically, this means that the company has a high probability for having a liquidity event, that is, either an IPO or the possibility of being acquired, as a means of providing an exit for the investors. This is normally a strong profile for angel investors, though even with the best selection processes most companies will evolve into what is termed a lifestyle company where private ownership and control, coupled with better than average annual growth rates, occurs. Thus, it is important for angel investors to structure their deal with incubator companies with the expectation that they probably will be successful but may well not create a near-term liquidity event. The good news is that the odds are in the angel investors' favor if they work closely with a successful incubator. They can also elect to become volunteers themselves for companies they are not investing in as a means of honing their own mentoring skills for the companies in their portfolio.

Bringing incubators and angel investors together creates a strong match, in which the company, the incubator, and the angel investor can all win.

What Do Entrepreneurs Advise?

In a study, "*The Characteristics and Value-Added Contributions of Private Investors to Entrepreneurial Software Ventures*," conducted by the Center for Venture Research, University of New Hampshire, by John Freear and Jeffery Sohl in June 2001, of 30 software company CEOs who had angel investors, friends were considered the most helpful resource in finding investors. Industry contacts/networks were in second place, followed by attorneys, other entrepreneurs, and accountants. Least helpful were bankers, followed by cold calls, investment forums, and professional associations.

Entrepreneurs were able to contribute many good, thoughtful ideas on how to find angels. The percentages represent how many of the entrepreneurs who responded to our survey cited that method as the best way. Figure 21.1 shows the results of our survey of entrepreneurs.

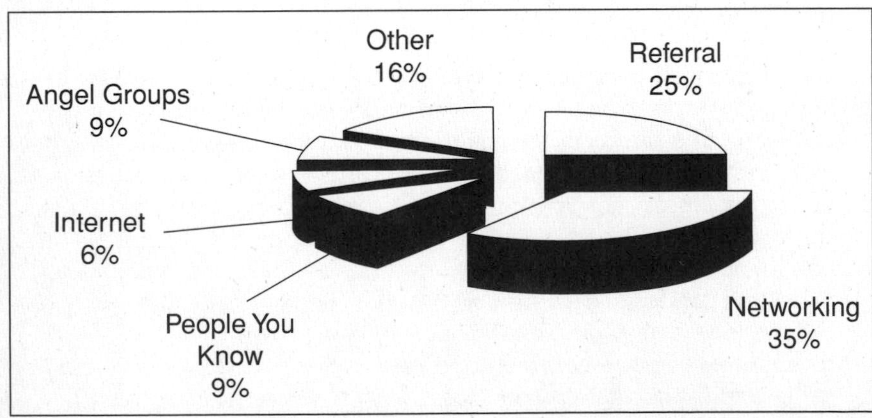

Figure 21.1 How to Find Angels

TO SOME ENTREPRENEURS, IT'S STILL A MYSTERY

"Still trying to find out the best way. . . ."

"I don't know."

The responses in Figure 21.1 show that most entrepreneurs know exactly how to find angels. They emphasized referrals and networking, they recognized that the Internet can be a good research tool, and the breadth of the responses show that they understand the need to employ multiple techniques to accomplish this. A relatively small number thought that angel networks or groups were the best way to go. In many areas of the country these groups are just forming or have recently formed and are not yet well known. And, many cities of significant size do not have any angel organizations as yet.

If entrepreneurs are so knowledgeable about how to find angels, why do they find it so difficult a task to undertake? It seems they know what to do, but not specifically how to do it. They cannot sit down and list the action steps involved in doing an angel search. Sometimes, they do not even know how to begin.

It is easy to say, "Get a referral from a service provider who knows angels." It is not so easy to ask, "How do I get a top-flight attorney or CPA to recommend my deal?" Or even, "How do I get in the door to talk to these people?"

Certain law firms gain the reputation of providing their clients with referrals to investors. But these prestigious firms don't accept just any client who walks in the door. They obtain clients through—yes—referrals.

The truth is that building an effective network that you can tap into when seeking capital requires effort over a period of time that could be months or years. You can't just begin to develop the contacts you need at the time you need the capital. Entrepreneurs who have taken the time to be active networkers in their business community over the course of their careers have a significant advantage over the entrepreneur who does not attend conferences, business association meetings and other events.

One of our clients read in a magazine article that the best way to find an angel was to obtain a referral to the investor from the CEO of a company the angel had previously invested in. The client did some research and contacted several CEOs who had been funded by well-known angels in California. The client received a rude awakening when these CEOs either would not take his call or told him, "I've never heard of you or your deal before. Why should I refer you to my investor?"

So the point of the process is not about obtaining a referral from these well-connected people. The objective is to gain the trust or respect of influential people, so you can utilize this relationship in obtaining a referral to an angel that is partially, at least, an implied recommendation of you and your company.

The angels, on the other end of this chain, are doing the same sort of networking, trying to find people they can trust or rely on to refer good deals to them. Without that network, they are just as lost as the entrepreneur who is looking for them.

The process is really about how loose social organizations are formed to move the deal along from the idea stage in the entrepreneur's head, to the point where it is a real company with real investors.

The sequence of successful networking with angels goes like this:

Entrepreneur gains the trust of key business people in their community.

These people agree to refer their deal to others they know.

One of their associates has gained the trust of one or more angel investors, and they pass the deal along to the angel.

The links in this chain are forged carefully and diligently over time.

Chapter Summary

- The first step in finding angel investors is to determine the profile of an angel who fits your company's needs.
- The next step is to build a network of business contacts that can lead you in the direction of the most suitable angels.
- Intermediaries may have many investor contacts, but their success in helping you find capital will depend on whether their investors are seeking a company specifically like yours.
- Business incubator organizations and angels often work together.
- There is no "Capital 911" for entrepreneurs to call.

CHAPTER

22

Making It Easy for an Angel to Find You

Using the Media

One way of linking up with angel investors is to let them know about the exciting things your venture is doing. Public relations, which includes publicity efforts, can help a start-up company in two ways: obtaining visibility and establishing credibility. With enough visibility, it is possible for angels interested in companies like yours to begin seeking you out.

ADVICE FROM AN EXPERT

Using Public Relations to Establish Credibility and Visibility: The Reality

Aimee Fitzgerald, President, Fagan Business Communications, Englewood, CO, aimeecolo@aol.com

Write news releases promoting the company and its products. Distribute those releases on a large-scale, mass basis. Call contacts and request stories. Wait for investors to take note and watch the funding flow in.

Sound good? If it really were that easy, Silicon Valley wouldn't be full of empty office space and dot.com might still be a good (and well-funded) form of business. Unfortunately, public relations is one of the most difficult professions to define and, as a result, to implement. When business managers think of public relations, they often think the term is synonymous with publicity, or that PR stands for press release. Understanding what public relations is—and isn't—can help a growing business use the discipline most efficiently for maximum results in establishing credibility and generating awareness.

Contrary to popular belief, public relations is not publicity, free advertising, or sales promotion. The real job purpose of public relations is to assist in developing relationships with a company's publics; hence the name, *public* relations. At its core, public relations is strategic and forms the base to develop a company's brand, image, and reputation.

And since it works with company messaging at the highest level—not just marketing or other functional messaging—the discipline is the heart of how a company presents itself to, and communicates with, its publics: investors, customers, employees, the business community, vendors, government entities, the news media, and any other groups that an organization impacts. When confined to one tactical area of news media relations, public relations' effectiveness is severely limited.

So, fortunately, the ways in which public relations can help a company become more visible to potential investors just happen to be the same ways it helps increase the company's awareness and credibility with all its publics:

Develop and Implement Key Messaging

Businesses will derive the greatest value from public relations by focusing on integrated messaging throughout their organizations. Top-level public-relations professionals are trained to help companies develop basic, simple, and concise key messaging. That means pushing to get to the core of what your business does, without the use of adjectives, fluff, or promotion—just the facts. Once you have two or three key points to first define, then to differentiate, your business, that can be readily understood in an elevator conversation, at a cocktail party, or by a reporter unfamiliar with your industry, you're ready to move on.

Implementing the basic messaging about what your company does throughout every communications vehicle you use, from e-mail and fax templates to proposals and investor presentations to your Web site, will do more than any news release ever will. When your company, however small, presents a simple, consistent message in everything it does, the impact on market awareness can be phenomenal. From outside the organization, even the smallest firm looks pulled together and buttoned down when it presents a simple, consistent message.

Develop and Implement Tactical Public Relations Programs That Support Company Objectives

At a tactical level, public relations includes not just news media relations, but community relations, investor relations, employee communications, and vendor/supplier communications. For start-up companies, news media relations is often not the best or most cost-effective method to create visibility. A community relations program that links a company with a nonprofit group or with a targeted industry trade show might be a better choice. A regular e-mail newsletter to customers, investors, and other interested parties may produce results faster with just the publics needed.

Use News Media Relations Judiciously

On a tactical level, it's important to remember that news media relations is the long-term process of developing working, news source-based relationships between members of the news media and company spokespersons. Publicity, another of the functional areas, is typically celebrity or event driven: bringing attention to a particular person or event for something unusual happening at the moment. For most start-up businesses, publicity has limited opportunity and value in terms of ROI.

Editorial news-media relations is only one part of a successful public-relations program; within that, only a minuscule portion of the work is involved in writing and issuing news releases. The real work comes in the research necessary to identify and understand targeted publications, and in developing ongoing working relationships with key reporters and editors charged with covering the company's industry. Similar to the sales process, editorial news-media relations generally do not culminate in much on the first contact; it takes time and constant effort to build. Remembering that news is defined by the reporter or editor, and that it is not promotion will greatly increase your chances of success.

Embrace Public Relations' Ability to Identify Critical Issues

One of the greatest values of public relations is to help companies identify where they may be vulnerable to scrutiny by their publics. Effective professionals can identify the potential effects of certain actions on the company's publics (before the media does), bring these issues to management, explain the risks, and provide alternative courses of action.

Building a Network

All the contributors to this book have emphasized the importance of referrals and network building in finding angel capital. But how do you really go about this? How does an entrepreneur get started?

ADVICE FROM AN EXPERT

Tips for Using Networking Skills to Attract Investors

Leni Chauvin, Founder, Business Referral Exchange, www.superstarnetworking.com

Sex, politics, religion, money. What have they all got in common? Well, they're topics many of us were advised by our parents not to discuss in polite company. Look at the first three subjects. With the relaxed mores of the latter part of the twentieth century, it seems the admonitions of our parents regarding these issues no longer ring true.

But when it comes to talking about our own money or the money of our close personal friends and associates, for all our sophistication and for all our worldliness, we're still as uncomfortable as we ever were. Think about it. When was the last time you asked a friend how much money they make? It's still a question that embarrasses most people. It's something we just don't want others to know. Money, after all, is just so darned personal. Sex, politics, and religion may have made it into polite circles as acceptable topics at a dinner party, but money is still a forbidden topic, even in this new millennium.

No wonder then, that entrepreneurs looking for investors are often stopped dead in their tracks. They become paralyzed with fear. They often overlook the best resource for funds available because they're too embarrassed to talk about money with their friends, relatives, or associates. They don't want anyone to know they might *need* money to grow their businesses. They wouldn't want people thinking they were *needy*, after all. Needing money and being needy are two separate things, and the sooner the entrepreneur understands that, the sooner he can get started with a plan of action that will help him tap into a resource that is already on his side.

Who am I talking about? The cold, uncaring banker in the glass tower at corporate headquarters? Absolutely not. I'm talking about the people the entrepreneur already knows. People who like, trust, and respect him already. People who *want* him to succeed. People who will likely want to be a part of his successes because they care about him. I'm talking about his sphere of influence, his circle of friends, his network.

Will everyone in your network jump at the chance to invest in your business? Absolutely not, but you can increase the odds of getting a little help from your friends if you:

Know whom you know. You can't begin to network for investors or anything else for that matter, until you know who is *in* your network. Make lists of everyone you know, how you know them, what you know about them, and who you have met through them.

Approach networking for investors as you would networking for referral business or a new job. It's really the same thing, after all. Change your mindset from looking for money to looking for business. That's really all you're doing. This will help take some pressure off of you.

Go about your search with a systematic plan of action, instead of jumping from person to person in a haphazard fashion.

Create visibility for yourself. Go to chamber of commerce functions, and such, on a regular basis so people get to know you. Going only once in a while will not allow you the opportunity to form strong relationships with anyone. It is from those relationships that your network will grow.

Join and become an active participant in a weekly business leads–exchange group limited to only one person per occupation. The ones I have operated have led to millions of dollars' worth of referrals for the members. These clubs are goldmines of opportunity for people in your position. Make sure you give lots of qualified leads to the other members. They, in turn, will want to make sure they continue to get those good leads from you and will help you find the investors you are seeking.

Look at all times as if you don't need the money. The hungrier you look, the less likely it will be that you will find an investor. If you look successful, you will attract what you are seeking. If you look down on your luck, you will attract a mass exodus from your vicinity.

Be clear about what you need and why you need it. Don't expect others to figure out how to help you.

Know your product or service inside out. Be able to answer any question, no matter how off the wall, with a succinct answer. Your prospective investor does not want to hear you droning on and on about your business. They just want you to cut to the chase.

Make your pitch a whine-free zone. Nobody wants to hear about the 10 banks that turned you down. They want to listen to someone positive and enthusiastic.

Tell the truth. Don't exaggerate, and be able to substantiate any claims you make.

Remember that money is still a touchy subject. Never push anyone beyond their comfort zone. It will come back to haunt you.

This above all else: Know WIIFM (What's In It For Me?). Think like your potential investor. Know how they can benefit from their investment. If they're sold on you they can easily become your strongest ally in helping you find other investors. If they think you've got something great, they'll want to recommend it to others and look good in the eyes of their network.

Conferences, Forums, and Trade Shows

Attending conferences and trade shows can be extremely beneficial for the entrepreneur seeking angel capital. These events could be on the subject of venture capital, or they could be trade shows focused on your industry. In either case, they are methods for getting closer to the elusive angel.

Most events set aside networking time where attendees can mingle and exchange business cards. The mindset to have when going to an event is not to meet your angel there. Rather, learn who the influential people are in the world of venture finance or in your specific industry who could be contacted at a later date. These people could be gateways to meeting angels. Making their acquaintance at an event is a good way to get them to take your phone call later on. The people you want to meet could be speakers at the event or major sponsors. If a law firm is a sponsor of a VC conference, there is a good chance that part of their legal practice is devoted to transactional work involving investors and entrepreneurs.

Actually pitching a deal at one of these conferences is difficult. You generally do not have the opportunity of getting the person's attention long enough to explain your venture adequately. The point of the exercise is to build your network of contacts and to pick up tips about how to raise capital for your venture.

Everyone you meet on an informal, social basis such as this could be a potential referral source. The person who is a stranger to you at the beginning of a conference could be a valuable acquaintance at the end.

Most people you will meet at the conference believe in entrepreneurship, and some of them may find your company and your story interesting enough to be a referral source. This highlights the serendipitous aspect of finding angels: You never know who might know whom until you ask.

The Strategic Research Institute, www.srinstitute.com, has a series of seminars devoted to private equity, and venture capital (among other topics). We have attended their Private Equity Conference presented in January every year and can recommend it. It is not inexpensive and it is an intensive three days, but worth the time and money.

Red Herring, www.redherring.com, has a series of conferences that are targeted toward entrepreneurs and investors, called Venture Market Regional Conferences. Even if your company isn't selected to present, the event can help you polish your own presentation, network, and learn more about where technology is headed.

There are other organizations that present conferences and seminars. The National Association of Venture and Seed Funds, www.navsf.org, has developed two workshops—one for angels, Seed Investing as a Team Sport, and one for entrepreneurs, Swing for the Fences—that are presented around the country.

Chapter Summary

- Publicity for your company can work wonders in helping you uncover previously hidden angels.
- Networking is a skill you can develop, if you are willing to put in the effort.
- Conference attendance can be a valuable way to build up your network of contacts.

YOU'VE FOUND AN ANGEL— NOW WHAT?

CHAPTER

23

To Invest or Not to Invest: That Is the Question

Angel Decision Making

When you watch an enterprise take shape from the beginning, when the venture is just an idea in an entrepreneur's head, and it progresses slowly and painfully into a viable entity, develops its products, obtains its seed capital, and moves forward, you draw the conclusion that the people who founded the company had no idea how difficult the whole process was going to be.

Perhaps it is important, even vital, that they didn't have any idea what they were getting into, because it might have prevented them from getting started in the first place.

We have worked with many entrepreneurs and many angels, and believe it is a remarkable talent to be able to identify a potentially winning management team. Venture capitalists say that they look for people with a track record of prior success, which is great. This is a luxury not available to most angel investors, because the majority of companies are not founded by people with one or two entrepreneurial successes they can point to. They might be people with a particular competence in one area. They might have good references and strong character. But they have not had any accomplishment with the difficulty factor of starting a successful company. Usually, this is their first venture, their first voyage into dangerous waters.

You can apply a certain investigative logic to analyzing the technology or the market. You can interview experts, talk to prospective customers. But how can an angel possibly understand what is inside each of the members of the management team? Who will thrive under the pressure, who will fold? Who can learn new skills on the fly so they can execute the many different kinds of tasks that are part of the management of a start-up?

Investors put money behind people, not just behind concepts. The whole key to the angel investing process is to be able to identify potential in up-and-coming, often young, people. It takes tremendous listening skills and the ability to ask the right questions. This may also be the reason angel groups are becoming so popular: They allow investors to reach a consensus, and an angel can listen and watch as an entrepreneur answers questions posed by another angel. The angel can ask his fellow angels for their reaction to the members of the management team and compare it to his own.

ANGELS VERSUS VENTURE CAPITALISTS

The spotlight in the VC industry is usually on cutting-edge technologies, those paradigm shifts everyone is always talking about. The VC firms chase after companies like these, with the result, as with any auction of a scarce commodity, that the price for the company's equity can, at times, often go sky-high.

Higher expectations by VC firms about rate of return leads them to rule out a broad range of potential investments, many of which are suitable for angels. Angels do not have the pressure to exit investments as quickly. These could include companies that are growing more slowly or are serving smaller niche markets. The typical angel only deploys a small fraction of their liquid assets to these early-stage investments. The remainder is in less risky assets, such as large or mid-cap publicly traded securities and income-producing real estate. For the VC firm, however, all the capital in their portfolio is earmarked for venture investments. They have to do painstaking analysis and screen through hundreds and even thousands of opportunities in order to find the premier investments, in their view.

Angels, though, can afford to take a bigger risk occasionally. Their decision could be based on something as simple as liking the individuals who founded the company, or finding excitement about the technology.

DEAL TALES: NOT TO WORRY, GOLFERS WILL INVEST IN ANYTHING RELATED TO GOLF

One of our clients had developed a new technology to aid in learning how to play golf. The founder of the company was a golf addict who was a successful salesman in his regular job, and a part-time inventor. The technology he developed seemed exciting: He had come up with the idea while trying to improve his own golf game and adapted a rather complicated communications technology to golf training. (We can't describe it in more detail than that because he had us sign one of those five-page nondisclosure agreements that prescribes nasty things that will happen to you if you divulge the secrets of the technology, even if you're captured by the enemy and tortured.)

The entrepreneur demonstrated this training aid at his country club, and invariably reported back that everyone thought it was: "neat," "cool," "super." He thought it was certain to get major funding. But from our point of view, in terms of finding venture capital for this enterprise, there were a few drawbacks:

The technology was very expensive to manufacture, leading to a high retail price and limiting the number of retail chains that would carry it.

Only a small percentage of golfers bother to take lessons consistently to improve their games, so it is questionable how many would purchase a training aid.

The entrepreneur had no prior experience operating or owning an early-stage company.

Golfers who carry too many gadgets in their golf bag look silly to their peers, like Rodney Dangerfield in *Caddyshack*. Image is very important to golfers.

So, what happened?

The entrepreneur wisely ignored the traditional VC firms and narrowly targeted his investment search to angels who are nuts about golf, just like him. He prepared a very professional business plan and product brochures to present to angels, and he did his pitch between shots while he and the angels played 18 holes. So, despite the apparent drawbacks mentioned, investor interest in his deal was very high. Wealthy golfers love their game so much that they put aside some of the investment fundamentals and let their passion for golf be their guide. The entrepreneur put into practice what we have been saying about constructing an ideal angel and then went out and found those who looked like that angel.

He got to play a lot of golf while looking for the capital, which is an added bonus. When the entrepreneur first showed us the technology, one of us, an avid golfer, got up from the chair and exclaimed, "Wow, this so cool. How does it work? I can't wait to try it." The other, a non-golfer, stayed still and said, "I don't get it."

You'll have to decide for yourself whether these angels were doing what all successful business people do from time to time, rely on gut instinct, the emotional reaction to a product, or were merely falling into the trap of performing "duh diligence" on their investments.

Critical Factors in the Investment Decision

We invited the subscribers of our newsletter to complete a survey of how they viewed angel investors. If you would like to subscribe to the Capital Connection newsletter, send an e-mail to listar@capital-connection.com with "subscribe cc-newsletter" (no quotes, of course) in the body of the e-mail. The subscribers are from all over the United States, and several are from other countries.

Entrepreneurs were asked to rank how they thought angels would rank the factors.

The Profit Dynamics Survey asked angels: What are the most important factors angels rely on to value a company prior to making an investment? They were asked to rank the factors from 1 (least important) to 9 (most important).

As you can see in Table 23.1, not surprisingly, quality of management was the number-one factor for angels, entrepreneurs, and venture capitalists. Stage of development, and industry, are ranked in last place by all three as well. What is interesting is the variance in the middle factors. Growth potential is ranked second by angels and entrepreneurs, and ties for fourth place with competition and ROI in the VC rankings. Product is ranked third by both angels and venture capitalists, but in sixth place by entrepreneurs.

Table 23.1 The Important Factors When Valuing a Company

Factors	*Angels*		*Entrepreneurs*		*Venture Capitalists*	
	Points	*Rank*	*Points*	*Rank*	*Points*	*Rank*
Quality management	7.1	1	5.5	1	5.4	1
Growth potential	4.7	2	5.4	2	4.2	4
Barriers to entry	4.2	5	5.4	2	4.1	7
Return on investment	3.9	7	5.3	4	4.2	4
Competition	4.0	6	5.3	4	4.2	4
Proprietary product	4.4	3	5.1	6	4.4	3
Market size	4.3	4	5.1	6	4.6	2
Stage of company	3.7	9	5.1	6	3.8	8
Industry	3.8	8	4.9	9	3.6	9

Entrepreneurs had very little variation in rank from the top factor to the bottom, only six-tenths of one point comprises the difference in the average rank from the top factor to the last-place factor. The range for angels is 3.3 points. Entrepreneurs considered quality of management the top factor, but not by much. With each of the factors, a significant number of entrepreneurs said it was most important, and a significant number said it was the least important. Even in the case of quality of management, roughly 40 percent of the entrepreneurs ranked it 8 or 9, and 30 percent ranked it 1 or 2 in importance. Well over half of the angels rated management as the most important factor, and 60 percent gave it a 8 or 9; only 10 percent gave it a 1or 2 in importance.

This lack of consensus can be viewed several ways. Entrepreneurs' experience with angels tells them that angels are very individualistic in how they analyze potential investments. It is up to the entrepreneur to determine what factors are most important to a given investor and make sure the factors are addressed in the discussions the entrepreneur has with the investor.

The data also showed that many entrepreneurs just aren't sure what factors are most important. Many of them gave all the factors a 6 or 7, for example, indicating all the factors were of significance.

The fact that entrepreneurs, who sometimes are accused of being too much in love with their product, ranked product uniqueness lower than other key factors, was certainly refreshing. Product narcissism can lead entrepreneurs to forget to explain a key factor to prospective investors: How are you going to sell this thing?

Table 23.2 shows that the top four factors for angels—quality of management, growth potential, product, and size of the market—are also the top four factors for venture capitalists. Two of those factors—quality of management and product—have the same ranking. The last two factors are also ranked the last two by venture capitalists. Venture capitalists ranked growth potential, competition, and ROI in fourth place, whereas angels rank them second, sixth, and seventh, respectively. Angels have a variance of 3.3 points, whereas venture capitalists have a variance of 1.6. It seems that venture capitalists do not differentiate as much as angels do.

Management is given a higher average point score by angels than by venture capitalists. Because angels invest earlier, it may be that the management team is even more important to angels than it is to venture capitalists.

So what does this mean for the entrepreneur?

Entrepreneurs need to demonstrate the quality of their management team, focus on the growth potential of their company, define their market and prove that the size of the market is large, and, of course, show that their unique product or service fills a need in the market. These tactics work well with both angel investors and VC firms.

Due Diligence

According to our surveys, angel investors say that on the average, they take 67 days to close whereas venture capitalists say they take 80 days, a difference of about two weeks. Is this because angels don't want to take the time to perform the same careful due diligence that venture

Table 23.2 How Alike Are Angels and Venture Capitalists?

	Angels		*Venture Capitalists*	
Factors	*Points*	*Rank*	*Points*	*Rank*
Quality management	7.1	1	5.4	1
Growth potential	4.7	2	4.2	4
Proprietary product	4.4	3	4.4	3
Market size	4.3	4	4.6	2
Barriers to entry	4.2	5	4.1	7
Competition	4.0	6	4.2	4
Return on investment	3.9	7	4.2	4

capitalists do or because they realize they do not have the experience or resources to do so? Venture capitalists have technical experts in their network they can bring in to evaluate the potential of an entrepreneur's technology. The angel? Probably not. Angels are often on their own.

Why is due diligence sometimes lacking in angel investments? Angels may not have lawyers or accountants who have due diligence skills, and the cost of having highly skilled professionals perform these services for an angel can add up very quickly. One of the benefits of angel groups is that the angels can divide up the due diligence tasks, so it is not so time consuming for any one angel, and you get the benefit of all the other angels' experience and perspectives.

In any type of venture investing, the investor is trying to make an educated guess about the risk versus the reward. Part of the entrepreneur's sales effort to the angel must involve helping the angel become comfortable that the level of risk is manageable. Think about how upset many investors become when there is a sudden drop in the stock market. Some people get angry, some lose sleep, some reach for stomach or headache remedies or more serious types of medication. The types of losses that are sustained in these situations are minimal when compared to venture investing: You can lose all the money you invested in a deal, and your money can be locked up with no potential for a return of any kind for a number of years.

Angels who invest as a group, whether a formal group that has regular meetings, or an informal group of friends, usually look for deals that at least one member of the group has specific industry experience or knowledge in. This helps makes the process of evaluating the risk/reward tradeoff easier, and allows the angel group to provide more valuable experience after the deal closes. One of the tenets of angel investing, which all successful angels have cited to us, is *invest in what you know*.

The angel's formidable task is to find a small company, a technology, a product, or a service that could become extremely popular with customers in a given niche, even though the entrepreneur may not have much data to support such a conclusion. The venture being presented to the angel may be in such an embryonic state that it is little more than an idea, and may not have accomplished any significant milestones in its development as yet. To the extent the angel understands the existing customer needs in the market or trends in a given industry, the angel's ability to spot a potentially winning solution to a customer problem is enhanced. The angels' understanding of the market allows them to envision the customer actually making the purchase decision.

In working with hundreds of entrepreneurs, assisting them in writing their business plans, there are two difficult parts of the plan to write effectively and convincingly:

1. Translating the theoretical marketing strategy in the plan to answer the question: Can you actually sell this product/service to a real live person and get him or her to pay you actual money for it?
2. Very few management teams have the coveted track record of success in prior ventures that investors want to see and take comfort in, so how do they explain why they will be able to pull off the incredibly difficult task of building a successful venture from ground zero?

Answering these two questions forms the heart of evaluating the risk of a venture. If the entrepreneur cannot articulate them in the business plan, and the angel does not have the analytical capability or staff members to investigate these questions independently, what happens? They fall back on the old, reliable gut instinct.

DEAL TALES: IS THAT RUMBLING IN YOUR STOMACH GUT INSTINCT OR MERELY INDIGESTION?

A very wealthy, very busy angel once hired us to find prospective investments for him. He had an ambitious goal of investing in five companies in the next year. This project seemed like great fun. He had given us fairly narrow criteria regarding the types of companies he wanted to invest in, so we weren't on a wild goose chase. We would find the company, write up a summary about its merits, and present our findings to the angel once every two months or so. We quickly learned how much an angel relies on his gut instinct to make these decisions. The deals we thought fit perfectly with his interests and experience he usually quickly dismissed. And he never could articulate exactly why he didn't like the ones he turned down. They just didn't feel right to him. We ended up presenting over 75 companies to him; he made only one investment. And we still aren't sure exactly why he liked that one deal so well.

Veteran angels will say that as they go along, they hone their due diligence skills, and also gain a better appreciation for the need for thorough due diligence. But there are other factors at play here before we can categorically state that VC firms' approach to due diligence is vastly superior to that of angels. First, there is a CYA aspect to all this investigation by the venture capitalists, and second, angels and venture capitalists have different goals.

The VC firm needs to perform this careful analysis not only because it probably leads to better investment decisions, but if an investment performs poorly or fails altogether, the VC firm has this documentation to explain what happened to the limited partners who supply money to the VC firm. It allows the VC firm to look like a prudent manager of the money rather than as people who guess about investments. A VC firm's decision to invest is made by a committee of the firm's partners; this spreads responsibility for the investment. An angel often makes the decision alone.

An angel may evaluate factors such as whether funding this venture helps the community as a whole by creating jobs, fostering community goodwill, and so forth because the entrepreneur is a respected or well-known member of the local community. A venture capitalist may live on the other side of the country from the entrepreneur, so these local factors are irrelevant to the decision-making process.

The venture capitalist is charged with finding the companies that will grow spectacularly quickly, and that have the potential for phenomenal returns for the institutions that provided capital for the VC firm to manage. The angel may be a person who built a nice little profitable company and sold it for $10 million. He could well be looking for other early-stage companies that could grow to modest, but undeniably profitable and valuable, levels. Obviously, there are more companies that fit that profile than the candidates for superstardom in the IPO market. The angel has built a company like this himself; he knows one when he sees one. This is particularly true for angels who invest in companies that are in the industries they are already familiar with from their own experience as operators of businesses.

With early-stage investments, angels cannot ever squeeze any significant portion of risk out of doing the deal, no matter how much painstaking due diligence they perform. Angels mitigate the risk as much as they can by investing in people who are known and trusted by people they know and trust, and by sticking to businesses not too unlike those they built and ran successfully. This method may not be as amateurish as some VC firms' partners would have us believe.

ADVICE FROM AN ANGEL WHO IS ALSO AN EXPERT

What Makes a Deal Attractive?

Bob Geras, President, LaSalle Investments, Inc., has been an active participant in the venture capital and angel community in Chicago for over 30 years.

Several often-cited fundamental characteristics of an interesting investment candidate are significant growth potential, quality management, reasonable valuation for the risks involved, and timely liquidity.

Usually, the most appealing investment opportunities, especially to professional venture groups, are the ones that offer the potential to achieve a significant scale of operations in a relatively short time. However, there are many other types of less dynamic situations that could also be very worthwhile. As a matter of fact, because the smaller, more mundane companies are often passed over by the big venture groups, there is less competition for them and, therefore, a better deal for the investor can usually be negotiated. The real question is:

How much potential reward is there for a given level of investment, risk, and effort, over what time span will this occur, and how does all this compare to other investment alternatives?

Significant Growth Potential

One attractive characteristic is the potential for the company to grow to a significant size in a few years. Attributes of a business with high growth potential are:

- Meaningful advantage in terms of technical know-how or lead time
- Market niche or segment in which these features or advantages *show a clear economic benefit to the customer*, such as higher quality, lower cost, or improved productivity
- Market whose size is already large enough or growing fast enough so that a believably attainable share could represent substantial sales for the company in a few years
- Availability of access to that market through established channels of distribution to readily identifiable customers
- High gross margins to allow for errors that inevitably occur in rapidly growing companies and to provide for substantial research and development to maintain a competitive advantage

Management

The company should have quality management with the drive, ability, and experience to make this growth happen. The existing team doesn't necessarily need to be presently complete, but the company should show the ability to be able to readily attract a full team with the qualities needed to build a successful company. These qualities include:

- Integrity
- Experience
- Knowledge
- Perseverance
- Leadership
- Creativity
- Stamina

In real estate the three most important ingredients for success are location, location, location. In venture capital investing it's people, people, people. If all the other ingredients are there, but you don't have the right people, the odds are stacked against you. No matter how attractive other aspects of the deal may look, remember that you can't make a good deal with a bad guy.

Good resumes are no insurance against possible failure. Always check into the entrepreneur's background. A successful prior track record is always a plus, but look beyond the surface facts. How much of the prior record was due to the entrepreneur's particular talents and efforts and how much was due to:

- Someone else's efforts
- A terrific product that sold itself
- Having been at the right place at the right time

After all, even a blind pig finds an acorn once in a while.

Also, how has the entrepreneur reacted during adversity? How did the individual function under extreme pressure, which is the condition under which most companies must grow? Is the entrepreneur a survivor? Did this individual keep other people's interests in mind at such times or only his or her own? What do the entrepreneur's former business associates, bankers, and investors think of him, his judgment, and his integrity?

An entrepreneur must also have an inclination to accept outside advice and listen to input from colleagues. A strong management team is crucial, because the business environment is continuously subjected to unexpected changes and management must be able to properly adapt in a timely manner.

Anyone can put a great story on paper, but how are claims verified? In addition to checking on the work histories of the key people as suggested, make use of resource networks of investors and/or consultants to find others with related experience or industry knowledge. Getting co-investors involved who may have more capacity than you for due diligence and experienced staff to monitor a deal once it is done, is another way to get proper pre- and postinvestment help.

Liquidity

There must be a good probability that the business, if projections are met, could be merged, acquired by another company, or sold to the public to obtain liquidity of angels' investments. If projections are not met, there should be other ways for angels to get out, such as a put option to the company or to the other shareholders.

Having registration rights for an IPO are not always the answer. If management doesn't want to go public, there are many ways they can undermine an underwriting effort. Multiple exit options must be thoroughly explored and provided for in advance to cover as many contingencies as can practically be addressed before the investment is made.

ADVICE FROM AN ENTREPRENEUR

Alexandre Gonthier, CTO, iPIN—Interactive Transaction Services

What kinds of questions did the angels ask you in the course of due diligence? "More than questions, they were essentially looking at getting a feel that we were race horses, I guess. At that stage, one bets on people, not so much on a product, or a client roster, or a business plan. They wanted to be convinced that we had the vision, drive, passion, focus, and execution capability that are required."

ADVICE FROM AN ANGEL

Steve Miller, Co-founder, Prairie Angels, www.prairieangels.org

Entrepreneurs wonder about what goes on in the due diligence process with angels. What happens when you decide to move forward with a company? "Different angels do their due diligence in different ways. Some want to find out as much as they can about the entrepreneur. They will look into previous employment history, into tax records, into credit history, just to make sure who they are dealing with, and about their management style and expertise. Some angels will be very focused on the market, to learn as much as they can about competitors out there, about the size of the market, to do as much verification as possible about potential customers. They may talk to potential customers and ask, 'Would you buy this, how much would you pay for it, how many other people out there are like you?'

"Many times there will be a management team committed to joining postfunding. Angels will want to talk to those candidates and find out whether they are really committed to this business, whether they are really going to quit their job and come to work for this start-up.

"Many angels will want to do verification on the technology, look into the status of any intellectual property, look into the status of how far along the invention is or if it is just an idea on a cocktail napkin. Every situation is different, because the companies are very different and the angels are different in their methods."

There seem to be parallels between angels' due diligence methods and those of VC firms. "Definitely. It's just that, because angels get involved at an earlier stage, there is not as much information available to them. There are some angels who will just write a check and not do any due diligence. If they are comfortable enough with the idea and comfortable with the management team, they are not going to spend their time doing a lot of due diligence.

"That being said, it's never a good idea to not do thorough due diligence, and these days that is a lot less likely to happen than it was a year ago.

"There were even institutional venture capitalists who didn't do any due diligence during the mania before March 2000. We have all learned that's not how you do business; it never should have been and it certainly isn't the way now. We are all much more patient writing our checks these days."

ADVICE FROM AN ENTREPRENEUR

Dave Westin, CEO, www.channelautomation.com

What is your opinion on angels' approach to due diligence? "There are two types of angels. The lead angel who gets friends and colleagues to go in with him or her. This individual will do the due diligence. The others investing with the lead angel are just doing that on faith. The lead angel's due diligence is virtually identical to the way venture capitalists do this. They are all high-tech guys, so that they've all been through the due diligence wringer with venture capitalists. They know the questions to ask and VC firms pretty much ask the same questions."

ANGELS ARE INDIVIDUALS, NOT INSTITUTIONS

A VC firm's decision to invest does not relate to the personal situation of the partners of the firms. Even if the partner working on the deal quit the firm, the deal could proceed. For individual angels, the personal situation of the angel often heavily impacts the outcome of the decision.

DEAL TALES: JUST SAY NO AND PUT THEM OUT OF THEIR MISERY

One of our clients came up with the innovative idea of throwing an angel's party to raise money for their software venture. One of the board members of the company had a beautiful, large home that he offered as the venue. The company invited wealthy individuals they had sent their business plan to, attorneys, and other service providers who worked with wealthy individuals looking for deals, and even members of the press. They produced a video on the company that played continuously in the living room. They even had a demo of the software for the investors to get hands-on experience.

It was a wonderful idea, really, because the management team got to talk about the company in a relaxed setting, and the investors, in turn, could offer constructive feedback and even had the opportunity to network and meet other interesting people.

As the evening neared a close, several of the angels expressed interest in talking to the company further.

The president of the company seeking capital followed up with one of these prospects every week or so, and kept hearing, "I'm very interested. Just give me a couple of weeks to finish some other things and I'll get back to you."

Unfortunately, though, the truth came out on the third or fourth phone call: The investor could not put any money in the deal because he was in the process of filing for divorce and his assets would be tied up until the legal process concluded.

The entrepreneur went away from this experience very puzzled. Why didn't the investor just come out and say this at the outset? Why did he string us along when he knew full well he wasn't going to invest?

We probably will never know the real reason. Did the investor's wife not yet know he was filing for divorce and he couldn't let the information out to the entrepreneur? Did he not want to face the fact he was going to lose a lot of money in the settlement and it boosted his ego to be courted by the entrepreneur?

This entrepreneur, for whom this was a first venture, quickly learned the lesson that angel capital is very much involved in the personal situation of the angel. All the crises that occur in an individual's life affect their investment decisions, whether the deal being offered is wonderful or not.

Chapter Summary

- Visceral reaction to the management team is an important element of angel decision making.
- Angels may invest in a company for the simple reason the product appeals to them.
- Entrepreneurs are very uncertain of what factors about a company make it most attractive to angels.

CHAPTER

24

The Mystery of Valuation

Fortunately it is not necessary to take a graduate course in financial analysis to understand how angels value a company. Many of them use remarkably simple valuation formulas. The absolutely simplest would be to say, "A start-up company in this size market with this type of technology is worth $1.5 million. If I put up $150,000, I should receive 10 percent of the equity." Before we scoff at this nonanalytical approach, we should consider that some angels view the financial projections for a start-up as essentially useless. So much uncertainty exists at a company's inception that it is almost impossible to guess what the company's revenues and earnings might be five years later when the company is sold and the investors exit and receive their returns. No amount of complicated financial analysis, using discounted cash flows or other tools, can yield any result the angel will be comfortable with. So the angel is saying that if the company is successful, the investors and the founders will both make a great return on their money and time. Let's not argue too much about the valuation right now, or put too fine a pencil to the numbers; instead let's concentrate on building the company, says the angel.

A number of angels even believe that playing too much hardball when negotiating the terms can result in a fracturing of the personal trust that the angel/entrepreneur relationship must be built upon.

Other angels do indeed rely on what is regarded as more traditional valuation formulas, however. The degree of sophistication they bring to this process varies from angel to angel.

A Simple Pricing Formula for an Early-Stage Venture

Let's say the projected earnings for the company on the projected year of exit are $1 million in Year 5. And the multiple on earnings a company like this one will command is 8. The value of the business at exit is therefore $8 million. If the angel's percentage ownership of the company is 15 percent, as an example, the angel will receive 15 percent of the $8 million, or $1.2 million. What was the investor's rate of return (ROI) over that time period?

> If you had initially invested roughly $115,000, your compound rate of return over the five years would have been 60 percent. This is the 10X rate of return that is often discussed as the objective of many early-stage investors, to earn 10 times your initial investment in 5 years.
>
> If you had invested roughly $225,000, your compound rate of return was 40 percent.
>
> And an initial investment of about $475,000 translated into a 20 percent return.

The longer you had to hold onto the investment before you exited, the lower your compound annual rate of return would be. In the preceding example, if the investor of $115,000 had to stay in the deal for seven years, the compound ROI would have been a little over 40 percent, substantially less.

ROI Expectations

Angels' expectations regarding ROI vary by the individual, of course. There are really two numbers involved here, the wished-for ROI, and the reasonably expected one. Our surveys of angels showed the average expected return was about 34 percent, but the expectations varied from 20 percent to 100 percent.

A recent study by the Center for Venture Research at the University of New Hampshire, in which software and other early-stage high-tech companies in the New England area that received angel financing were surveyed, reported that investors were seeking a seven-in-seven return: seven times their money over an expected holding period of seven years. This translated into an expected 32 percent return. These results showed both great patience on the angels' part—willingness to stay in the deal for seven full years, and rather modest ROI expectations. Recall the data from Chapter 1 that showed early/seed-stage investors actually earned an average compound rate of return of 65.5 percent over the last five years.

An entrepreneur making calculations about the projected value of the company in five to seven years, the amount of equity given up to angel investors, and the return that results, must be able to demonstrate to angels that participating in his or her venture can result in an ROI of at least 30 percent to 40 percent or more.

TAKING A LARGE BITE OF REALITY SANDWICH

We have in our office a business plan from an early-stage technology company with what appears to be a viable, patent-protected technology that could capture a large share of its market. They say they raised $1.2 million of Series A capital for 2.2 percent of the company. They reached a few benchmarks in research and development with the capital and now want a Series B round of $10 million for 5 percent of the equity.

If 2.2 percent of the company was worth $1.2 million, the company was valued at more than $50 million. If 5 percent is worth $10 million, they now believe the company is worth $200 million. In the current environment, that is outside the range of valuations that most similar-stage companies are commanding from VC firms. Will angels be able to see this, or will they tend to go along with the valuation provided by the company? Particularly since another group is already on record putting in the $1.2 million at the $50 million valuation. How could the entrepreneur possibly justify a valuation like this to an investor? Or asked another way, what planet is this entrepreneur from?

The University of New Hampshire study cited earlier reported much more realistic valuations in software company deals in New England that actually closed:

> The average first round of financing was $1,230,000. For that, the company gave the investor 24 percent of the equity in the company.
>
> The second round of investments averaged $2,071,000. After the second round, the founders still retained majority control (54 percent) of the equity in the company. Thus, the second round of investors received 22 percent of the equity.
>
> A 24 percent stake for $1,230,000 means the company was valued at $5.125 million, not $50 million. And after the second round of investments, the valuations were roughly $10 million, not $200 million.

In a study of start-up companies in New Hampshire, the Center for Venture Research reported that premoney valuations received by these companies had a huge variation, from $1 million to $55 million, with an average of $11.2 million. In this study, the average amount of equity the investors received was 30 percent.

ADVICE FROM AN ENTREPRENEUR

Alexandre Gonthier, CTO, iPIN—Interactive Transaction Services

How did you and the angels arrive at the valuation for the business? Was this difficult? "Pretty simple: We wanted $5 million premoney, they offered less, and we accepted. A basic rule of thumb is $1 million/founder."

How long did it take the angel(s) to decide to invest, from the time they met you? "Thirty days (as opposed to 90 to 120 days with venture capitalists)."

What factors about your business were most important to them in deciding to say yes? What was most attractive? "What was attractive to them was:

Drive, passion, focus, and execution capability of the founding team

Type of company (infrastructure software)

Size of the opportunity, upside of the business plan

Absence of strong competition—timing was good

Global vision—dual presence from day one in the United States and Europe."

One area where an individual angel many times cannot possibly be as well versed as an experienced venture capitalist would be in the valuation of early-stage companies. The venture capitalist simply has access to much more data about comparable deals, companies that have gone public, and other benchmarks that can be used to establish the current market value of the equity of a start-up company.

ADVICE FROM A VENTURE CAPITALIST

Kirby Cochran, Partner, Red Rock Ventures, www.redrockventures.com

When you see a company come in and you see that it has already received an angel investment of, for example, $500,000, do you look at the company a little more favorably? Is this investment a validation of the concept and maybe they've been able to achieve a few milestones using this angel capital? "It is, but, at the same time, venture capitalists are very concerned about how they raised the money and at what valuation. That is one of the biggest problems in raising follow-on money. Angels are not sophisticated investors, so they don't understand about getting a deal done and exit strategy. You have to look at whether the valuation was fair and reasonable. We see deals daily in which the valuation is wrong. The entrepreneur funds a company, then goes to get angel investment. Angels by definition are friends, family, acquaintances—high net worth people the entrepreneur has come in contact with. These people are typically not sophisticated when it comes to understanding how you value a deal and how you enable that deal to attract follow-on financing.

"I saw a company recently that was putting a valuation on a basic startup, a minimal revenue company. I heard about it through an angel, so I asked the angel, 'What is the valuation of the company you are investing in?' He said, 'I'm not sure what you mean, but 1 percent of the company is purchased for $750,000.' I asked, 'Is that pre- or post-money?' He said, 'Well, what does that mean?'

"Let's say a company raised $1.5 million, so they sold 2 percent of the company and have a postmoney valuation of $75 million. Now you, as a venture capitalist, take a look at the company's pro formas and you see the projected revenues in year 1 are $2 million and a projected loss of $1 million. You have to go back to your valuation models on what the market has already done with similar type companies. This company is selling for 37 times revenues, because you can't put an earnings multiple on it. Now you look at the second year and see the revenues are projected to be $10 million, resulting in a $4 million profit. Now it is being sold for 17 times end of year 2 projected profits.

"You find that, in order to execute their plan, they have to raise $7 million in year 2. Well, angels are not the type of people to put in $7 million, so the company has to go to the venture capitalists for the money. The first thing venture capitalists are going to ask is, 'What's your valuation?'

"A venture capitalist is a fund manager, and a fund manager is responsible for achieving a certain internal rate of return that satisfies the institutional investors in their fund. The venture capitalists' return is achieved at exit, and there are four alternatives:

1. Is it an IPO candidate? The reality is that only 1 in 600 companies that get VC financing ever go IPO. So the idea that the exit strategy is an IPO, is remote.
2. Is it being acquired by a larger company that has stock or cash it can use to purchase the company?
3. A cash on cash return, an EBITDA (earnings before interest, taxes, depreciation, and amortization) cash return model.
4. You go out of business.

"Those are the only four strategies for being able to get out of a deal. The venture capitalist is going to do some basic capitalization-valuation models on the company. You want to find what comparable companies trade for in book-value multiple. What do they trade for in multiples of earnings, and in multiples of revenue? Venture capitalists look first at what the valuation model is for publicly traded comparable companies, and then they go to MergerStat or some other type of database and find out what the private deals are going for in this industry group, what companies have been sold and acquired and at what price. Then the venture capitalists take these valuation models and overlay the company's pro formas.

"They say, this company should trade for *X* price if it were an IPO, or if it were acquired, it would be worth *X* amount. Now what the venture capitalist has to do is take discounts from this number for quality of management, and probability of success in getting the company to execute their plan.

"It would be interesting to ask other venture capitalists how many companies they have seen hit the business plan that was originally given them on a top line (revenue) and bottom line (pretax profit) number. I've been in the business 20 years, and my response is zero. I've had companies hit their top line number, but never their bottom line number.

"There are some rules of thumb. Usually A round investors want to see a valuation of under $10 million because they typically want to put $3 to $5 million into a company. They almost never want to see a valuation of over $20 million.

"So back to our example: They brought the money in at a valuation of $75 million; they sold 2 percent of the equity for $1.5 million. They now are going for the $7 million and they sit down with the venture capitalists who knock some sense into their heads by saying, 'Look, your valuation is out of whack. and we're going to give you a $7.5 million premoney valuation, and we're going to give you $2.5 million in capital for a postmoney valuation of $10 million.' In order to bring this money in, the entire group of existing stockholders has to take a 90 percent dilution in the value of their equity.

"The venture capitalists are going to buy on a postmoney valuation basis, 25 percent of the company. So right away, the original investors have been crammed down 90 percent."

How do the original investors react to that? "How do you think they'll react to that? Before, they had 1.5 million shares out of 75 million. Now, they own 90 percent less of that. After they get done with this deal, they are diluted another 25 percent with the new money coming in. There's an alternative, though. If management understands this, they'll protect their original investors, and say, 'Look, you still own $1.5 million worth of stock out of the $7.5 million valuation.' So now instead of owning 2 percent on a premoney valuation, these original investors own 20 percent. Management had owned 98 percent of the deal, but now they own 80 percent. And they have probably split the pie among themselves and given options to employees, so the effect of this dilution on them is magnified. If the management does not have a large enough stake, they start losing incentive to be involved, they'll be out looking for another deal to be involved with."

Undermotivated management would translate into a lesser chance the company would succeed. "That's right. It's not just a funding perspective. You have to look at management. So, it would have been easier if management would have gone into the deal and said, we're going to raise our first money at a $4 million or $2 million valuation, and we're going to sell *X* amount. A lot of times companies want more money than they should have or need at the outset. It is better to take less money, just the amount you need to execute your plan. So instead of that $1.5 million, let's say they just went after $500,000. And now when they come in and do the next valuation, they can offer the venture capitalist a valuation of $5 to $7 million premoney. Then they get a valuation on a B round of $10 to $12 million. You have the big venture capitalists who say, 'Unless we can put in $5 to $10 million, we aren't interested.'

"Let's say your angel round came in at a $2 million premoney valuation, and they put in $500,000. Your second or A round comes in at $5 million valuation. So what your original investors say is, 'Great, we made 100 percent on our money.' Now a B round of $10 million comes into the company. This takes them up to a postmoney valuation of $20 million. Now, we can go out for an IPO for a $50 million pre-money valuation and raise $30 million. This is a realistic example of how you accomplish exit strategies. I don't care if someone buys the company for $80 million, I don't care if we go IPO. If you follow the mathematics, the company has succeeded, it's been capitalized, there have been exit strategies, and internal rates of return have been hit.

"At an IPO of $50 million, the B round investors have made 150 per-pcent on their money, and done it in under a year.

"This all goes back to: How was the company started, what was the original capitalization and valuation?"

The whole thing can get screwed up at time zero. "That's right. And that's why people should come to Redrock Ventures. We're there to help structure the capitalization of the company, not just to give money.

"All experienced venture capitalists have an understanding of these numbers.

"When entrepreneurs start a company, they have to be careful how they raise the seed money. Did they raise it from more than 35 nonaccredited investors? Did the investors rely on a private placement memorandum (PPM)? Was the PPM written by a law firm that has errors-and-omissions insurance to cover any of the mistakes management might have made in the PPM? Was an audit included, were there financials in the PPM? Who did the audit? As funders, we look at all these things, because if the entrepreneurs did not raise the money correctly, they have potentially created liability for the company.

"The company can make their problems the venture capitalists' problems. When it comes time to file the prospectus for an IPO, you could have all sorts of problems. You may have to go back and get recision rights from first investors, and that can make a deal look ugly.

"Venture capitalists have to be concerned with all these things. Did the entrepreneurs just write a business plan, and the people who invested just relied on the plan to invest? How were the subscription agreements filled out? Did the entrepreneurs raise money in one of the states where the PPM has to be filed for two weeks before they could raise the money?"

Isn't it true that all these errors can open up the possibility of the angel or original investors being able to demand their money back if things don't work out? "And guess who they're going to come back after. The deep pocket venture capitalists who are on the board. So now the venture capitalist has to help the company defend the lawsuit."

In our experience, many entrepreneurs have such a zeal to get

the money and get going with the company that they ignore a lot of these legal/organizational issues. Some of these people don't undertake the effort to get the right legal advice from the beginning. "They get an attorney who doesn't put them into an LLC, or puts them in an incorrect domicile where they file. Then they charge them excess fees. I generally do not have a good impression of attorneys in this process because most attorneys don't have an understanding of the funding process and they mess up the company."

The founder of a start-up may not know how to find a really top-flight attorney. "Yes, they're generally dealing with some hack."

ADVICE FROM AN ANGEL

Steve Miller, Co-founder, Prairie Angels www.prairieangels.org

Do you believe that angels get more skilled at valuation as they go along? Is there a learning curve to this activity? "I think there is probably a learning curve involved. It's not just in picking the right deals, but in structuring deals correctly, getting the right terms. By right terms, I don't mean making the deal onerous on the company in favor of the angel. The right terms for an angel deal should be those that are not only fair to the angel and the company, but also give the company the best shot at getting additional funding in the future.

"It could be very easy to structure a deal that has fantastic terms for the angel investor but no venture capitalist or institutional investor would ever touch the deal because of the terms the angel has struck."

Then it becomes a traumatic event to go back in and fix the structure of the company. "Most later-round investors would just pass and move on to the next deal rather than take the time and make the effort to try to fix the mess the previous investors may have left."

Valuation of an early-stage company is a big mystery to many entrepreneurs. Do you have a philosophy about valuation? "Valuation is an art, not a science. Every deal is different in terms of how you get to valuation. It needs to be fair, and entrepreneurs need to have an eye toward future rounds of funding. It may be that the entrepreneur and the angel agree that the opportunity is worth $10 million premoney. If the venture capitalist in the next round thinks the thing is only worth $5 million, then it's only worth $5 million."

Do you see entrepreneurs coming to your group having done their homework about what marketplace valuations really are? "Some have done their homework. I may not agree with their perspectives. Others have no clue. It runs the gamut. Certainly, I would prefer to be dealing with someone who has done their homework, not just on the valuation question, but on everything. What their competition looks like.

What are the holes in the management team that they need to fill. What the market opportunity is. All of those are clues about how good the management team is. If they don't have a clue about what valuation is, it is a definite red flag.

"That being said, entrepreneurs may be basing their valuation on multiples of what publicly traded companies are at, of what they think their earnings will be in year 5. But at least it forms a basis to have a discussion with them, as opposed to someone who says, 'Well, my Aunt Bertha told me my idea is worth $10 million, so she gave me an investment based on that.'

"We should include the angels here, too, though. There are really smart angels out there who have done their homework about valuation and know what they are talking about, and there are really dumb ones out there too."

ADVICE FROM A VENTURE CAPITALIST

Eric Janszen, Managing Partner, Osborn Capital LLC, www.osborncapital.com

What should entrepreneurs keep in mind when negotiating the value of their company with angels, if they expect to also require venture capital in the near future? "To acquire venture capital you must first survive. In the recent past, entrepreneurs fretted about getting too little for their company. Those that worried too much about that are now out of business. In the old, old days in 1995, when Jeff Osborn first started angel investing, he'd get 10 percent to 20 percent of a company for $100,000. When prices rose north of $2 million premoney for seed-stage deals, Jeff and I stopped investing. They reached as high as $10 million for backing two unseasoned guys and their dog. In the future we'll get 10 percent to 20 percent of a company for $50,000. That's the nature of postbubble asset deflation. Whatever price you are offered today is likely to be better than the price you will be offered tomorrow."

ADVICE FROM AN ANGEL WHO IS ALSO A VENTURE CAPITALIST

Patrick Soheili, Barrington Partners, Silicon Valley

Some venture capitalists think that angels being involved with a company at the seed stage can cause unrealistic valuations when the company seeks its next round of funding. What is your view? "If a venture capitalist walked into a deal in which angels were involved, the price was already established. There was a markup, an 'up round' from the original founders of the company. The venture capitalists were paying a price higher than they would have paid otherwise. To a large extent, this has changed. There is much more reality to valuations—and to these markups—today.

"Angels sometimes lack the sophistication, if you will, for putting the right price on the deal. Some of the venture capitalists' complaints might be warranted. Imagine you or me as angels. We do this as a hobby, something we do on the side. We don't ask, 'Is this a great deal? Is it the right deal? Is it competitive? Is this good for the company long term? Could it hamper the company from getting the next generation of financing that would come in? Could it deter the VC firm from coming in?'

"Angels may not subscribe to *Venture One* because it costs too much money. Angels don't talk to that many venture capitalists, so they don't necessarily know what the market value of a given deal is. They don't have a big net and don't spend as much time talking about the value. They don't share data with other investors and compare. So, to some extent, the venture capitalists' opinions are right.

"But, to a large extent, to avoid that problem, you could open a bridge round where the price would be established by the venture capitalists when they come in. The angel could get a warrant position in the company, at a discount, based on that price. The angel came in earlier, took more risk than the venture capitalists coming in now, so they deserve to be compensated for that. But the ultimate price would be set by the venture capitalists, the professionals."

Chapter Summary

- The valuation of a company in an angel round can impact the company's ability to receive follow-up funding.
- Valuation is not a matter of following prescribed formulas; it is a highly subjective process, an art not a science.
- Angels do not necessarily have sufficient data needed to arrive at a reasonable valuation of an early-stage company.

CHAPTER

25

Coming to Terms

Remember a deal's not a deal until the check clears. Entrepreneurs sometimes erroneously think they have a deal with an angel and may start actually making commitments to spend the funds before they are received.

Term Sheets

THE GOOD NEWS: ANGELS TEND TO KEEP IT SIMPLE

Angel investors typically do not present entrepreneurs with overly complicated deal structures or laundry lists of lengthy terms and conditions, especially when compared to venture capitalists. However, there is no set pattern of terms an entrepreneur might be able to anticipate from an angel, either. Angels express their individuality in the kinds of terms they propose. Angels may be interested in having representation on the company's board of directors. This does not mean that if you have eight angels in your company, you will have to seat all eight of them on your board. But the lead angel would certainly ask to be given a seat.

When a company is at its earliest, seed stage, the terms tend to be the least complex. As the company grows and the second or third group of investors comes in, the terms of each subsequent financing grow in size, scope, and the number of lawyers' fingerprints on them.

Investors craft the term sheets to reflect these sorts of concerns:

I need a seat on the board so that I can ensure my voice is heard in determining the company's strategy.

I need protection from having my ownership severely diluted in the subsequent rounds of financing.

I may want the first right to purchase shares held by the other angels in the deal before they are sold to an outside party.

I want to make sure my shares are included when the company registers to make a public offering, so I can exit the investment.

Another term that may appear could be the stages at which the capital will actually be provided to the company, often as certain milestones are reached. Venture capitalists often inject the capital in stages as well.

DEAL TALES: YOU'RE ALMOST 50 YEARS OLD, YOU SHOULD KNOW BETTER

A number of years ago, we were asked by an entrepreneur who had a consumer-products manufacturing company, to help him with his marketing strategy. We came in and helped coach his marketing department in preparing a plan document. He was selling product, and things were going OK, but he had pretty well exhausted his own (considerable) resources and wanted to have someone else come in and share some of the risk with him. This fellow had access to all sorts of wealthy individuals by virtue of being a member of an exclusive country club. He did all the right things: good business plan, active networking to find investors, he was excellent at presenting and patiently answered all of the investors' questions. He had also been successful in other ventures. It should have been a relatively painless process to find capital, but it happened to be a tough time: The stock market was down, money was tight.

The only offer he got was from the "devil in a blue suit" variety of angel. Two minutes with this guy and you could see he was an obnoxious, horrid, conceited jerk. After three minutes with him, your estimate got worse. The angel's attorney produced this incomprehensible, 100-page agreement with all sorts of language about bad things that would happen to the entrepreneur if he didn't meet some very stringent milestones and performance benchmarks after funding. It seemed odd to us an angel would have something that complex already prepared. Angels are supposed to want to go in and *help* companies. Angels like to keep things *simple*, we had heard. We urged the entrepreneur to check him out thoroughly before signing anything. The due diligence uncovered that this angel was involved in scores of lawsuits, all as the plaintiff. He even sued his dog for excess barking. Well, we finished our marketing plan document, sent the company an invoice for our work, and never heard back from them. A few months later we heard that the angel had come in and taken over the company, kicked the entrepreneur out of the company, and taken the entrepreneur's stock, all courtesy of this investor's cadre of lawyers.

Just for kicks on a slow afternoon, we sent the angel, now the CEO of the company, a demand letter for payment of our fee in writing the marketing plan. His lawyer swiftly faxed back, "We have no recollection of your alleged work product. We owe you nothing." Very truly yours, Slither and Slime, Esq.

MORE GOOD NEWS: COMMON IS PREFERRED OVER PREFERRED

The first capital a young company receives usually takes the form of common equity, the same class of shares the founders hold. Thus, the founders and the angels are on equal footing. Later rounds of financing may involve convertible preferred stock. Preferred stock grants the holder certain additional rights, including payment of dividends before the common shareholders, and priority claim to be paid in the event the company is sold or liquidated. The convertible feature means that the shares can be exchanged for the common shares that would be sold in a public offering; this is the path for the convertible preferred shareholders to exit, in other words.

Venture capitalists like the convertible preferred shares, naturally.

Structure of the Deal

The angel investor often provides the first capital that goes into a start-up company. In general, the negotiation process for this round of funding tends to be far less complicated than the second and third rounds. However, an experienced attorney is still a vital participant in the process, helping the entrepreneur understand the options available in structuring the deal.

ADVICE FROM AN EXPERT

Angel Investor Deal Terms

Stephan J. Mallenbaum, a partner at Jones, Day, Reavis & Pogue, one of the largest global law firms, where he leads the Venture Capital/Technology Team.

Angel investors are, by definition, not investment professionals. So angel investment terms vary widely, from simplistic common stock purchases, sometimes based on no more than a handshake and a check, to convoluted nonstandard arrangements that can actually prevent a company from securing future funding.

Even the term *angel investor* covers a lot of ground. Some angels are parents or relatives, basically well meaning and hoping for some financial return, but hardly smart money. Others are prestige investors, primarily seeking bragging rights to ownership of a sliver of the tech boom; these investors might have invested in a restaurant or in a thoroughbred racehorse in decades past. Finally, there are the quasiprofessionals. These investors may have a high degree of business acumen, or perhaps a strategic connection to the market, but do not have the full array of networks, resources, and business savvy that professional investors typically bring to a deal.

For the company, the point of an angel investment is to get the business or technology launched, to get to a compelling story that will be of interest to professional investors and the capital markets. From the angel's side, it is to give the company enough business fuel—cash—to enable the founders to take the company to that next level, and then to let the professionals boost the company, and the angel's investment stake, to success. Thus the overarching rule for both sides in an angel transaction is to structure a straightforward deal that will get cash to the company, basic protections to the investor, and no impediments to future rounds of professional financing. This is not the time for either side to try to make a killing; otherwise the opportunity itself may be killed.

If the company valuation is too high, venture investors may lose interest, either because they perceive that the founder is unrealistic, or because they recognize that a downround will be difficult to sell to existing angel investors. If the valuation is too low, the founders' equity interests will quickly be diluted to a low level, and the investors will recognize that the founders may not be adequately motivated to drive the company to success. If a company issues common stock to an angel investor, it's probably unfair to the investor who provides hard cash, as against the founders' sweat equity. On the other hand, a complicated preferred stock instrument, packed with registration rights, multiple liquidation preferences, protective provisions, super voting rights or similar features can be an impediment to future financing because first round professional investors typically expect that their preferred stock rights will be absolute, or at least senior to all other classes of stock.

Other provisions that sometimes appear in angel deals are absolute nonstarters and will have to be eliminated before there is even any serious discussion with professional investors. These include nondilutable equity interests, options to acquire the company or to acquire underlying technology, put rights, and rights to participate in management—which, of course, should be done on the basis of merit, not on the basis of investment.

Another feature often seen in angel transactions is the floating, or variable, valuation. The company and the angel investor reason that, because they are not deal professionals or valuation professionals, neither should take the risk of fixing a valuation. So the investor acquires a convertible security that converts into whatever security the company ultimately issues to professional investors in its first professional financing round, usually at a discount, of say, 15 percent. The discount is to reflect the fact that the angel invests early, and, therefore, assumes more risk. In effect, the professional investment sets the terms and the price of the angel round. Although this approach avoids negotiating a valuation and terms that may later prove to be inappropriate, it can itself create obstacles to a future transaction. For example, venture investors typically would not want angel investors to hold the same security that they do, because that might create fiduciary duties. Similarly, the venture investors will typically want absolutely senior registration rights, voting rights, and liquidation preferences, undiluted by angel investors who may convert into the same security. Finally, from the point of view of the angel investor, the typical prenegotiated 15 percent discount may not adequately reflect the risk he assumes, particularly where the company advances significantly in its business development before the venture capitalist invests and sets the valuation.

So what does a well-crafted angel investment structure look like? That, of course, depends on the company and the investors. But a good starting point might be a convertible preferred stock with a liquidation preference equal to the amount invested, voting rights on an as-converted basis with the common shareholders, and no special dividends, control provisions, or prohibitions on the issuance of senior securities. As for valuation, work backwards: Estimate the valuation that a VC investor is likely to attribute to the company at the time the company is ready for VC investors, and reduce that amount by a factor of 2 (at least in the market conditions prevalent in Spring 2001). That will give the angels a reasonable opportunity for appreciation in what is, after all, a very risky investment, while giving the company plenty of headroom to do its next financing, and even another angel round if necessary.

The views set forth herein are the personal views of the author and do not necessarily reflect those of Jones, Day, Reavis & Pogue.

How Long Until Closing?

We asked entrepreneurs: How long do you think it should take to close a deal with an angel investor from the time the investor receives the plan?

We also asked angels how long it actually takes them to close, on average. And we asked the same question of VC firms.

Our Profit Dynamics, Inc. surveys revealed that angels say it takes them an average of 67 days to close. Forty-five percent said it takes them between 31 and 60 days, 30 percent said between 61 and 90 days. Eighty-one percent said they close in 90 days or less. Just over 50 percent closed in less than 60 days. In contrast, only 19 percent of the venture capitalists said they closed in less than 60 days. The average closing time for venture capitalists was 80 days.

Entrepreneurs underestimate the time it takes angels to close by nine days; they believe angels ought to be able to get the job done in 58 days. A significant number of entrepreneurs, 24 percent, believe a deal should close in less than 30 days, whereas only 6 percent of the angels said they usually close in less than 30 days. Only 1 percent of venture capitalists said they usually closed in less than 30 days. Figure 25.1 compares the very different perspectives of the groups.

ADVICE FROM AN ANGEL

Luis Villalobos, Founder and Director, Tech Coast Angels, www.techcoastangels.com

How long do negotiations take between your group and an entrepreneur? "The fastest deal we've ever done, from start to finish, was a weekend. The slowest was 10 months. A typical process is three to four months, from the time the people would submit their plan over our Web site."

Is this variance due to the complexity of the technology or to stumbling blocks that occur along the way? "The one that took 10 months had a lot of problems with the business model, so over that 10-month period the entrepreneur revised the business model fundamentally

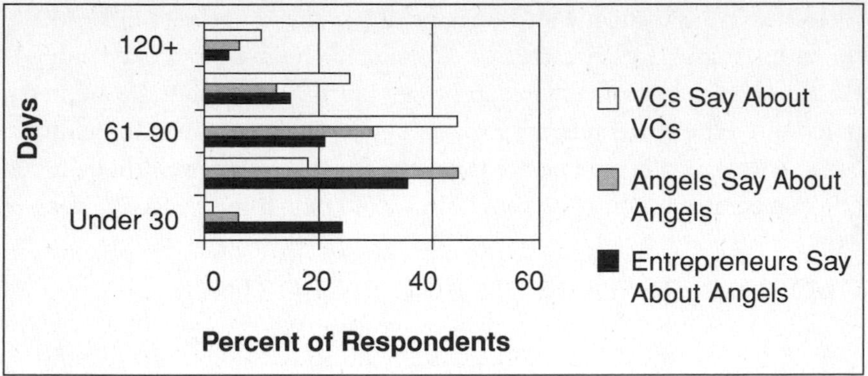

Figure 25.1 How Long Until Closing?

> three or four times. It can be a case where we are comfortable that the business model can be executed successfully. Other times there could be some technical due diligence required that can take time. Some deals immediately capture people's attention; others end up being more on the back burner."

In a study begun in June 2000 of start-up companies in New Hampshire, the Center for Venture Research found that entrepreneurs said that an average of five months elapsed between the time the angel and the entrepreneur met and when the deal closed, in a first round of financing. The negotiation time decreased in subsequent rounds of financing. In our experience, this seems a bit longer than we have seen.

Not allowing enough time to raise capital from angels, or from VC firms for that matter, is one of the major mistakes made by entrepreneurs. They end up becoming very frustrated with the investors, and in some cases it could cause the venture itself to be negatively impacted if the entrepreneur runs out of seed capital before the angel round of capital can be raised.

And it should be noted that there are two parts to the time it takes to raise money from angels: the time it takes to find the angels, and the time it takes to close the deal. Many entrepreneurs find that both parts, when combined, can take three, six, or nine months—or more.

Entrepreneurs cannot always affect how quickly the process goes, no matter how vigorous their efforts. Investors go at their own pace. We had one entrepreneur client that kept saying that if we could just get him in front of an angel, he could get the angel to agree to invest then and there, because he was such a good salesman and could make an impassioned speech he called the power close. Unfortunately, the angel who was most interested in his company took an approach to due diligence similar to Peter Falk's famous TV character, Lt. Columbo. The investor poked around, then poked around some more, and asked just the right questions to pretty much shred the entrepreneur's logic and point out the flaws in his venture. Since he wasn't prepared to overcome the investor's very well thought out objections, no amount of power closing could help him salvage the deal.

CLOSING REMARKS ABOUT CLOSING

ADVICE FROM AN ENTREPRENEUR

Alexandre Gonthier, CTO, iPIN—Interactive Transaction Services

How did you feel when the deal closed, you received the capital, and you realized you had a partner in place? "We felt great! We were running out of our initial cash, and had no choice but to close that round. For two weeks, we were virtually bankrupt, as we had managed to meet payroll the month before, but had no more money to meet payroll again that month. And when you don't meet payroll, it is over, as your employees are your only asset at that point. So we closed our round, partied for a few days, and started doing board meetings every month to really start leveraging our new partners, and to start making progress at a faster pace."

Chapter Summary

- Angel investors, because they invest in early-stage companies, tend to use less-complex term sheets, and when angels present entrepreneurs with overly complicated proposed deal structures, that can be an advance warning of trouble.
- Angels generally seek to purchase shares of common equity in the company.
- Entrepreneurs underestimate the time it will take to close a deal with an angel investor.
- After receiving an angel round of financing, it is permissible to party for a few days.

CHAPTER

26

Entrepreneurs Who Attracted Angels to Their Company

A Discussion with the Founders of Reason, Inc.

Reason, Inc. (www.reasoninc.com) is the nation's only full-service wireless-device management company, helping organizations manage their wireless products and services. Reason's flagship service, Reason for Wireless™, is a comprehensive Web-based system integrating help-desk service, procurement management, and billing management. Reason for Wireless provides companies with the industry's largest library and database of information on wireless devices from all major manufacturers and carriers, and is fully customizable. Reason is based in Aurora, Colorado.

We talked with Chris Hotz, the President of Reason, Inc. and the CEO, Jeff Kohler.

Why did you think your company would be attractive to angel/private investors?

Chris Hotz: "Our market is very large, and our business model makes sense. We focused on a clear revenue model (ours is recurring) and worked very hard on trying to be clear, simple, and consistent in our message. We stayed in our comfort zone (wireless) so we believed that our industry knowledge and credibility would be attractive to investors."

Jeff Kohler: "We have a business plan that is easy to understand, has a recurring revenue stream and a road to profitability, and we're experts in the wireless industry. Anyone who has ever dealt with wireless understands the great pain involved, so they are willing to look at solutions. Also, wireless was, and still is, a booming industry."

How did you prepare your presentation for the angel/private investors?

Chris Hotz: "We spent very long nights writing our business plan, focusing again on clarity with a lot of detail. That plan became the roadmap for our presentation. After all, we didn't want potential investors to hear one thing and read another. We took the key points of the plan, put them on PowerPoint slides, and practiced, practiced, practiced. Ironically, in several of our initial meetings, the potential investors didn't even want to see the presentation. They wanted to hear it directly from us."

Jeff Kohler: "Chris and I did a huge amount of planning on the business model and financials, we practiced presentations, and we worked hard to simplify, simplify, simplify. This way, if we only had 15 minutes with a prospective angel investor, they could still walk away with a clear understanding of who we are, what we do, why we do it, and how we make money."

Did you face any challenges in finding the angel/private investors? How did you find them?

Chris Hotz: "We were very fortunate in finding our angel investors. A personal friend of Jeff's, who is well connected in the local community, was enamored with our initial business model and made some key introductions. From there, it was not difficult to convince them to invest. Don't get me wrong, though. These are very savvy investors, and we did our job in convincing them that our plan was a good one. We also secured an introduction to a group of marquee NFL players through another friend and through contacts we had at the company for which we both worked before starting Reason. That was a big win for us, because 28 percent of our angel round came from a group of three NFL players. They, too, are savvy. As you can imagine, highly paid athletes get approached by countless investment opportunities, so they are not an easy sell."

Jeff Kohler: "Yes, personal relationships and networking."

Many companies have a fear of disclosing confidential or proprietary information to angel/private investors. Was that a problem for you? If so, how did you overcome it?

Chris Hotz: "We never had a problem disclosing any information with our potential investors. The only things we did not share were names and/or dollar amounts of other angel investors who did not wish to be identified. We were always very careful with details of how we will spend the money, because it is important not to give too many specifics. Our intention was never to mislead anyone, but recognize that business models can change to a great extent in the early stages of a company's development. We never wanted to mislead our angels."

Jeff Kohler: "Disclosing confidential or proprietary information was not an issue for us, because we did not really have anything too proprietary, given that we're an execution play. In other words, we're not out there developing proprietary next-generation software or relandscaping technology as we know it. What we offer is a way to manage a company's wireless products and services; it doesn't do anyone else any good unless we, ourselves, get out there, knock on doors, get the system deployed, and make sure it works.

"In addition, even if someone had the entire version of our business plan in hand, it still would not give that person the ability to do what we do. The wireless business is too complex, and unless you've lived it and breathed it for years and years, you're most likely going to miss the mark anyway."

Did you actually meet with the angel/private investors that eventually invested in your company? If so, what was that first meeting like? Who attended, what questions were asked, what would you have done differently?

Chris Hotz: "We met with about one-third of our angels. The first meeting, with one of the individuals, was actually very good because we prepared for a long time. We met at the potential investor's home, in his basement, and used a PC and projector to give our PowerPoint presentation. The investor had invited friends, one of whom ended up investing as well. The questions generally focused on what we thought the return on their money would be, how long it would take us to be profitable, and our background and who we were. They wanted to make sure we didn't blow their money. This type of meeting was typical. Because we had such a high participation rate per meeting, I can't say what I would have done differently."

Jeff Kohler: "I'd say we met with almost half the angels who invested in Reason. First meetings were almost always casual, with a laid-back atmosphere. Many were at restaurants or in their homes or offices. I never met one person I didn't like.

"One first meeting was especially memorable. A Denver Broncos player came to my house to talk to us about joining in with other NFL players to invest. We had prepared nice fruit and sandwich trays for the meeting. Just before we went to serve the food, my dog ate both trays in their entirety, and then sat there and breathed on the prospective investor the whole time. And my four-year-old daughter asked the man why he was in our house. He invested anyway.

"At most of these meetings, it was just the prospective investor(s) attending. Questions focused on what we do, our backgrounds, and how we'll make money. The most-repeated questions: 'Who are your competitors?' 'What is your experience?' 'What is your exit strategy?' "

What made you decide to go with the angel/private investors who eventually did invest?

Chris Hotz: "They had money to invest. All the introductions we had were to top-quality, high net worth individuals. We looked at angel money as a way to get us to the next level (VC dollars), and not as a means of building a board of directors. (In fact, none of our current board members have been angels.) So our only requirement was that they met the criteria in our private placement memorandum and had money to invest."

Jeff Kohler: "In general, angel investors typically help a company obtain a better valuation, they don't require board seats, and they mean fewer barriers to entry. As for our own angels, they had the ability to invest to help us get to a level at which a venture capitalist would become interested, because we'd built something and others were buying into the concept."

What contribution, besides money, do your angel/private investors bring to your company?

Chris Hotz: "They can make introductions to other potential investors, venture capitalists, and prospective customers. Some of our angels are well-recognized in their respective communities, so they add credibility to our business. It is very nice to be able to say: '(So-and-so) is an investor in Reason.' Other prospective investors like to know they are in good company and not making a poor decision."

Jeff Kohler: "They have helped us with networking—meeting other prospective investors and prospective customers. Their names often provide a bit more credibility for the company."

How active are the angel/private investors in the day-to-day management of your company?

Chris Hotz: "Our angels have no impact on our day-to-day operations at all."

What impact has having angel/private investors in your company had on the venture capitalists you approached for your second round of financing?

Chris Hotz: "In our case, the recognizable names of the angels helped raise credibility slightly, but in the long run, venture capitalists don't really care who the angels are (unless, of course, it's someone like Bill Gates!). So I'd say our angels did not have much impact on the decision of our venture capitalists to invest. The most important contribution of the angels was giving us the ability to get to the position where our business was attractive enough to approach venture capitalists."

Jeff Kohler: "The angels help validate the concept. If the names are big enough—and many of ours were—they can lend some credibility to both you as an individual and your business. This really is nominal, though."

Anything unique, different, or unusual about your experience with angel/private investors?

Chris Hotz: "I think the NFL connection is unusual. The lead NFL player in our angel round is an amazing man. He is very intelligent, humble, and offers his help to us anytime. He actually gave us tickets to the SuperBowl and introduced us to his agent, who is one of the most well-known NFL agents in the country. He did this to give us the opportunity to meet additional prospective investors."

Jeff Kohler: "I think the evolution of the story with them is interesting. I had gone to Pittsburgh on behalf of my previous company to talk to all the Pittsburgh Steelers after a practice, in their meeting room, about investing their money in wireless companies instead of bars and restaurants. They all loved the idea, but didn't know what to do from there. After the meeting, one of the players followed up with me, and arranged a meeting with some of the other players. They really wanted to pursue the idea, but didn't know anyone they really trusted and felt they could trust to run a wireless company. It didn't go anywhere at that point, but later on, when Chris and I formed Reason, it just came together. The rest is history. The Steelers' connection is also what prompted a Denver Bronco to invest. I think that if there hadn't been an NFL players' connection, my dog's sandwich-eating spectacle could have hurt the deal. Now, interestingly, one of our angels works with a VC firm in the off season. So we now have an avenue into other areas of funding."

What advice would you give to entrepreneurs who are looking for angel/private investors?

Chris Hotz: "No matter how excited the investors are, no matter how fast they say they can get you a check, it will *always* take at least twice as long as you thought to get the money in the bank. I would also suggest that you make it very clear in the beginning that it is your business, and you will make the management decisions. You are not looking for managers or board members, just some seed money. By establishing these things early on, we never encountered the problem of angels showing up at the office and disrupting operations—a situation I've heard has occurred more than once at some companies!"

Jeff Kohler: "Network as much as possible, be humble, know your business inside and out, and be able to talk about it and present it simply. If you've got a good background or a good referral, you'd be surprised how big-time people are willing to talk to you. Getting them to part with their money, however, is an entirely different story. Everything takes twice as long as you'd initially think."

LIVING WITH AN ANGEL

CHAPTER

27

Advantages of an Angel Investing in a Company

Call them value-added services or nonmonetary benefits—the idea is that the angel investor's involvement with the company after putting the money in can reap rewards for the company down the line. Some how-to-be-an-angel seminars even promote the idea that the angel can offer these services as a means of obtaining more equity for a lower dollar investment.

Expertise and Contacts

Angels often have accumulated a wealth of valuable contacts over the course of their business careers. These contacts can help the company in obtaining new customers, particularly corporate customers. The contacts can be used to recruit the best technical talent available in today's highly competitive labor market. The angel may have contacts with other financing sources, and we have already mentioned that angels often bring other angels with them into a deal. Suppose the company needs some consulting assistance or advisory-board talent. The angel may be able to spin through his or her Rolodex and find just the right individuals and contact them more quickly by going through fewer channels than if the entrepreneur tried to do this alone.

In the past, angels may have had to negotiate with creditors, potential customers, or joint venture partners, financial sources, or members of the financial community, such as investment bankers. The entrepreneur may be unfamiliar with any or all of these types of negotiations and may benefit from the counsel of the angel.

ADVICE FROM AN ENTREPRENEUR

Dave Howard, CEO, 1Vision Software, Inc (www. 1visionsoftware.com)

How important has been the nonmonetary contribution of the angels (advice and contacts)? Could you give us some specific examples of how they helped you? "One angel is currently working to establish distribution channels for 1Vision products in Asia. (He is located in Asia and has business contacts in that region.) One firm provided assistance with business development activities, development of corporate strategy, and implementation of tactical-level operation plans. Our angels have assisted with early product and concept research on 1Disk.com, 1Vision's on-line storage service, and with the generation of project plans for the product."

What factors about your business were most important to them in deciding to say yes? What was most attractive? "The most attractive feature was our expertise in storage management and the unique patented features of our storage management technology. 1Vision's foundation is its patented Persistent File System (PFS) technology, which provides the industry's most universal, intuitive, and simple way to manage and protect data files. PFS technology represents the first major breakthrough in file management technology in more than a dozen years. Applications of this unique technology represent the greatest barrier to competition."

The management complexity of a venture increases exponentially as the scope of the venture and the number of employees grows. The angel may know how to advise the entrepreneur on how to monitor the business from a financial control standpoint. The angel may have been involved in the industry for many years and may have a vision of the direction the industry is likely to take.

The angel has probably much more experience in motivating employees and in selecting them and evaluating their performance.

The most often mentioned value an angel provides sounds nebulous, but it involves a general understanding of business, an I've-been-there-before, or even I've-seen-it-all, attitude. The angel can then serve as a person to bounce ideas off of, and may even encourage the struggling entrepreneur during down times.

In the opinions and views that follow, however, it becomes clear that there is by no means any agreement about how much added value an angel brings to start-up ventures, or even whether it is valuable at all.

ADVICE FROM AN ANGEL

David Burwen

What is your view about the value-added services angel investors provide to companies they invest in? "I think that if you have a very experienced and strong management team in the company, the investors do not add that much value to the company beyond the money. A weaker or greener management team can benefit from the input from an experienced angel or venture capitalist who is willing to spend significant time with the company.

"The really experienced teams with good product ideas typically do not do angel rounds; they simply get initial funding from venture capitalists. It is often the weaker teams that end up approaching angels because they are not going to be attractive to venture capitalists until they get further down the road and prove that they have the capability to build their business.

"There is a wide range of angel investor backgrounds. I represent the type of angel who worked in key positions in several start-ups and was a founding executive of a very successful software start-up. I represent a kind of angel who has the experience to help a start-up beyond providing money. There are other angels who are simply financial types—maybe they are in the leasing business or they inherited a lot of money and sort of dabble by investing in new companies.

"An angel who has a leasing company can help the company with a leasing line of credit. In this way they add a little additional value beyond the money. However, the other financial types usually do not have the experience to provide strategic or operating assistance. They might be helpful in securing future venture capital, depending on their contacts.

"I typically get involved at one of two different levels with start-ups. One level is as a passive investor where I am simply part of the group of angel investors. I'm not leading the deal, I'm just putting money into the financing. After the closing, I occasionally talk to the CEO and usually make some suggestions that may be helpful. This is a kind of casual advice.

"The other level is where I am very much involved in the start-up phase. I help the entrepreneur to raise the initial money. And once we raise the initial money, I help the CEO figure out how to get the company going—what is the vision, what is the strategic focus, what does the business model look like? There are often a whole group of strategic issues that must be clearly defined and articulated. The company needs to know where it is heading. If you don't know where you are going, any path will do. This involvement can be as a board member and/or as a consultant spending a lot of time with the company. I've done both.

"One of the key ingredients for success is focus. When you start a company, many things come up that can absorb an entrepreneur's time. A start-up has limited resources, and must be able to use its time effectively. If it wastes it on nonessential matters, it won't be successful. Inexperienced entrepreneurs often don't understand well enough how to invest their time. Angels can help keep them on track.

"For experienced entrepreneurs, there is value to having an angel, such as myself, who has been through the start-up phase before, in multiple situations. I have a broad perspective on ways companies develop successfully, and ways they fail.

"One problem of being a minority shareholder is when the angel sees the company going in the wrong direction. He or she can often not change the course of events. If you are going to be effective as an angel, you must have the influence to move the company in the right direction. This means either having financial control or, if not, sufficient respect of the CEO and board of directors to heed your advice."

ADVICE FROM AN ANGEL

Brent Townshend

As an angel, can you see tangible evidence of your contribution? "Most companies do not take the angels' advice straight out; it gets filtered through a lot of different perceptions and the entrepreneur's own ideas. The best you can hope for is pushing them in the right direction. It doesn't happen very often that you tell them what to do and they actually do it.

"With some companies, they say they want value-added investors, people who will contribute. Then you write a check and never hear from them again. Others are really serious about involving the investors in what they are doing."

Does the company seek out the investor's contribution, or does the investor volunteer contributions? "I am usually very busy. I have my own company and invest in a number of companies, so unless they ask me, I am not pushing myself on them. Other angel investors are much more proactive, though. I can see both sides. With my own company, I have raised money from both venture capitalists and angels, and sometimes it is a little annoying to have the angels involved too much. At a distance they may have good ideas in terms of the big picture, but when they start to look too much at the details, they don't know enough about the details to really be constructive there.

"If you take a small amount of money from a large number of angels, you end up spending a lot of time maintaining those relationships with the angel investors. Then, when they call up and say, 'I have this great lead for you,' you can't say, this isn't really in our strategic direction. You have to follow up the lead. If you have a lot of little angels doing that it can be distracting."

ADVICE FROM AN ANGEL

Craig Johnson, Chairman, Venture Law Group, www.vlg.com

Does having an angel investor in a company validate the company for future financing? "That depends who the angel is. Absolutely it does if you can bring in a very successful entrepreneur whose very presence adds to the luster of an unknown group of founders. One of the most common ways that I help companies get started, before they go for venture financing, is to try to find an individual who has a golden record of success in the related industry to what the company is proposing to do, and see if I can interest that individual in making an investment and perhaps becoming involved as a director and advisor. It helps immeasurably to have such a person involved.

"I call it the leaning-forward effect because venture funds make their decisions at Monday-morning meetings, and each partner will be sponsoring a certain number of new investment opportunities that the partners will discuss. There are generally 8 to 12 people sitting around the table discussing opportunities, and people have to make decisions very quickly about whether to pursue a given investment opportunity or not. It helps a great deal, especially in a less obvious opportunity in which the entrepreneurs are not brand-name people starting their sixth successful company, if a general partner presenting the opportunity to the other partners can say, Oh, this well-known angel is involved in this company or is on the board and has made a $2 million investment.

"These highly-regarded angels add tremendous credibility. That causes the other partners at the table to lean forward because they want to hear more. Everyone knows that high-profile angels don't have to get involved with a company—they have many alternative uses for their time. So if they commit their time as well as their money, it must be something pretty interesting."

Because most angels have had prior experience building their own company, they know many techniques for negotiating with customers, joint venture partners, or financing sources on favorable terms for the company. They may know how to implement a financial control system to help manage the company's growth. They may be able to assist with interviewing candidates to fill out the management team, or in evaluating resumes that are submitted. It is in that general category of operations—how the various parts of an enterprise fit together—that an angel can be most valuable to an entrepreneur, who may not have that generalized experience. This is the contribution that is somewhat hard to describe, but it is the idea of having been there before, having made tough decisions and having been able to anticipate the challenges a company faces as it develops. One person described this to us as being a "hard-nosed type of guy."

ADVICE FROM A VENTURE CAPITALIST

Kirby Cochran, Partner, Red Rock Ventures,
www.redrockventures.com

Angels have told us that they get a lot more involved in a company and helping it, and they mention that venture capitalists don't provide that same level of hands-on help. Is that fair? "That's fair, sure. But quite frankly, that hands-on involvement could end up being a detraction. You get some stupid angel in there that gives bad advice, or feels like it's his company. Again, angels are not sophisticated money, and generally they have egos so big they wouldn't fit through a double-car garage door."

Angels say they rely more on their instinct about the people in the company in making the decision to invest, rather than extensive due diligence. "That's unfortunate, because most people's instincts are wrong."

The entrepreneur also has to get a good feel of how much of this experience and time the angel is likely to devote to the company. Will the angel remain enthusiastic even if the fledgling venture goes through some hard times, or will he view the investment as disappointing and devote his time elsewhere? If the equity the angel is given is partially based on how much nonfinancial assistance they can contribute, the responsibilities of the angel need to be spelled out clearly in advance of the deal closing.

How can entrepreneurs get these value-added services from angels? The first step is to tell the angel what kind of help you need.

ADVICE FROM AN ENTREPRENEUR

Dave Westin, CEO, www.channelautomation.com

Have the angels performed as you expected in terms of adding value? "Quite honestly, most angels do not add value. We have a ton of smart money in our deal, a lot of the *Who's Who* in the Valley. Everyone's so busy with their own projects, their own careers, I would estimate that most of our investors have put money in 10 or 15 other companies, so it's not like we are the only venture they are dealing with.

"At the end of the day, if you are looking for an angel to get key goals done for you, you are in more trouble than you think, because you have to have it within your core team to execute the fundamentals of getting your product out, getting your first few customers, getting the first alliances negotiated.

"If you are looking for the angel to do that for you, it's probably not going to happen. They may say they are going to do everything in the world for you. A few angels of ours have been extremely solid with relationships we could leverage. But not all have."

If you had the opportunity to take $2 million from dumb money or $1 million from smart money, which one are you going to take? "I would take the $2 million. You need the money to grow the business. As an entrepreneur, part of your job is to network effectively; you can pick up good advisory people as you go.

"You use the $2 million to achieve milestones and then bring on additional people. With just the $1 million, you could be in continuous fund-raising mode. What I learned is, when the money is available, take it.

"Angels do not add as much value as they would have you believe. They are trying to say, 'We add so much value, we should get a break on valuation (more equity for a given amount of money).' But the reality is, they have their own companies, jobs, family lives. Wealthy people travel a lot. They may not be available to help you."

ADVICE FROM A VENTURE CAPITALIST WHO IS ALSO AN ANGEL

Frank A. McGrew IV, Managing Director, Paradigm Capital Partners, Memphis, TN, www. memphisangels.com

Having Memphis Angels participate in the financing of a company gives it additional validation later on? "Right. We are a little different than some angel groups because we are a full-time professional organization with a VC fund associated with it. Angels typically pick one deal a year, get involved with it, put a couple hundred thousand dollars in it.

"We have the ability to not only get involved with a company, but bring professional resources to bear, seven days a week if necessary. I think beyond that we also have the ability to bring in other venture capitalists later on because we understand that model as well.

"It was easier to be an entrepreneur in terms of raising money in 1999 and early 2000. As times have changed, the market has become more competitive. We went into this with our value proposition realizing that we had to get more actively involved in the businesses."

ADVICE FROM AN ANGEL WHO ALSO IS A VENTURE CAPITALIST

Patrick Soheili, Barrington Partners, Silicon Valley

You like angels to be involved, because it represents a validation of the company. "Many times companies come to us (our VC firm) and we introduce them to angels. We say, 'Go see this guy or that guy, and see what they think.' To a venture capitalist, if angels get involved, it shows that experts in the field believe in this thing. Remember, most venture capitalists have been out of the industry from an operational perspective for a number of years. We have been out of the day-to-day operations. Most angels are either still in the industry or very recently separated from the industry. This means their contacts, their expectations, their understanding of what customers want, and what the product/service is solving for customers are all more recent. The angels have a much more realistic picture than venture capitalists might."

The talents, contacts, and capital angels bring can be a powerful catalyst for the company's growth.

Specifically what can an angel do for the entrepreneur?

ADVICE FROM AN ENTREPRENEUR

Alexandre Gonthier, CTO, iPIN—Interactive Transaction Services

How important has been the nonmonetary contribution of the angels (advice and contacts)? Could you give us some specific examples of how they helped you? "Gil Amelio was our first angel investor, and he took a board seat from the very beginning. He was instrumental in helping us shape the industrial vision that we have followed, in bringing credibility when we needed a lease line from Comdisco (the lender asked to speak with him on the phone). When it came to the due diligence phase with the venture capitalists (Accel Partners and Sutter Hill Ventures), who invested in our first professional round, we also sought his guidance and presence in the VC all-partner meeting. In these meetings a company presents to the entire partnership, which then approves or does not approve an investment. In addition, Mr. Amelio has always been available to introduce us to Fortune 100 executives in the United States."

DEAL TALES: NO GOOD DEED GOES UNPUNISHED

We worked with a marketing company that purchased the license for a technology from an inventor in another country. The license came up for renewal just at the time the founders were out looking for angel investors. This license was crucial to the value of the company because the products the company marketed could not be produced without it. We asked several times whether there would be any problem obtaining the renewal from the inventor, knowing that inventors can be a bit flighty at times. The founders said, "Oh, no. There will be no problem. The inventor is a friend of ours. He thinks we're great."

The angel happened to be going to the inventor's country on business, and graciously offered to conduct the negotiation with the inventor on behalf of the company, even before the transaction was completed for the angel to invest in the company. The angel was a highly skilled negotiator in matters such as these, the founders of the company were not. So the angel and the inventor met. A strange thing happened. The inventor was so impressed with the angel he decided to quadruple the compensation he wanted for the license, both an up-front fee and a royalty. His offer was very much out of line with reality. Why did he do this? He met the angel, and decided that if a wealthy individual takes the time to meet with him about this tiny company's license, the tiny company must be on the verge of making a lot of money. And he wanted his fair share. The negotiations turned acrimonious, and the company ended up losing its license, losing a lot of its value as a result, and on top of that, the angel was scared away from investing.

One of those lose–lose situations. The company loses a great opportunity to grow their business, the angel loses a potentially great investment.

Did they make a tactical mistake by telling the inventor about the angel coming in? Wasn't the angel's efforts at negotiation precisely the type of value-added service angels are so good at providing to early-stage companies? Or was the inventor just capricious? In the uncertain world of entrepreneurship, even when all the ingredients for success, including capital, are in place, the outcome is by no means assured.

Chapter Summary

- Because they understand what it takes to build a successful enterprise, angels may be able to add valuable experience and contacts to an early-stage venture.
- The involvement of an angel who is highly regarded by venture capitalists can facilitate the company receiving a second round of financing down the line.
- There is considerable debate about whether angels really add as much value as they say they do.

CHAPTER

28

Working with an Angel after the Close

Reporting to the Angels

Maintaining a positive relationship with angel investors depends to a great extent on keeping them informed about the company on a timely basis. This allows the angel a comfort level that the members of the management team are being good stewards of the capital, and lets the angel cheer the company on as it reaches important milestones. And as we already pointed out, if the angel is to provide contacts or assistance to help the company over hurdles, the angel first needs to know what the hurdle might be, well enough in advance, that the needed contacts or assistance can be lined up.

It is recommended that even very young companies implement a systematic reporting process, both for internal use in managing the business and also to generate the information that angel investors need to see.

ADVICE FROM AN ENTREPRENEUR FROM THE EAST COAST

What is your philosophy about working with angels after the deal closes? "Have a very open and honest relationship with investors. We have over 30 investors in our company. Make sure you send, minimally, a quarterly letter to all the investors but then on a monthly basis contact the lead investors and let them know what is going on within your organization, your accomplishments, and challenges you are facing, so that they may be able to look for contacts and relationships you may be needing down the line.

"Ninety-five percent of the guys we have dealt with have been extremely solid. Don't ask them to do the work that you, the management team, should be doing yourselves. You are getting the most upside. I find my friends who are entrepreneurs saying, 'This guy is going to be my white knight, and get this done, or that done.' That puts a huge risk on the company. Unless the angel has nothing else to do, they don't have the time to do all these things."

ADVICE FROM AN EXPERT

Investor Reporting Packages

Nigel A.L. Brooks, President, The Business Leadership Development Corporation

Ernie L. Recsetar, President, Stirling Capital Corporation

Robert J. Moss, Business Development Partnership, Inc.

There is an old expression is business: You get what you measure. Therefore it is extremely important that investors agree with entrepreneurs before a deal is funded about what the future performance measures will be. It is also important that they agree on the format, content, and frequency of the investor reporting package—the vehicle by which the performance measures will be reported to the investors by the entrepreneur.

Historically, the only major form of investor reporting was income tax-related, especially in the days when investments in early-stage businesses were tax sheltered. The primary reporting vehicle was schedule K-1 of the business income tax return.

During the era of huge investments in technology-related businesses that occurred during the late 1990s, investors assumed that they would get a rapid and significant return on their investments. Many did not pay attention to investor reporting at all.

Sadly, the bubble burst, leaving many investors stunned about how their proceeds were used or misused by entrepreneurs.

Unlike public companies, which must comply with Securities and Exchange Commission reporting requirements such as 10-Q and 10-K, reporting standards for private companies are essentially nonexistent placements, other than tax reporting.

Whereas some angel investor groups, VC firms, and institutional firms may have well-defined investor reporting packages, most do not. When they do exist, these packages may vary according to the level of involvement that the investor has in the business after the deal closes.

For example, an investor who becomes a board member should be well informed and receive board-member packages that contain financial statements and other pertinent data.

Other than tax reporting, passive investors may not receive any form of investor reporting package at all, unless they specifically ask for it.

Based upon our experience in providing capital advisory and management consulting services to a wide variety of public and private businesses, we believe that it is absolutely essential that entrepreneurs and investors agree to an investor reporting package before a deal is funded.

Our experience demonstrates that entrepreneurs become more accountable and are more proactive in responding to early indications of problems when they are required to prepare such packages; prevention is better than cure. Our experience also demonstrates that investors are more likely to participate in future rounds of funding when they are well informed about the historical performance of a business.

We recommend that entrepreneurs and investors establish monthly, quarterly, and annual reporting cycles. However, the entrepreneur should not be unnecessarily burdened to produce elaborate reports—just sufficient information to keep the investors realistically informed.

In the monthly cycle, we recommend that the investors receive a status report, supported by financial statements, that describes the current issues facing the business and the current status and/or resolution of issues from the prior period. The report should succinctly present the financial condition and should focus on exceptional conditions. The status report focuses on actual performance as opposed to probable performance based on projections.

In the quarterly cycle, we recommend that the investors receive a performance report, supported by financial statements that describe trends and status by key indicators. The key indicators will vary according to the nature and development stage of the business. Businesses that are in major development stages will focus on project indicators, but all will include indicators of ongoing performance. We recommend that trends be tracked over time, ideally three years, noting seasonal fluctuations as appropriate.

The quarterly performance report should include the monthly status report.

In the annual cycle, we recommend that two sets of reports be prepared. The first is a fiscal year-end report and the second is a performance assessment conducted three to six months after the fiscal year end.

The fiscal year-end report includes the monthly status and quarterly performance reports with a more in-depth analysis of the business.

We believe that a sound investor reporting package process will improve the relationship between an investor and entrepreneur and lead to improved business performance.

Angels view these reports not just as a summary of what has happened, but as a kind of distant early warning system of possible trouble on the horizon. It is particularly disconcerting to investors to find out that the company is going to run out of money this Friday, for example. Why not alert the investor to a potential cash shortfall well enough in advance so further funding can be obtained?

ADVICE FROM AN ANGEL

Brent Townshend

What sorts of reports do you like to receive from a company after you invest? "The best is a quarterly written report with financials, balance sheets, and income statements, a discussion of major events that are happening, and what they are looking at in the future. Three or four pages is fine. I don't want a huge thing to read, just to know about the important things going on. When things are not going according to plan, I like them to point this out early as opposed to saying everything is beautiful for four quarters in a row, then the next quarter they tell you, 'We need more money or we aren't going to survive.'

"At minimum they need to point out the good and the bad—we planned on doing this, but we're short here. Too often, they only tell you the good things about deals they signed with customers, things like that. They don't mention all the other things they were planning on doing that have fallen apart.

"You need to be honest with the angels. You have the investment; it is not to your advantage to paint too rosy a picture in case it does go badly and you have to ask them for more money. It is much better to be consistently realistic with the angels."

Exit Tragedies: What Happens When an Investment Goes Bad?

We have discussed how angel investors face a high degree of risk. It's easy to look at risk as an abstract concept, a characteristic, like saying the sky is blue (or gray for those of you in the Midwest). But the harsh reality is that risk means, for all practical purposes, that when you make the investment you kiss the money goodbye. There is a risk of outright failure, that the company will not last and all the equity investors will most likely be left with nothing. But another troublesome risk is illiquidity: Even if the company is going gangbusters, you can't get any money out of the investment, any return, for a lengthy period of time, even up to five years. It's not like a CD where early withdrawal means you lose points of interest. It means there is no practical way to get any of your investment out.

Here are some of the alternatives for investors when they see an investment going rapidly downhill; each one is painful.

- Replace the founders on the management team and/or change the board of directors.
- Put in additional funding themselves.
- Raise additional funding from new investors.
- Take part in the day-to-day operations of the company.
- Sell the company or merge it with another entity.
- Let the company run out of cash and close the doors.
- Sell the assets of the company, including intellectual property.

It's easy, of course, to have 20-20 hindsight, but the best angel investors are not just those that pick the big winners, but those that avoid the really big losers. And because angel investors usually have a minority position in a company, they have to convince the founding shareholders to go along with any of these alternatives.

ADVICE FROM AN ANGEL

Bill Krause, Mentor Capitalist

Could you describe a situation about a company that should never have been funded? "Sure. A company that was founded by entrepreneurs who had very little, if any, business savvy. I really wouldn't even call them entrepreneurs. I would call them opportunists. Either young graduates out of engineering school or MBA students who had an idea that the Internet could make a crappy business into a better business. What I mean by that is that retail, by its nature, is not a crappy business, but a very difficult business.

"In fact, the Internet is a technology that enhances existing retail business. It is not a substitute for traditional retail. So pick almost any B2C (business-to-consumer) Internet company, and that was a flawed concept from the outset. Including Amazon. One of my colleagues had this great insight. The period of time in a company's history when they have the highest gross margin is in the early stages. That is when their competitive advantage is at its peak. Over time, gross margins have only one way to go, and it's down. So you take Amazon, and their gross margins have only one way to go, down. If they had a business that couldn't make money when their margins were at a peak, how do they plan to make money when their margins begin to decline? Then they have this mound of debt to pay off. There are only two ways to pay off debt, and both require profits. Either you pay the debt off through equity financing because you're profitable and have equity financing available, or you have enough profits to service the debt. I submit that Amazon will eventually be acquired by a major retail chain."

ADVICE FROM AN ANGEL IN CALIFORNIA

What happens when a transaction goes bad? The company is failing. The management team isn't what you thought it was going to be. "As an angel investor, you're stuck. If you've written the check, there's really nothing you can do. You can try to persuade, you can try to influence, but fundamentally, you are going to have to ride the investment. Also you will find that the checkbook is closed. Other angels that might have come in for a follow-on round, won't. The venture capitalists will not jump in. One common financing sequence might be angels in the first round, venture capitalists and a few angels in the second round, venture capitalists thereafter. So if an angel investment goes south, typically it means there will not be any further investment coming in and the company will eventually close its doors.

"In the dot.com space, we are witnessing weekly a half-dozen or a dozen companies closing their doors. That means the preceding six months has been a terrible journey for these companies. They are struggling to find money. There is not money to be had in most cases. They are peeling away employees, laying off sequential layers of employees. People are going on half-salaries. These are companies that have not necessarily gone astray because of mismanagement. It is just a major consolidation of a market that grew much larger and faster than it should have. A process of unwinding that is very messy and unpleasant."

Protection of Legal Agreements

It sometimes seems to entrepreneurs that investors try to make the legal documentation of the deal too lengthy and detailed, almost as though the investor doesn't trust the entrepreneur. After all, the entrepreneur argues, we are both all fired up about this company, and we're going to be working closely together for years. Why do we need all this legal work done? Whatever happened to deals with a handshake?

The reason for all this legal protection for the angel is that the perceived value of any outsider's contribution to a venture—investor, service provider, whomever—inevitably declines over time. In the beginning of a venture, when the money is absolutely critical, the investor is the entrepreneur's best friend, and the entrepreneur will promise almost anything to the investor about how they will be rewarded when the company is successful. But let's say the company goes along and is successful. The entrepreneur will attribute the success more to all the effort he put in and the good decisions he made, rather than to the value of the money, advice, and contacts from the investor. This is only natural: Ego is a necessary aspect of being an entrepreneur, because out of ego comes the belief you can succeed. The verbal promises made when the deal was being negotiated may well turn out to be worthless.

The angel needs to have the promises converted into paper form, as much as is practical to do, so they aren't lost as memories fade over time.

The solution for angels and entrepreneurs is that both sides need to be represented by attorneys with an understanding of business and a certain amount of creativity. It's not just compliance with securities laws that is involved; it is a matter of creating documents that express the needs and concerns of both parties.

ADVICE FROM AN ENTREPRENEUR

Dave Westin, CEO, www.channelautomation.com

How do you determine if a given angel will make a good partner? Do you do reverse due diligence on them? "You really have to.

If not, you do a disservice to your company, because little issues will pop up later on down the line. It's better to have all expectations, beyond just the term sheet, clarified at the get-go, versus having to continually deal with issues such as, the angel requesting that you enter into a partnership with a company, even though it may not be in the best interest of your organization, because your angel sits on their board.

"There's a lot of that kind of thing that goes on in the angel investment community."

So, the first step is to ask a lot of questions and get to know the people? "Without a doubt. The big mistake a lot of people make is thinking angels are there just to put in money. That may not be the belief of the angel, who thinks, 'I put in this money, now I want to add value to it.'"

How much of this needs to be put in writing versus just hashed out person-to-person? "The problem is that most of this stuff isn't worth anything in writing. It's really an oral understanding. What differentiates really excellent teams is the ability to work through issues quickly. None of this needs to be in writing, It needs to be verbally communicated and understood. Because at the end of the day, the angel can't do anything, either. He has no real leverage point other than your goodwill. Depending on the personality, if you say no to them, you can get some vindictive angels. The person may say, 'Hey, I'm no longer on the board, I hope the company goes down.' You get all types.

"Personalities play a huge role. You have to make sure the angel who invests believes in not only the concept or the product, but also that the management team can take the company to the next level. If they don't believe that, they shouldn't invest, because they will meddle so much in the internal operations—fix this, you need to add that, and so on. Things that may not be necessary, because they aren't there from a day-to-day basis.

"They may not have good relationships with certain members of the management team, so they want them replaced with their buddies or themselves."

How can the entrepreneur be assured the investor will follow through on promises to help? "The way I handled it, I gave specific advisory agreements to angels. If we got a customer through them, it would be worth X amount of stock, for example. If I needed them to do something above and beyond, they would be compensated. It respects the angel's time. It gives them avenues to add some additional upside to their investment. I showed them all my objectives for the organization, partnerships we needed, things like that, and if they facilitated the objectives, great. Everyone benefited."

To Meddle or Not to Meddle

Angels usually have significantly more real-world operations or business experience than the founders of the companies they invest in. The angel who observes the management team steering the company in the wrong direction faces a real problem of determining how much assistance to offer to get things back on track. Doing nothing is not a viable option for most angels, who, after all, are used to being deeply involved in their own companies. There is also the concept that you have to let the little birds fly out of the nest at some point.

ANGELS' VARYING LEVELS OF INVOLVEMENT

Angels' desired level of involvement in a company can vary significantly. The roles they play after investing could range all the way from 1 to 6:

1. Invest, and remain completely passive, with little contact with the founders of the company.
2. Invest, take a board seat, and advise or assist the founders if they seek out the advice.
3. Invest, take a board seat, and agree to be a formal advisor or mentor with prescribed duties.
4. Invest, take a board seat, and assume a full-time executive role with the company.
5. Invest, take a board seat, and become CEO.
6. Invest, obtain a majority position, and control the board of directors.

Most angels prefer roles 2 or 3, but some are willing to settle for role 1. Many entrepreneurs wish for 1, but may really need 2 or 3, whether they realize it or not. Roles 5 and 6 are the entrepreneur's nightmares, of course. Fortunately, most angels have no interest in taking on full-time CEO chores, nor do they seek out majority control of the company.

ADVICE FROM AN ANGEL

Tom Horgan, Acorn Technologies, San Diego, CA

Let's say you spot some obvious problems with the management team, how much do angels get involved in recommending other people be added to the team, or that the management structure be reorganized? Venture capital firms quite often require that certain changes be made. What kind of clout do angels have in that regard? "Since we operate as a network, we would have a strong say. We firmly believe that we bring expertise in along with capital. We haven't had to do this so far, but I know we would operate in that mode, should it be required."

ADVICE FROM AN ANGEL

Brent Townshend

Isn't it hard to resist getting more involved in the actual management of the company when things start to go badly? "It is hard to resist. The first thing you feel like doing is to look at the numbers and say, you should cut this, do this, do that. The best advice angels can give is more at the high level, rather than looking at the details. Angels can point out, you're going to run out of money in six months, you need to scale back expenditures because it may be difficult to go out and raise additional funds. Or you need to concentrate on getting these customer contracts signed up. This is better than going into very fine details about running the show.

"I don't think it is the place of the investors to start taking managerial roles. There are situations, though, in which angels can end up in more operational positions if the company is lacking in some skill area, and one of the angels has that."

What happens when one angel gets very involved with the company? Do the other investors feel as though they are being left out? "Usually there is not much interaction between angels. The company talks to them individually, but they don't really talk to each other. They probably don't know that one angel is extremely involved. I am quite happy if I see one of the angel investors focusing on the company, because I think he's looking out for my interest as well."

Patience Is an Important Angel Virtue

Angels get a lot of personal satisfaction when they see their companies succeed, and the success is partially due to the time and effort they put in. They also understand that they have to be patient with the companies as they progress toward whatever the profitable exit event for the angel investors may be.

Chapter Summary

- Prompt reporting of key developments at the company to the angel is vital in maintaining a positive relationship with angel investors.
- The expectations of both the angels and the entrepreneurs must be expressed prior to closing, but it is difficult to reduce all these expectations to written documents.
- Angel investors frequently face painful decisions about what to do with a failing company they have invested in.
- Angel investors must decide when and how much assistance to provide their companies that are struggling.
- Angels must be extraordinarily patient in order to follow their investments to an exciting conclusion.

CHAPTER 29

Tales from the Venture Vault

Horror Stories and Advice from Entrepreneurs and Angels about Why Things Go Awry

Sometimes, the relationship between the angel and the company ends in disaster. This may be due to market forces that come to bear on the company and kill it. Or the perpetrator may be one of the principals in the deal himself. No matter what, it can be a bloody mess, as these contributions we received attest. Understandably, most of these entrepreneurs and angels did not want to be identified. Don't read these too late at night, or at least make sure all the doors and windows are locked.

Boo.

(SCARY) ADVICE FROM AN ENTREPRENEUR

"I once had a communications company, and I had financing from an angel investor as a cosigner on a long-term loan for $100,000 and on a line of credit for $150,000. I had paid off the long-term loan rather quickly (a 10-year loan in three years) and was revolving my line of credit. I had paid off the loan because my angel had expressed an uneasiness in the rapid change in my industry (he didn't understand my business). When I needed a short-term increase in my operating line (three months) to purchase the material for an unusually large project and needed the angel's guarantee with the bank, I was unable to get it. A year later, I had paid down my line of credit to $100,000 and was being forced to move because my local market had collapsed. I was unable to borrow any more money to make the move and ended up going broke. I still owe my angel $100,000 and all of my suppliers an additional $50,000. If the angel had just cosigned the loan as he promised the company would be around today."

ADVICE FROM AN ENTREPRENEUR

"Three of us got together to form a B2C (business-to-consumer) startup. We set up a corporation and went about finding ten investors at $50,000 per unit. We sold one unit, then we were referred to a fellow who had (and still has) a successful business in an unrelated B2B (business-to-business) market. This guy liked our business plan and offered to buy the remaining nine units. We agreed to sell, and things were up and running. We did the research and development, but since this angel held controlling interest, the venture never got off the ground. The problem was that Daddy Warbucks, being unfamiliar with the company's market, thought the marketing efforts that worked in *his* business would be sufficient in ours. He sold to a very small, easily reached market that was used to paying high prices for their goods. Our start-up had a much larger retail target market that was used to paying low prices and was very expensive and time-consuming to reach. He went through several marketing managers and invariably replaced each one, just as sales were ramping up, mainly because he just didn't understand how the new company *needed* to market its services. In the end, when his total investment passed the $2 million mark he pulled the plug and tried to sell the business, which never happened."

ADVICE FROM AN ENTREPRENEUR

"A couple of guys started a company and hired me as their chief architect. The research and development was completed, but the single angel investor turned out to be a total control freak and just about ran the business into the ground before it ever got going. From time to time, he would withhold bank transfers in order to gain leverage from the founders; he did a bunch of other underhanded things in order to wrest a controlling interest of the business from the founders.

"Eventually, the founders located a White Knight who came in and nullified the effect of the first investor, but this guy also became a problem later on. Initially, he fired everybody and brought in his own people; they spent nearly two years completely reinventing everything we had done, and eventually ended up with a very similar product. The good news in this scenario is that the second investor was able to get the company acquired and all the other investors were cashed-out. The founders are off doing other things today, but they both say that if they had it to do over again, the one thing they would not do is issue voting stock to the angel investors.

"The moral of this story: If you're going to get angel investors, be sure you have at *least* three of them after the initial round of funding and that you hold at least 50 percent control and there's 25 percent stock left for later offerings, and/or issue nonvoting stock to the angels, as they're very likely to turn into devils later on."

ADVICE FROM AN ENTREPRENEUR

"I started a sporting-good manufacturing business. We completed the patenting of several of our designs and began making inroads with retailers as well as with direct mail sales. An angel approached me about a 50-50 partnership: He agreed to put in $3 million of expansion capital to take care of the marketing program. Because our sales were pretty minimal, he secured the investment on my shares of the company, with certain sales benchmarks that had to be reached. Three months leter, he installed his own guy as CFO, who began to withhold the funds we needed to order materials and finance large orders. Pretty soon we fell so far behind plan that the angel's lawyers served me with papers that I was in default of our agreement and my stock belonged to the angel. He had terrific lawyers, and in no time, I had lost my company and all the time and money I had put in. You should never sign an agreement specifying targets you have to reach when the managerial decisions you make do not determine the outcome. Afterward I learned he had made the investment for the sole reason to acquire the patents the company owned. He didn't care about growing my company at all."

ADVICE FROM AN ANGEL

"I invested $600,000 in a start-up educational technology venture. The entrepreneurs burned through this capital much faster than expected, and said they wanted to fly in and meet with me about a change in the capitalization of the company. In the meeting they said they had found an institutional partner who was willing to put $5 million into the company, but my ownership was going to be diluted down to almost nothing. The entrepreneur said the market for the product was so hot that, when the effect of the new capital kicked in, my tiny new percentage would be worth much more than the larger share I owned before. It seemed interesting to me that a market that was so cold to their product that they used all of my capital and still had not lined up any major customers, was suddenly going to become so hot. To me, their presentation was just a dog-and-pony show on behalf of the institutional investor, and I asked them what had happened to our partnership, based on mutual trust, that we formed when I made my investment. Loyalties can certainly switch quickly when $5 million becomes available. I also told them to get out of my office."

ADVICE FROM AN ENTREPRENEUR

"When I first started to raise money for my company I was introduced to a husband and wife from a wealthy family who were well known in the angel community. They generally took participatory roles in companies they invested in. In addition to money, part of their added value was that they were supposedly experts in developing one of my planned channels of distribution. They had done it before in another industry and they were willing to invest in the venture and help me develop the channel.

"As we went through the process, they had promised to invest an equal amount of money as I had, and the wife's name went into the business plan as the VP of sales. As we were closing our first round of funding, they started telling me how much they wanted in terms of equity and salary from the new venture. Basically their plan was to take all the money allocated for the entire management team for themselves, and they wanted twice the amount of equity that I was getting for the same amount of money.

"After a few heated days we decided it was best that we part company (about 1 week before we were to close on our first round). This is when it got interesting. Three weeks later they called me and stated they still wanted to develop the channel for me on a much different deal. Still wanting to develop the channel, I began negotiating a channel agreement with them and gave them a great deal of material related to the channel and how we would manage and develop it.

"For many of the same reasons the investment part failed, we failed to get an agreement for them to develop the channel. Still thinking they were nice but greedy, I agreed to walk away and didn't think anything of it.

"Two weeks later I went to lunch with one of my biggest competitors in the area. When I went to his office I noticed their very familiar fax cover sheet. It turns out that they had taken all of my materials, repackaged it as their own, and presented it to my regional competitors."

ADVICE FROM A VENTURE CAPITALIST

Larry Kubal, Managing Director, Labrador Ventures

"Labrador Ventures invests in early-stage information technology companies. With an average initial investment of $2 million in a company, Labrador minds the early-stage funding gap between angel investors and larger venture capitalists, and works with both groups of investors throughout the life of a company.

"Labrador has worked with many excellent angel investors who have added great value to our portfolio companies. One recent experience, however, led us to remind our entrepreneurs that angel investors often do not have the same focus, discipline, or financial stamina that venture funds do, especially those angels who enthusiastically joined the tech bubble at its height.

"Here is just one example of angel investing that happened to turn into a difficult situation for the entrepreneur. It is by no means meant to be broadly representative, but rather illustrative of the type of problems an entrepreneur can encounter. One of Labrador's portfolio companies was raising a Series B round during the last year, when the follow-on financing market was especially difficult. Labrador was the lone VC firm in the deal and was accompanied by several significant angel investors. These angels had initially represented themselves to the company as willing, deep pockets ready to participate in future financing rounds. The company was progressing at a normal pace. Both angels reneged on their commitments when the anticipated need for the Series B financing arose. Labrador offered to bridge the company. The angels were invited to participate in the bridge or to draft their own terms and lead a bridge. They declined both and attempted to block the company from accepting the bridge because it would be dilutive to their positions given their nonparticipation.

"The entrepreneur felt betrayed by these angel investors who not only withdrew their financial support but became obstructionist. In this case the investor group became dysfunctional and damaged the prospects of the company. Building a company in the current environment is in itself a major challenge. Nonsupportive or obstructionist investors, of any type, increase the challenges faced. Because the focus, discipline, and financial stamina may be different between angels and VC funds, entrepreneurs should be careful when evaluating their financing options."

ADVICE FROM AN ANGEL

"One case involved an individual (the founder) who was one of the most tenacious and persistent people I've ever known. Unfortunately, he managed to alienate every single vendor and contractor we dealt with, including me. He got funding from several angels, burned through the money, and then started accusing his contractors and vendors of ripping him off. The angels sided with him in hopes of getting something, but all they ended up with was a couple of judgments from lawsuits some of us filed against the company. He finagled things so all the assets got transferred to another company and the investors were left holding the debts. One of the angels now controls the carcass of the original corporation."

Chapter Summary

- Angel investors can abruptly become disenchanted and withhold badly needed funding, effectively killing the company.
- Angels sometimes misdirect the company because they believe their way of doing things is the only way.
- Slowly, inexorably, angels may take over the business right in front of the entrepreneur's eyes.
- Angels may make promises they do not intend to keep.

- Angels may obstruct the company's ability to obtain financing in the future.
- Entrepreneurs also may fail to keep promises they made to an angel who was their only financial ally when the company started.
- Entrepreneurs may waste the angels' money and manage the company right out of business.

THE FUTURE OF ANGEL INVESTING

CHAPTER 30

Making the Angel Investment Market More Efficient

The Financing of Early-Stage Companies: It's a Wacky World Out There

After you have talked to enough players in this marketplace—the angels, the venture capitalists, the service providers, the entrepreneurs—you come to a surprising conclusion:

Everyone thinks, when it comes to investing in early-stage companies, that their way is the best way and the other guy is, well, not too bright. They are smart, probably brilliant; the other guy is, unfortunately, clueless.

Silicon Valley angels view themselves as the elite corps of angel investing. Angels in the other parts of the country are not nearly as skilled at this as they are. It is almost as if they wonder why the other guys even bother.

Silicon Valley isn't alone in this rather haughty attitude. When one of us mentioned to a well-known angel in Southern California that we have angel groups in our hometown, it sounded as though he chuckled. We quickly changed the subject before this could be confirmed.

Venture capitalists think angels are amateurs and they are the pros. Venture capitalists sometimes argue that angels can actually mess up companies' chances of getting VC investment further down the line because of the poor job they do on valuation of the company.

Some of the organized angel groups think they have the process down cold. They choose the best deals. They get the highest rates of return. Other groups? They'll probably lose a lot of money and fold, the superior groups say.

And, there are definitely individual dumb angels and smart angels. How do we know this? The angels say so. Investors decry the fact that entrepreneurs sometimes hire incompetent service providers to advise them, which ends up causing the company problems and slowing down its development. But the reason is, of course, that incompetent service providers tend to be somewhat less expensive.

Entrepreneurs draw the conclusion that many investors, angels, and venture capitalists are not too smart, especially those who decline to invest. "They just don't get it," say the entrepreneurs, as though discussing hopelessly slow learners in an Algebra I class.

Why this reluctance by all parties involved to give anyone but themselves even the slightest credit for knowing what they are doing? Why do so many of these people have to keep congratulating themselves on being the best at what they do?

If you look at the actual results of investing in early-stage companies, we see that this activity involves a constant learning process. No one is infallible. In the speculative frenzy in 1999 and part of 2000, when investors were chasing after deals that in many cases turned out to be really bad ideas, not even the largest VC firms, it seems, were immune from making blunders. Perhaps some of these people think that if they keep saying they are superior at early-stage investing, eventually it will be so.

The Problem Is All in the Geography: A Tale of Two Valleys

One of the main reasons that many regions of the country do not have adequate sources of entrepreneurial financing is simply a matter of how the region is perceived by investors. A second reason is that the more something is repeated the more it is viewed as a fact.

Silicon Valley views itself as having:

- The brightest technical minds coming out of the best universities
- A terrific lifestyle and climate
- A wonderful infrastructure of service providers to assist early-stage companies
- Fine communities to raise a family
- A fabulous pool of successful executives to draw upon
- The greatest concentration of venture capital in the world

These things are repeated so often, we all know them and accept them. Now let's look at how investors view Phoenix, Arizona, the Valley of the Sun. We surveyed venture capitalists around the country and asked them why there is not more venture capital flowing into our state, and specifically our largest city.

"Lack of infrastructure, talent, and senior management support."

"Arizona is not known to have abundant senior executive talent, dynamic proven high-tech entrepreneurs, nor an infrastructure that supports the type of technology start-up companies that venture capitalists would invest in."

"No critical mass of high-tech companies and labor pool with the right skills and general infrastructure to support high-tech activities."

So, Phoenix' explosive population growth in the last 10 years is due to dummies and incompetents moving there.

"It's not a tech hub; unlike Austin or Denver, there are not many successful tech companies or tech-centric universities spinning off talent."

"You need to have the entrepreneurs with good ideas in order to attract venture capital."

Wait, though. Don't you need venture capital in order to become a tech hub?

"It is not one of the big hubs where VC money is located. It's off the beaten track."

"We generally take board seats when we invest in companies, and the travel time outside of the Bay Area becomes problematic for monthly board meetings. Takes too much time for most VCs to travel there."

Dear VC: Phoenix hasn't been off the beaten track since the railroad came through last century.

"Not enough local capital, especially early stage."

"No seed/angel capital: no network of high net worth individuals that will seed startups (angels)."

This observation is true: much more angel activity is needed.

"No access to a wealth of VC firms. If you are in Silicon Valley, you get on the freeway and drive 15 minutes and you can visit 50 different venture capitalists."

"Probably the lack of a local VC industry."

Now we get it: Phoenix doesn't have enough capital because it doesn't have enough capital.

How Do People in Phoenix View Silicon Valley?

Silicon Valley housing costs are ridiculous; where we live, you can still get a three-bedroom house in a nice neighborhood for under $200,000. There, if you only have $200,000 you might as well sleep in your car.

The weather there is damp and cold; ours is warm and sunny nearly year round. In fact, venture capitalists spend upwards of $500 per night to stay at our resorts in the winter. (The locals wait until summer and get the same rooms for $75).

They have power blackouts; we have surplus electric power because we built a nuclear power plant ahead of when we needed it. You see, we believe in harnessing advanced technology here.

There, it can involve a two-hour commute to go a distance that would take 25 minutes in Phoenix.

We aren't simply touting our own community here, because what we've said could be stated for many places around the United States. But it seems that communities can be their own worst enemies when they don't stand up and refute these erroneous characterizations. The venture capitalists are certainly open to be convinced that their opinions of a given area are wrong. But more communities need to try.

Suppose you are a person living in the Midwest whose family made a fortune in the 1920s and 1930s. You are 45 years old, full of energy, with $10 million of your own capital you invest in the stock market, as your primary activity. You may be curious about angel investing but two things hold you back: You have been taught that your area is not a spawning ground for innovation, so there are no good deals to be found. There are no other organized angels in your area to network with, to refer deals back and forth, and to learn the angel investing ropes from.

So because the major VC firms ignore your area, angel investing is weak there, too. Angels take their cues to some extent from the VC firms. Areas with lots of VC activity tend to have more conferences or meetings on the subject of investing, where curious angels can listen and learn. Angels want to cultivate relationships with VC firms, who will be tapped for the subsequent rounds of the company's financing. Angel-founded companies then end up being located near the VC firms.

The problem is, VCs' perceptions filter down to the angels. We have in our city many, many millionaires who own expensive winter homes and have no idea of the investment opportunities in private companies that are there.

Articles have appeared on the subject of how more capital for early-stage companies needs to be made available in large, prosperous cities like San Antonio and even Chicago. The problem is widespread.

The truth is there is no real geographic superiority: Angel investing can be successfully done all over the United States. You need an environment that fosters innovation, such as universities. You need business people who have built or sold successful companies and now have capital, time, and experience to devote to helping start-ups. But an equally important element is the careful, even painstaking, analysis of the market, the technology, and the competition of a prospective investment.

Overcoming that perception problem is not easy. Angels fill in the gaps in regions that are capital deserts. But they have to be more organized and educated about the process. Clearly, it is not reasonable that the ingredients of entrepreneurial success only exist in a small area in California.

Some of the venture capitalists, thankfully, did give us hope:

> *"All you need is a great idea positioned in an attractive and growing market space and a quality management team with domain expertise. If you've got these, it doesn't matter where you are. The money will find you."*
>
> *"With regard to attracting capital, companies simply have to have good businesses. Good businesses attract capital, no matter where they are located."*

Broadening Angels' Investment Interests

Even with angels having more visibility and becoming easier to contact through angel networks and through the Internet, many entrepreneurs with nontechnology ventures are still faced with an almost insurmountable challenge to obtain capital for their venture, namely the perception that these ventures have inherently lower potential return on investment, and are, therefore, less attractive.

We tend to view proprietary components of a technology, such as aspects of it that can be patented, as the best means to establish a competitive advantage and barrier to entry in a market. These advantages can result in a high return on investment down the road. Over the course of the last 15 years, we have seen numerous instances of ventures that are well planned and have sound management teams having difficulty gaining interest from investors simply because they were involved in service, distribution, entertainment, consumer products, and other areas in which it was not easy to articulate what the competitive advantage could be. Many of these companies could have particularly benefited from the expertise that angels provide: operations experience, distribution know-how, financial-management expertise.

Entrepreneurs with nontech ventures have felt left out in the cold, even when the VC market was hotter than it had ever been. Many of these ventures have high enough margins to create the opportunity for significant cash flow and return on investment. But we have all been taught that technology is the only way to go.

Several years ago, we knew of one entrepreneur who started a commercial cleaning service and one that started a company that made vitamin supplements based on high-tech formulas that promised to make us all into immortal, gorgeous, perfect beings. The commercial cleaning service, if it had been able to obtain capital, would have grown rapidly. It was operating in a market experiencing a high rate of growth in commercial office space, and the management team had a great competence in delivering a high rate of service with relatively low labor and materials cost—high margins in other words. There isn't anything new or sexy about a commercial cleaning business, however, and the angel investors yawned over this deal. The company continued to make money, however, with or without the angel capital.

The high-tech vitamin formula company, however, got a ton of angel capital, attracted celebrities to its board, and promptly learned, even with proprietary formulas, it costs a fortune in marketing costs to tell all of America how to become immortal, gorgeous, perfect beings. They blew through the capital, went bust, and closed their doors.

It is true that historically the home-run investments for venture capitalists have typically been based on a technology. But in the cases just mentioned the seeming barrier to entry, the proprietary formulas, was less useful than the real barrier to entry—delivering top-flight service to the customer and maintaining high margins. Many times it appears that investors don't view the latter barrier as any kind of barrier at all, and that is why they decline to invest. The lessons we drew from these situations were: (1) angel investors should keep an open mind and look at a broad range of opportunities, and not just try to be mini-venture capitalists chasing the next hot technology; (2) getting rid of dirt will always be a growth market in America.

Angel capital is truly the lifeblood for many different kinds of ventures, not just high tech. We need to find ways to help these nontech ventures get more visibility and to help them get their message across.

EXPANDING THE AVAILABLE BASE OF ANGEL CAPITAL

In order to bring more angels into this market, there needs to be many more educational programs around the country on the nuts and bolts of finding companies and conducting due diligence. Many universities have programs on entepreneurship, in the hopes of spawning new companies out of the research done at the university, but the other side of the equation, the investor, is ignored. Great ideas for high-tech companies cannot come to fruition unless more angels become involved in providing seed capital. Right now, there are only a handful of people who speak on the subject of angel investing around the country.

Even more basic than education is awareness. It is surprising how many financial advisors who work with high net worth individuals, including account executives at brokerage houses, have little or no knowledge of private equity for early-stage companies. They couldn't even answer basic questions their clients might have on this subject.

We need more people experienced in private equity to take on the challenge of organizing an angel network in their community. Many cities have no angel networks at the present time; others that have one might be able to support five. There is some evidence that a single network can become too unwieldy with more than, say, 100 members. It is no easy task putting together an active network, but in some ways it is as important as other economic development efforts undertaken by a community to stimulate job creation or foster high-tech development.

Because many angel networks have formed very recently, they are just beginning to flex their muscles and step up to the plate with capital. Their numbers of closed deals will undoubtedly grow markedly over the next few years.

MORE WAYS FOR ANGELS AND ENTREPRENEURS TO MEET

Formal networks are terrific vehicles for angel investment, but they do not address all the capital needs of the entrepreneurs. There need to be more ways for angel investors and entrepreneurs to meet in informal, social settings where an initial contact can be made. The problem with networks and venture capital conferences is that so much screening of companies goes on before they arrive at the few who will actually be introduced to the members or present at the conference. The screening is highly subjective and many times good companies are overlooked, because for one thing some entrepreneurs are good at formal presentations and others just sweat and stammer through the whole thing. But you put these same entrepreneurs in a room of investors, with some cold beverages and hors d'oeuvres, and they can talk all night.

COACHING FOR ENTREPRENEURS

In our experience, many entrepreneurs fail to obtain funding simply because they cannot articulate their message; they cannot distill the advantages of their venture in terms the investor can relate to. The result is they get a polite decline or they are eliminated from screening processes of networks and capital conferences, and don't even get adequate feedback in order to improve the message next time. A great service that management consultants could begin providing would be coaching assistance to entrepreneurs about how to get ready to talk to investors. This involves much more than catch phrases like *elevator pitch.* It is being prepared for the questions investors will ask, having your business plan virtually memorized. Many angel networks do this coaching, but again, not that many companies get selected to move along the process with these networks.

We have done role playing sessions with entrepreneurs, in which we play the rich guys contemplating an investment in their company and they play themselves, and it is very interesting how this preparation builds the entrepreneurs' confidence.

HARNESSING TECHNOLOGY AND INVOLVING THE PUBLIC EQUITY MARKETS

In comments from angels in this book, we have seen that there is skepticism that Internet matching services for angels and entrepreneurs will ever generate a large amount of investment. But it seems as though there ought to be ways of getting the Net working on networking for angels seeking out deals and entrepreneurs seeking out angels. Hopefully, bright minds are thinking up innovative solutions right now.

Many of the business models of matching services are really just taking finder's fee services to the Internet; they are transaction based. What would really help entrepreneurs would be having a means to develop a dialogue with investors through the Internet, and starting them on the process of learning what investors want. That initial contact with the angel investor is the most difficult bridge for most entrepreneurs to cross. But the questions would be how such a service could generate revenue.

The public equity markets can also contribute to the growth of angel capital by allowing individuals to invest small amounts of money in a public venture fund that would make investments in private, and sometimes early-stage companies. This is a great way for individuals to get their feet wet in venture investing. They can monitor the progress of the public fund's portfolio of companies, and learn more about how to select early-stage companies for investment. From a macro perspective, this also increases the total pool of capital for early-stage companies, because any investor who can afford the share price of the public stock, which might be $25, could indirectly make angel investments, not just the wealthy individuals or accredited investors.

RECOGNIZE THAT TO SOME EXTENT, RAISING CAPITAL WILL ALWAYS BE DIFFICULT

Because many entrepreneurs express frustration with the difficulty of obtaining capital and the time it takes to do so, it is natural for them to wish for ways the process could be streamlined, such as the Internet matching services, to give entrepreneurs faster or greater access to the vital funding they need.

The problem is that many angels say this streamlining won't help.

The struggle to find investors, the time-consuming process of constructing a business plan to present, the slow and sometimes painful due-diligence process—all of these serve as a kind of natural selection process that results in the best (or at least the better) deals being funded more often than not. And along the way, business models are honed, and management teams are strengthened. Some angels liken this to almost the struggle a bird goes through to hatch. If you can't make it out of the egg, how well are you going to do out there in the competitive marketplace? After all, after you come out of your shell, your problems are just beginning . . .

They also insist that successful angel investing is a very personal process—the angel and the entrepreneur making a one-on-one evaluation of each other that includes extremely subjective factors, even nonbusiness factors, such as "Do I like this guy?"

Increasingly, what can be overcome is the hidden nature of this whole market, and the need to be already well-connected to wealthy people in order to attract investment. Angels are taking a cue from their VC brethren and becoming more visible. Formal angel groups—with phone numbers that can be looked up, addresses that can be contacted, Web sites that can be accessed—are shortening the time it takes to get in front of investors.

Closing the deal, though, will always involve a certain amount of agony, as we have learned from those who make a serious effort at being angels.

Chapter Summary

- Participants in early-stage investing tend to tout their own abilities highly and disparage those of others.
- The lack of capital in some parts of the country is due to investors' incorrect perceptions, not the lack of sound investment opportunities.
- Angel investors can sometimes overlook non-high-tech companies that have great business models and growth potential.
- There are many new ways linking angels and entrepreneurs together, but we need more of everything: more angels, more networks, more innovative vehicles for investment in early-stage private equity.
- Despite recent and likely future innovations to make attracting angel capital easier, it will continue to be a process that tests entrepreneurs' endurance.

CHAPTER

31

Outlook: What a Wonderful World It Could Be

The Story of a Start-Up as Told in the Year 2010

People ask him how he did it: Build a $2 billion company in just five years from 2006 to 2010. His answer is, "I don't think I'm any genius. We're just in a golden age for entrepreneurs, and let me tell you, it's a lot better than it was just ten years ago."

Probably the turning point came when the Seed Capital Stock Exchange (SCSE) was formed in 2005. This, as you remember, allowed companies looking for first money streamlined access to wealthy investors without the time-consuming and expensive process that a public stock offering used to entail, and it gave investors liquidity as well. When his company was listed, all 1 million shares he was offering at $15 per share were purchased in five days, so he could focus on the business instead of spending all his time out there meeting with venture capitalists. In fact, he turned down four offers from venture capitalists to invest. "You guys contacted me too late," he told them, smiling.

Of course, it didn't hurt that the Dow had hit 30,000 that year, and there were more than 40 million millionaires out there looking for hot new investments.

The next thing he did right was to purchase the latest artificial intelligence business simulator software. This $895 package ran his business model against 10,000 other recent start-ups and predicted there was an 87 percent chance his business would succeed. He tweaked his business plan a while, and ran the program again; this time it said 95 percent. Then he was ready to launch. "They tell me people used to rely just on gut feelings and spreadsheets. Seems kind of primitive to me," our entrepreneur adds.

At this same time, the government was doing its part, too. The Capital Formation Act of 2003 completely eliminated the capital gains tax on any investment made in a company less than three years old. Two years later Congress appropriated funds to partially underwrite the cost for cash-strapped entrepreneurs to have the patent and other legal protection work done for their new technologies.

Our entrepreneur's company wasn't even that unique an idea—he found an interesting niche market and offered the products to consumers through the Internet. "I came up with this idea way back in '99, but the money people told me dot.coms were dead. Dead, dead, dead, they said."

What was his response? "I came back with consensus forecasts that showed there would be 2.5 billion people shopping on the Net by 2009."

What happened then? "They still turned me down. Go figure."

How Things Have Changed: When Returning to Normal Is Viewed as Negative

1999	*2001*
$50 million valuation of start-ups	Valuations falling from first round of financing to the second
Investors chasing B2C Internet companies	Investors trying to keep the 1999 companies alive
Everyone wants to be an angel	Many angels wish they had taken up another hobby instead

Hot deals are cool ideas on cocktail napkins	Hot deals are established companies that have reached milestones
Entrepreneurs too optimistic about chances of obtaining capital	Entrepreneurs are too gloomy about chances of obtaining capital
Angel networks popping up everywhere	Empty place settings at the dinner meetings
Media think angel investors are geniuses	Media think angels are dumb
VC firms think they know everything about private equity	VC firms think they know everything about private equity

(There are some constants in the universe.)

Now the reality: Investment in private companies by both angels and venture capitalists has been steadily, and at times rapidly, increasing over the past 10 years. In 1999, there was a tremendous spike in activity driven by exuberance over e-commerce on the Internet. Now, over the next several years, investment will most likely return to a more normal level, but a level that is still high relative to what it was even five years ago.

ADVICE FROM A VENTURE CAPITALIST WHO IS ALSO AN ANGEL

Frank A. McGrew IV, Managing Director, Paradigm Capital Partners, Memphis, TN, www.memphisangels.com

What do you think the outlook is for angel investment in the next few years? "Angels are here to stay, as evidenced by the tremendous amount of wealth that has been created by the run-up of the bull market and a lot of people wanting to recycle their capital. There is no typical angel. Some may tighten their reins and stop making incremental investments. Some may do smaller amounts per deal. From the overall perspective, there have been a lot of angels who have made a lot of money funding start-ups. Sometimes they do it for financial gain, sometimes to occupy their time. There are a number of objectives for any entrepreneur to understand before taking money from angels. Are they patient? Are they trying to get in at the lowest price possible and get control of the business? Are their interests aligned with those of the entrepreneur?

"It will be harder for companies to get second-round funding completed. Some venture groups have time constraints working with existing investments. They aren't looking for new ones. They say, 'we don't need to go to the orphanage to look for children, we've got enough of our own to look after.'

"I think people have revised their expectations about angel investing and venture capital in general. It was not uncommon for angels to make 10 to 15 times their money in as little as two years in the past. The amount of dollars going into angel investing has compressed."

ADVICE FROM AN ANGEL

Bill Krause, Mentor Capitalist

What do you think the next two to three years will bring us in venture finance? "I think you will see a return by entrepreneurs to that fundamental: They get started because they have a passion for the cause. I think venture capitalists will return to a sane approach to building businesses, and they will appreciate the fact that too much money can be just as dangerous as too little money. You don't instill the discipline in the company to make the tough choices when you have so much money you don't need to. Venture capitalists have been guilty of giving companies too much money in order to accelerate a process that takes three to five years. It didn't work.

"Venture capitalists will begin to make sure that when their companies are ready for the public market, they are really ready. Companies will have to have predictable revenues and have profits behind them when they go public, not just projected in front of them."

If you were going to give one piece of advice to an entrepreneur just starting to look for capital, what would it be? "Persevere pursuing the best venture capitalists you can find. They are people who are in the business of building businesses for a living. Everyone else is an amateur on the sidelines. The most fortunate thing that can happen to an entrepreneur is to get funding from the best and brightest venture firms they can."

ADVICE FROM AN ANGEL

Steve Miller, Co-founder, Prairie Angels, www.prairieangels.org

How do you see angel investing changing? Is there anything that could be done to make this process more efficient for the entrepreneur? "We have seen times when seemingly anything could get funding, then we saw a period when the cure for cancer couldn't get money. I think the pendulum will come to the middle. We will get to a place where good, solid businesses with good management teams will get funded at fair valuations. No matter what happens with the stock market, there are always going to be entrepreneurs with good ideas who want to start companies and there will always be angel investors who want to invest in those companies. The quantity of capital fluctuates depending on the markets.

"It's always a good time to be an entrepreneur with a great idea. The cream rises to the top and gets funding even in the worst of times. It's still a lot of work. We won't see the mania again, but that's good."

ADVICE FROM AN ANGEL

Brent Townshend

What do you think the future of angel investing will be? "There has been a short-term downturn in angel investing. Many angels made their fortunes in tech stocks and when the public markets decline, their paper wealth declined as well. So it is tied to the stock market.

"Angels that still have a lot of money, however, are still very interested in making investments because there are a lot of good deals out there. Companies today are more solid with more reasonable valuations than those a year ago."

ADVICE FROM AN ANGEL

Luis Villalobos, Founder and Director, Tech Coast Angels, www.techcoastangels.com

What is your view of the angel investing environment for the near-term future? "The short answer is: It is going to be fabulous. There has never been a time like the present for angel investing. The valuations are terrific from the angel's standpoint. A lot of the people who were in angel investing because they wanted to do a quick flip on an IPO are no longer around. I think the thing most people have missed is that we keep hearing about what went wrong with early-stage investing in 2000 and early 2001 (when the Internet bubble burst). Nothing went wrong. That is how our entrepreneurial capitalist system works. You have to have the lure of huge, huge profits in order to attract the hundreds of thousands of entrepreneurs who will work away in garages, and take vastly reduced salaries, in order to launch their ventures—and then most of them don't make it. The economy would not stand for subsidizing the wages of all these people trying to build their dreams.

"The current Internet wave gave us e-Bay, Amazon.com, Yahoo!, and AOL, as well as things like Google that are not yet profitable but will be terrific. It had very positive outcomes, and that's what we need as angels and entrepreneurs to fuel our desire to participate.

"Angels look for real passion in the entrepreneur to fulfill a dream, to deliver a product or have some technology enter the market. The fact they want to make a profit is good, but if the profit motive is all that drives them it is a big turnoff. We have entrepreneurs who focus on how quick they are going to make an exit for us and for themselves; I think their motives are misplaced in that case. What we really want is somebody who is really about building a business long-term, and wants to deliver value to customers."

ADVICE FROM AN ANGEL

Ken Deemer, Tech Coast Angels, www.techcoastangels.com

What do you see for angel investing in the future? "The last few years have been an abnormality in a lot of ways, all up and down the investment chain. For a while it seemed like anyone with half an idea could get funded by venture capitalists or angels. It has sort of come back to where it had been. Angel investors have been around forever. The longer-term trend looks very strong for angel investors, for groups like Tech Coast Angels and others, where investors can find others with similar interests and collaborate, share the risk and share the work. This opportunity has not been widely available until very recently."

ADVICE FROM AN ANGEL

Steven P. Subar

What is your view of the current angel investing environment? "I'm optimistic. Part of that is colored by my own personal experience. This is a buyer's market. The different ways of structuring deals work right now to the benefit of the investor. Whether it is liquidation preferences, or ratchets, or different kinds of terms you would like to see for your own protection—the climate is such that you are taking less risk. You are saving time, because the deals that didn't make sense where the valuations were based on something like the number of Herman Miller chairs they had in the office—those deals you aren't seeing anymore.

"These days there is no shortage of good new ideas for early-stage investors to consider. From the standpoint of how quickly someone would realize a return, those economics have changed substantially, which just means you need to change your planning horizon. This comes back to the deal terms and structuring the deals in such a way to accommodate the longer time horizon. If you are in the deal longer you need a higher rate of return.

"You have to recognize the economy ebbs and flows. The past several years were an aberration, but everything tends to the norm—unless you believe something has fundamentally changed, and the economy won't continue to grow over the long term, that technology is not going to continue to play a significant role in increasing productivity, and the United States won't continue to be a leader in doing all of that. To me, that would be a hard position to take. If you are in angel investing for the long term, there isn't anything to be concerned about."

What Can We Really Expect in the Future?

The pessimists say that the hot days of VC investment are over, and that angels have mostly flown from the scene. The investment landscape is littered with the broken dreams of failed dot.coms.

Nonsense.

To give up on the funding of early-stage companies is to give up on the American economy itself, because the technical innovation that is supported by investors who take these considerable risks becomes the foundation of our economic growth in the future.

Greed infected this marketplace for a while, but the patient survived. You might argue the patient came out stronger.

ANGELS ARE THE ULTIMATE OPTIMISTS (NEXT TO ENTREPRENEURS, OF COURSE)

It is safe to say that angel investors will always be with us, in good economic times and bad, whether the stock markets are soaring or plummeting. The activity is too beguiling, too absorbing. Investing in early-stage companies is definitely something that gets in your blood. When we began the interviews for this book, the press coverage about venture capital and the outlook for finding capital had turned extremely negative. We expected to talk to angels who reminisced about the good old days when rates of return were high and there were plenty of good deals to be had. We thought that perhaps we would hear from angels who had become disgusted with this type of investing altogether, and had no intention of financing a start-up ever again.

But we heard no such thing. We heard about learning from mistakes and being more cautious. The angels, from billionaires on down to the merely affluent, no matter what region of the country, told us they were very much still in the game.

ADVICE FROM AN EXPERT

How Angel Investing Has Changed and Its Future

Jeffrey E. Sohl, Director, Center for Venture Research; William Rosenberg, Professor, Whittemore School of Business and Economics, University of New Hampshire

The history of high-growth start-ups is a history of equity financing. From the time when Alexander Graham Bell received financing from two angels to complete his early experiments on the telephone, through the expansion of the Body Shop in 1976 with equity capital from a private investor, to today's world of angel-backed high-tech ventures, the angel market has experienced much growth. Recently, we have witnessed an explosion in angel financing. With this rapid expansion many of the tried-and-true angel ABCs (attitudes, behavior, and characteristics) have been tested. Stories abound of finding the deal on Monday, investing on Tuesday, and going public on Friday. While market gyrations have been noted by the research conducted by the Center for Venture Research for the past two decades, none have been as heavily reported in the media as this last one. As the forest begins the inevitable culling, we see a return to the core values that have driven the angel market. Gone are those investors with only cash, replaced by the angel who provides value-added investing and the experience of building companies, not just exit strategies. Patience is back in vogue, with angel holding periods determined more by the maturity of the company and management team than by the need to force liquidity for the sake of instant gratification. Investing in industries that an angel is familiar with, and is in the position to conduct meaningful due diligence, replaces the need to jump on board with the next big thing—whatever that thing may be. A return to reasonable valuations, from both the entrepreneur and investor perspective, will only add to both the sanity and stability of the angel market. We will pass through some bumpy roads and volatile cycles, and these are of vast interest from a research view. Market changes provide a tremendous learning platform. The vital role of business angels continues to be critical, and the know-how and capital of angels remain largely untapped resources. While much is known about the angel market, there remains a great deal to learn. I for one will enjoy these exciting times ahead.

ADVICE FROM AN ANGEL IN ARIZONA

What is your philosophy about angel investing? "I put around $100,000 in each deal at first, and I know that by the time I am finished with the company I will have put in additional funds to help the company move forward or do something like guarantee a credit line for the company. Mentally, I write off the investment after I make it, because you have to accept the fact that it is likely you will not get anything back. Out of six investments, I hope that one will be a substantial winner. And there is a lot of hoping involved, to be sure.

"I could never quit making these investments, though. It is too much fun."

Perhaps one of the reasons angels are so persistent is that to be an angel is to make a statement of your own individuality. It is very much an individual risk. When a midcap public company goes on a rocket ride and doubles in three months, you can certainly congratulate yourself if you purchased your shares at the bottom and rode to the top. Thousands of other people made the same decision, however. You were just one of many. You may have been advised to buy the stock by any one of the thousands of financial advisory firms in the United States.

However, your decision to put $100,000 in a fledgling software company working out of a 1000-sq.-ft. office suite is very different. You may be the only person who believed in the company and the management team. They may have been turned down by a hundred different investors before they found you.

When this company takes your money and your advice and turns it into a venture that grows and grows, it becomes a personal victory for you, the angel, as well. You took a lonely, individual, risky, courageous position that other investors would not. When this little company becomes larger and attracts $10 million of investment from a world-class venture fund, part of the credit goes to you and you alone. Even if the entrepreneur, flushed with success, doesn't necessarily recognize your contribution—you do. You know.

Angels separate themselves from the pack. They don't run with the thousands who react to buy and sell recommendations from brokerage houses, or the latest pronouncement from the Federal Reserve. They are alone in their offices, with limited, sometimes scanty, information to rely on. And they go to their checkbooks and put their money behind someone else's dream, a company no one has ever heard of before. Angel investing requires an extraordinary leap of faith.

Whatever their motivation was—even plain old greed—the end result is all that counts. And the end result is that tiny lights most of us can't even see can become supernovas in just a few short years. Wealth is created, but more importantly, our ability to imagine is unleashed. And out of that imagination, our economy is continually reborn.

Maybe for an entrepreneur, the appearance of an angel is miraculous after all.

Chapter Summary

- Best of luck to you in finding that special angel.
- We know they're out there.

APPENDIX

Experts Who Contributed to *Attracting Capital from Angels*

Bruce Borup, *Advice on Presenting to an Angel Network* (page 192), is assistant professor of entrepreneurship and chair of the Business Administration Department at Alaska Pacific University. His educational qualifications include an L.L.B., an M.A. in marketing, and a Ph.D. in business. Bruce's expertise is in start-up management with 15 years as a founder and lead entrepreneur of several different companies. Bruce has served in the military as an infantry officer, ranger, and arctic paratrooper. He is on the advisory boards of several local high-tech start-ups and is a board member of Alaska InvestNet, Alaska's capital-matching organization. Bruce is the Sam Walton Fellow for Free Enterprise at Alaska Pacific University, managing the SIFE team—business sudents who perform entrepreneurial outreach within the local community.

Bob Bozeman, *Foreword* (page ix), is a recognized expert in the field of angel investing and entrepreneurship. His management experience includes 12 years as CEO/president or general manager in software, information technology/services, and computer supplier industries (including Vetronix Sales Corporation, Altos Computer Systems, and Natural Language Incorporated) and five years as vice president in a very high-growth Fortune 100 corporation contributing to growth in revenue from $50 million to $2.7 billion (Wang Laboratories). He also founded two high-tech businesses (Library Systems and Bozemans', Inc.). He graduated from the University of Cincinnati (Distinguished Alumnus Award) and Northeastern University and is a member of the guest faculty for the University of Michigan, teaching "Angel Investing: Principles and Techniques of Investing in Private." He is a member of the board of directors for Hipbone, Metasound, Searchbutton (acquired by Mondosoft); an advisor for BristleCone Ventures, LP; Compass Capital, LLC; and GAC Capital; and general partner of Angel Investors, LP (both Funds I and II) and Genesis Capital II, LP.

Nigel A.L. Brooks, *Investor Reporting Packages* (page 274), is president of The Business Leadership Development Corporation (www.bldsolutions.com), and has more than 25 years' experience as an entrepreneur, line manager, project manager, and management consultant. He established Java Centrale–Metrocenter, a European-style gourmet coffee cafe and catering business, and was senior vice president of technology strategy and reengineering, American Express Company; vice president, Booz-Allen & Hamilton, Inc.; and partner, Arthur Andersen and Company, S. C. (Andersen Consulting). He has experience in North and Latin America, Europe, the Far East, and Australia.

Paul E. Burns, *Intellectual Property Protection* (page 118), is a shareholder in the law firm of Gallagher & Kennedy in Phoenix, Arizona, where he concentrates his practice in intellectual property, technology-related business transactions, and litigation and dispute resolution. He obtained his B.S. in computer science, magna cum laude, from Boston College, and his J.D., magna cum laude, from Boston College Law School. He is co-founder and president of the Arizona Internet and E-Commerce Association, and serves on the board of directors of the Arizona Technology Incubator. Mr. Burns is registered to practice before the United States Patent and Trademark Office, and is a member of the bars of Arizona, California, Texas, New York, Connecticut, Massachusetts, and the District of Columbia.

Leni Chauvin, *Tips for Using Networking Skills to Attract Investors* (page 214), is founder and president of BRE Business Referral Exchange (www.superstarnetworking.com), a business coaching and training company aimed at helping clients obtain more business, a solid client base, and plenty of referrals. With over 20 years' experience in sales and marketing, Leni knows which (phone) buttons to push to get things done. Through weekly leads-exchange meetings, individual and group coaching, teleclasses, writing, and corporate training, Leni guides people to bcoming successful.

Aimee Fitzgerald, APR, *Using Public Relations to Establish Credibility and Visibility: The Reality* (page 211), president, Fagan Business Communications, Englewood, Colorado, (aimeecolo@aol.com). Aimee began Fagan Business Communications in 1984, serving consumer and business-to-business clients on regional, national, and international levels. The business focuses on positioning and message development, with consistent, integrated implementation. Areas of specialization include editorial news media relations, community relations, and investor relations for high-tech, recreation/tourism, and financial services industries. Aimee has worked as a senior manufacturing planner for Digital Equipment Corporation, and as a systems consultant for Arthur Andersen and Company. She holds a bachelor of business administration degree, with honors, from the University of Notre Dame, and an M.B.S. degree, with highest honors, from the University of Minnesota. She is an accredited member of the Public Relations Society of America, and serves as a national assembly delegate and board member for the organization's Colorado chapter.

Beth Gallob, *Ready, Fire, Aim Is for Amateurs: Or Why You Need a Marketing Plan* (page 143). Gallob Communication (www.gallobcomm.com), has more than 20 years experience providing technical, marketing, and corporate communication for global high-tech companies in a wide range of industries, including telecommunications, networking, hardware, software, and e-business. Prior to launching her marketing communication and consulting firm in Phoenix, Arizona, Beth successfully built and managed communication groups for a number of Minnesota-based companies. Her areas of expertise include developing marketing strategies, implementing integrated marketing programs, and creating award-winning marketing communication materials ranging from corporate overviews, product brochures, and customer success stories to press releases, advertising copy, and Web content. Beth manages the Marketing Special Interest Group for the Arizona Software & Internet Association and contributes a monthly marketing-oriented article to an e-mail newsletter for entrepreneurs. She has a B.A. from Metropolitan State University, Minneapolis.

Bob Geras, *What Makes a Deal Attractive?* (page 230), is president of LaSalle Investments, Inc. An active participant in the venture capital and angel community in Chicago for more than 30 years, he has been termed "a virtual Renaissance man of entrepreneurship" in a *Chicago Sun-Times* interview and "one of the Big Three 'old timer' angels in Chicago" in a cover story by *iStreet*. Recently he was listed as one of the "Internet 100" by *Crain's Chicago Business*. Many venture capitalists, accountants, attorneys, and other consultants call Bob when they have a client who needs a good dose of mentoring as well as some seed or early-stage money for a young company. This is not only because Bob has been at it for so long, but also because he has extensive line operating experience as an entrepreneur, turnaround specialist, and real estate developer in addition to having been a longtime investor in a wide variety of deals. LaSalle Investments will often raise additional money from other investors when the company is ready for it.

Randy Haykin, *Foreword* (page x), managing director, iMinds Ventures, www.iminds.com (a.k.a. Outlook Ventures), 415-547-0000. Randy Haykin founded iMinds in 1995. iMinds is a venture management firm that specializes in delivering hands-on assistance, customer connections, and funding to seed and early-stage companies, particularly in enterprise software and software infrastructure market areas. He has represented iMinds on the boards of Impulse! Buy Network, eCircles, eTeamz, Voquette, Pakana, QBiquity, and Longilent. Prior to iMinds, Randy held various senior sales and marketing positions in the high-technology arena over the past 15 years with high-profile companies such as Yahoo!, Viacom, Paramount, BBN, IBM, NetChannel, and Apple Computer. He served as the founding vice president of marketing and sales at Yahoo! and as interim VP of marketing at NetChannel, which was successfully acquired by America Online in 1998. He also served as part of the core team that launched America Online's Greenhouse, a successful venture incubator.

Christopher D. Johnson, *Pennies from Heaven* (page 117), partner, Squire, Sanders & Dempsey L.L.P. (www.ssd.com), has practiced for more than 20 years in the corporate and securities areas, with significant experience in initial and subsequent public offerings, private placements, mergers and acquisitions, corporate reorganizations and restructurings, public company securities law compliance, venture capital finance, and corporate governance. Mr. Johnson was a member of the executive council of the state bar of Arizona's Securities Regulation Section from 1979 to 1995 and served as its chair from 1994 to 1995. He has been a member of the boards of directors of the Enterprise Network and the Arizona Technology Incubator, and he currently serves on the planning committees of the Arizona Venture Capital Conference and the Arizona Software Association Investing in Innovation Conference. Mr. Johnson is a frequent author and lecturer on corporate and securities law topics.

Woody Maggard, *The Angel Investor and Incubators* (page 206), is president and CEO of the Arizona Technology Incubator. Recent activity includes being an advisor and consultant to a $100 million venture accelerator fund; a consultant to Summit Ridge Partners in Santaquin, Utah, for the development of a 2,200-acre mixed-use residential development that will have a seed fund, incubator, technology park, and wired community; chairman of NETeXc Information Services, Inc., a Delaware-based Internet company; co-founder and co-owner of LearnDaily.com, a Utah-based Internet company; and chairman of a trading compay for 9 years. With extensive senior management background in private, public (county and city), quasi-public, and university sectors, principal roles have been directing the development of world-class commercial, industrial, and research projects; development of technology-based business and research in research park and innovation and commercialization centers; and directing research institutes. This includes experience in providing facilities for projects such as DuPont's multibillion-dollar twenty-first-century initiatives in the life sciences, including agrobiotech, pharmaceuticals, and biotech.

Stephan J. Mallenbaum, *Angel Investor Deal Terms* (page 250), leads the venture capital/technology team at Jones Day, one of the world's most recognized and largest law firms. He focuses on the unique business and legal issues of high-growth and technology-driven companies, including capital formation, strategic acquisitions, and the exploitation, financing, and marketing of technology products and services. He counsels clients in complex technology-driven transactions, including venture capital transactions, acquisitions, financing, public offerings, strategic partnering, and multiparty transactions. He is adept at bringing practical business solutions to complex transactions and is experienced in driving complex, multiparty transactions to successful conclusions. He works closely with companies in developing successful business strategies and commercializing technology from a global perspective. He is a graduate of Massachusetts Institute of Technology and has more than 20 years of experience in the emerging growth and technology sector.

J. Casey McGlynn, *The Differences Between Angel Investors and Venture Capitalists* (page 152), is a partner at Wilson, Sonsini, Goodrich & Rosati (www.wsgr.com). He heads one of the largest new venture practices at the firm. He is a nationally recognized leader in the representation of start-up and emerging growth technology companies in the health care and information technology industries. Mr. McGlynn has helped hundreds of emerging growth companies to meet their financing needs through introductions to an extensive network of angel investors, financiers, venture capitalists, corporate partners, and investment bankers. Mr. McGlynn joined WSGR in 1978 and has been a member of the firm's executive, nominating, and compensation committees. He is a frequent contributor to magazines and newsletters focused on angel and venture investing. He is also a frequent speaker on issues relating to the organization and funding of new ventures. During January 1998, Mr. McGlynn formed a small venture fund focused on angel investing. Since that time he has formed several subsequent funds focused on seed investing with total capital exceeding $200 million. In the past three years, he has helped a significant number of entrepreneurs with funding and mentoring to transform their ideas into successful VC-backed businesses. As of December 31, 2000, nine of his fund's portfolio companies have completed IPOs and 19 have been acquired. Mr. McGlynn received his B.S. and J.D. degrees, with highest honors from Santa Clara University.

Robert J. Moss, *Investor Reporting Packages* (page 274), has over 12 years of sales, marketing, and corporate finance experience providing several hundred million dollars of commercial financing and funding commitments to clients in a myriad of industries. Currently holding the position of director of sales and marketing for Business Development Partnership, Inc., he previously served as vice president of business development for Stirling Capital Corporation from 1997 to 2001, established proprietary financial programs for the promotion of a nationwide network that fosters capital and corporate advisory services, and implemented new financial products, services, and strategies that provided results.

Ernie L. Recsetar, *Investor Reporting Package* (page 274), is chief executive officer of Stirling Capital Corporation, (www.stirlingcapital.com). Stirling Capital Corporation is a relationship-based commercial investment and merchant banking company specializing in providing capital solutions to referred business clients ranging from small to midsize and public companies involving financing amounts from $1 million to $100 million. Mr. Recsetar has been involved in approximately $12 billion of underwritings and fundings. This involvement includes: serving on credit committees, negotiation, documentation, structuring, workouts, and litigation. While at Greyhound Financial, Mr. Recsetar oversaw the operating expenditure of $100 million over a five-year period. Even though not having direct marketing responsibility, Mr. Recsetar generated business volume and profits exceeding many of Greyhound Financial's lines of business.

Susan F. Shultz, *The Board Book* (page 126), established SSA Executive Search International, Ltd., in 1981. SSA (www.ssa.com) conducts searches locally, nationally, and internationally. SSA is the U.S. partner of Morgan and Partners Group, Europe, an executive search group with offices in 11 countries, and also has search affiliates in Asia and Mexico. SSA has a division devoted to the recruitment of directors for corporate boards and helps growth companies, both public and private, structure, strengthen, and diversify their statutory and advisory boards. SSA is a member of the National Association of Corporate Directors and Directorship. SSA also identifies international affiliates, consults on various international projects, and conducts seminars on human resources, strategic affiliates, and boards of directors.

John Sizer, *How Can an Advisory Team Be an Asset When Looking for Investors?* (page 130), has 17 years of experience in public accounting and is the partner in charge of the local audit and advisory practice for Deloitte Touche Tohmatsu (www.deloitte.com). A CPA, he has extensive experience in serving emerging growth companies, as well as SEC registrants.

Jeffery E. Sohl, *How Angel Investing Has Changed and Its Future* (page 311), is director of the Center for Research and William Rosenberg Professor, Whittemore School of Business and Economics, University of New Hampshire.

Quinn Williams, *Angel Investing Has Evolved in the Last Decade* (page 201), is a senior corporate and securities partner for Snell & Wilmer, a law firm with offices in Phoenix and Tucson, Arizona; Salt Lake City, Utah; and Orange County, California. He heads up the firm's emerging business and venture capital practice groups. Mr. Williams has extensive experience in public and private securities offerings and has served clients in a broad range of industries. A major component of Mr. Williams' practice is private equity and venture capital firms that invest in high-growth technology companies. He is the founding chairman of the Arizona Technology Incubator and the Arizona Venture Capital Conference. In addition, Mr. Williams is active in a number of community organizations and currently serves as a board member for Arizona Innovation Network, Arizona Technology Incubator Fund, Governors Regulatory Review Commission, Greater Phoenix Economic Council, Scottsdale Charros, and Scottsdale Partnership, along with serving on the board of several other nonprofit companies. Mr. Williams has been a recipient of the Ernst & Young Entrepreneur of the Year Awarad and of the Small Business Administration (SBA) Financial Services Award.

Index